ROGUES

MERIDIAN

Crossing Aesthetics

Werner Hamacher

Editor

Translated by Pascale-Anne Brault
and Michael Naas

Stanford
University
Press

———————

Stanford
California
2005

ROGUES

Two Essays on Reason

Jacques Derrida

Stanford University Press
Stanford, California

This book has been published with the assistance of the
French Ministry of Culture—National Center for the Book.

"The 'World' of the Enlightenment to Come (Exception,
Calculation, Sovereignty)" was published in *Research in
Phenomenology* 33 (2003): 9–52. Reprinted here with
permission of the publisher, Koninklijke Brill
NV, Leiden, the Netherlands.

Printed in the United States of America
on acid-free, archival-quality paper

Library of Congress Cataloging-in-Publication Data

Derrida, Jacques.
[Voyous. English]
Rogues : two essays on reason / Jacques Derrida ;
translated by Pascale-Anne Brault and Michael Naas.
p. cm. — (Meridian)
Includes bibliographical references.
ISBN 0-8047-4950-7 (hardcover : alk. paper)
ISBN 0-8047-4951-5 (pbk. : alk. paper)
1. Legitimacy of governments. 2. Sovereignty.
3. National state. 4. Rule of law. I. Title.
II. Series: Meridian (Stanford, Calif.)

JC497.D47 2005
320.1—DC22
2004016072

Original Printing 2005

Last figure below indicates year of this printing:
14 13 12 11 10 09 08 07 06 05

Typeset by Tim Roberts in 10.9 / 13 Adobe Garamond
and Lithos Display

Rogues was originally published in French in 2003 under the
title *Voyous: Deux essais sur la raison* © 2003, Éditions Galilée.

Contents

Acknowledgments   ix

Preface: Veni   xi

PART I: THE REASON OF THE STRONGEST
(ARE THERE ROGUE STATES?)

§ 1 The Free Wheel   6

§ 2 License and Freedom: The *Roué*   19

§ 3 The Other of Democracy, the "By Turns":
     Alternative and Alternation   28

§ 4 Mastery and Measure   42

§ 5 Liberty, Equality, Fraternity, or,
     How Not to Speak in Mottos   56

§ 6 The Rogue That I Am   63

§ 7 God, What More Do I Have to Say?
     In What Language to Come?   71

§ 8 The Last of the Rogue States: The "Democracy
     to Come," Opening in Two Turns   78

§ 9 (No) More Rogue States   95

§ 10 Sending   108

PART II: THE "WORLD" OF THE ENLIGHTENMENT TO COME
(EXCEPTION, CALCULATION, AND SOVEREIGNTY)

§ 1 Teleology and Architectonic:
The Neutralization of the Event   118

§ 2 To Arrive—At the Ends of the State
(and of War, and of World War)   141

Notes   *161*

Acknowledgments

We would like to thank the College of Liberal Arts and Sciences and the University Research Council at DePaul University for their generous support of this work. Our thanks also to Ginette Michaud, Steve Michelman, and the members of the winter 2004 graduate seminar "Sovereignty and Democracy" at DePaul University for their many helpful suggestions. Finally, we must express our deepest gratitude—yet once again—to Jacques Derrida, for his patience, guidance, and friendship. Although he does not always make a translator's work easy—rogue that he is—he does always make it enriching and enlivening. Once again, he will have given us this gift.

The Wolf and the Lamb

The strong are always best at proving they're right.
Witness the case we're now going to cite.
A Lamb was drinking, serene,
At a brook running clear all the way.
A ravenous Wolf happened by, on the lookout for prey,
Whose sharp hunger drew him to the scene.
"What makes you so bold as to muck up my beverage?"
This creature snarled in rage.
"You will pay for your temerity!"
"Sire," replied the Lamb, "let not Your Majesty
Now give in to unjust ire,
But rather do consider, Sire:
I'm drinking—just look—
In the brook
Twenty feet farther down, if not more,
And therefore in no way at all, I think,
Can I be muddying what you drink."
"You're muddying it!" insisted the cruel carnivore.
"And I know that, last year, you spoke ill of me."
"How could I do that? Why I'd not yet even come to be,"
Said the Lamb. "At my dam's teat I still nurse."
"If not you, then your brother. All the worse."
"I don't have one." "Then it's someone else in your clan,
For to me you're all of you a curse:
You, your dogs, your shepherds to a man.
So I've been told; I have to pay you all back."
With that, deep into the wood
The Wolf dragged and ate his midday snack.
So trial and judgment stood.

—La Fontaine

Preface: Veni

The strong are always best at proving they're right.
Witness the case we're now going to cite.
                    —La Fontaine, *The Complete Fables of Jean de la Fontaine*

What political narrative, in the same tradition, might today illustrate this fabulous morality?[1] Does this morality teach us, as is often believed, that force "trumps" law? Or else, something quite different, that the very concept of law, that juridical reason itself, includes a priori a possible recourse to constraint or coercion and, thus, to a certain violence? This second interpretation was, for example, Kant's, and it did not necessarily represent the point of view of the wolf. Nor, for that matter, that of the lamb.

First of all, with regard to the couple *force* and *law*, from where do we get this formidable tradition that long preceded and long followed La Fontaine, along with Bodin, Hobbes, Grotius, Pascal, Rousseau, and so many others, a tradition that runs, say, from Plato to Carl Schmitt? Do we still belong to this ever-changing yet imperturbable genealogy? Before even speaking of force, would justice be reducible to law [*droit*]?[2]

What about law [*Quoi du droit*]? And what about who [*qui*]? One says in French *qui de droit* to designate a subject who has rights [*droits*] over . . . who has the ability or right to . . . who has the power of deciding on. . . . But just who has the right to give or to take some right, to give him- or herself some right [*droit*] or the law [*droit*], to attribute or to make the law in a sovereign fashion? Or the right to suspend law in a sovereign way? Schmitt defines the sovereign in precisely this way: the one who has the right to suspend law.

Two lectures here seem to echo one another.[3] They perhaps answer one another, just as Echo might have feigned to repeat the last syllable of Narcissus in order to say something else or, really, in order to sign at that very instant in her own name, and so take back the initiative of answering or responding in a responsible way, thus disobeying a sovereign injunction and outsmarting the tyranny of a jealous goddess. Echo thus lets be heard by whoever wants to hear it, by whoever might love hearing it, something other than what she seems to be saying. Although she repeats, without simulacrum, what she has just heard, another simulacrum slips in to make her response something more than a mere reiteration. She says in an inaugural fashion, she declares her love, and calls for the first time, all the while repeating the "Come!" of Narcissus, all the while echoing narcissistic words. She overflows with love; her love overflows the calls of Narcissus, whose fall or whose sending she seems simply to reproduce. A dissymmetrical, unequal correspondence, unequal, as always, to the equality of the one to the other: the origin of politics, the question of democracy. If I seem to be insisting a bit too much on these *Metamorphoses*, it is because everything in this famous scene turns around a call *to come* [*à venir*]. And because, at the intersection of repetition and the unforeseeable, in this place where, each time anew, by turns [*tour à tour*] and each time once and for all, one does not see *coming* what remains *to come*, the *to-come* turns out to be the most insistent theme of this book. "Veni!" says Narcissus; "Come!" "Come!" answers Echo. Of herself and on her own. We all know what comes next.[4]

Unless these two addresses, here coupled together, leave, as if abandoned, an open correspondence. A correspondence to come and left hanging, open, unsettled and unsettling [*en souffrance*].

Delivered just a couple of weeks apart, close in their themes and in the problems they treat but destined for two very different audiences, these lectures seem to invoke a certain *reason to come*, as *democracy to come*—in the age of so-called globalization or *mondialisation*.

The concepts of "reason" (practical or theoretical, ethical and juridical, as well as technical), the concepts of "democracy," of "world" and especially of "event" (the arrival or coming of "*what* comes" and of "*who* comes") belong here to a whole skein of problems that could hardly be undone in a preface. But without forming a "system," a certain interweaving remains an unyielding necessity and its analysis a task. That is, at least, the hypothesis being put to work here. One of the most visible guiding threads for such an analysis would be the huge, urgent, and so very difficult question, the old-new enigma, of *sovereignty*, most notably nation-state sovereignty—whether it be called democratic or not.

What is "coming to pass" or "happening" [*arrive*] today in technoscience, in international law, in ethico-juridical reason, in political practices and rhetorical strategies? What happens when we put to work within them the concept and the name of *sovereignty*, especially when this concept and this name, in the power of their heritage and of their ontotheological fiction, appear less legitimate than ever?

What is happening to the notions of the "political" and of "war" (whether world war, war between nation-states, civil war, or even so-called partisan war)? What happens to the notion of "terrorism" (whether national or international) when the old phantom of sovereignty loses its credibility? For this has been happening for longer than is often believed, although it is happening today in a new way and at a different pace.

This situation was certainly not created, and was not even really revealed, by that supposedly "major event" dated "September 11, 2001," even if those murders and those suicides (though many others as well) media-theatricalized the preconditions and some of the ineluctable consequences of this situation; and even if the structure and possibility of the so-called event were constituted by this media-theatricalization.

The word *voyou* has a history in the French language, and it is necessary to recall it. The notion of an *Etat voyou* first appears as the recent and ambiguous translation of what the American administration has been denouncing for a couple of decades now under the name "rogue state," that is, a state that respects neither its obligations as a state before the law of the world community nor the requirements of international law, a state that flouts the law and scoffs at the constitutional state or state of law [*état de droit*].[5]

This language thus retains a certain privilege when we are questioning what is being *made* of *mondialisation*—a questionable and itself very recent translation of *globalization*. The experience of translation orients us here, and precisely through the English language, toward what might be called, in a few words, the "question of the United States," the question of their "right of the strongest," their "law of the jungle [*droit du plus fort*]."[6] Hegemony? Supremacy? A new figure of Empire or imperialism? Should we be satisfied with this vocabulary, or should we, with no compass to orient us, seek something else?

As in another recent work, "The University Without Condition," this text ultimately proposes a difficult or fragile distinction.[7] I consider it scarcely possible yet essential, indispensable even—an ultimate lever. When it comes to reason and democracy, when it comes to a democratic reason, it would be necessary to distinguish "sovereignty" (which is always in principle indivisible) from "unconditionality." Both of these escape absolutely, like the absolute itself, all relativism. That is their affinity. But through certain experiences that will be central to this book, and, more generally, through the experience that lets itself be affected by what or who comes [*(ce) qui vient*], by what happens or by who happens by, by *the other to come*, a certain unconditional renunciation of sovereignty is required a priori. Even before the act of a decision.

Such a distribution or sharing also presupposes that we think at once the unforeseeability of an event that is necessarily without horizon, the singular coming of the other, and, as a result, a *weak force*. This vulnerable force, this force without power, opens up unconditionally to what or who *comes* and comes to affect it. The coming of this event exceeds the condition of mastery and the conventionally accepted authority of what is called the "performative." It thus also exceeds, without contesting its pertinence, the useful distinction between "constative" and "performative." Along with so many other related distinctions, beginning with theoretical versus practical reason, the scientific versus the technical, and so on.

The common affirmation of these two lectures resembles yet again an act of messianic faith—irreligious and without messianism. Rather than a "religion within the limits of reason alone" (still so Christian in its ultimate Kantian foundation), such an affirmation would resound through another naming of *khōra*.[8] A certain reinterpretation of Plato's *Timaeus* had named *khōra* (which means *locality* in general, spacing, interval) another *place* without age, another "taking-place," the irreplaceable place or placement of a "desert in the desert," a spacing from "before" the world, the cosmos, or the globe, from "before" any chronophenomenology, any revelation, any "as such" and any "as if," any anthropotheological dogmatism or historicity.

But what would allow these to take place, without, however, providing any ground or foundation, would be precisely khōra. Khōra would make or give *place*; it would give rise—without ever *giving* anything—to what is called the coming of the event. Khōra receives rather than gives. Plato in fact presents it as a "receptacle." Even if it comes "before everything," it does not exist for itself. Without belonging to that to which it gives way or for which it makes place [*fait place*], without *being a part* [*faire partie*] of it, without *being of it*, and without being something else or someone other, giving nothing other, it would give rise or allow to take place.

Khōra: before the "world," before creation, before the gift and being—khōra that *there is* perhaps "before" any "there is" as *es gibt.*

No politics, no ethics, and no law can be, as it were, *deduced* from this thought. To be sure, nothing can be *done* [*faire*] with it. And so one would have nothing to do with it. But should we then conclude that this thought leaves no trace on what is to be done—for example in the politics, the ethics, or the law to come?

On it, perhaps, on what here receives the name *khōra*, a call might thus be taken up and take hold: the call for a thinking of the event *to come*, of the democracy *to come*, of the reason *to come*. This call bears every hope, to be sure, although it remains, in itself, without hope. Not hopeless, in despair, but foreign to the teleology, the hopefulness, and the *salut* of salvation. Not foreign to the *salut* as the greeting or salutation of the other, not foreign to the *adieu* ("come" or "go" in peace), not foreign to justice, but nonetheless heterogeneous and rebellious, irreducible, to law, to power, and to the economy of redemption.

PART I

The Reason of the Strongest
(Are There Rogue States?)

For a certain sending [*envoi*] that awaits us, I imagine an economic formalization, a very elliptical phrase, in both senses of the word *ellipsis*. For *ellipsis* names not only lack but a curved figure with more than one focus. We are thus already between the "minus one" and the "more than one."

Between the "minus one" and the "more than one," democracy perhaps has an essential affinity with this turn or trope that we call the ellipsis. The elliptical sending would arrive by e-mail, and we would read: "*The democracy to come: it is necessary that it give the time there is not.*"

It would no doubt be on my part, dare I say it, a bit *voyou*, a bit roguish, if not *roué*, were I not to begin here by declaring, yet one more time, my gratitude.

Yet one more time, to be sure, but for me, yet one more time ever anew, in a way that is each time wholly new, yet one more time for a first time, one more time and once and for all the first time. Not once and for all, not one single time for all the others, but once and for all the first time.

At moments like this in Cerisy, having to face a repetition that is never repeated, I feel the urgent and ever more poignant necessity of thinking what this enigmatic thing called "a time" might mean, as well as, each time, the "re-turn," the turn [*le tour*], the turret or tower [*la tour*], turns and towers, these things of re-turn, this cause of an eternal return even in the mortality of a day, in the undeniable finitude of the ephemeral.

Perhaps I will do little more today than turn, and return, around these turns, around the "by turns" and the "re-turn."

I would thus be, you might think, not only voyou, or roguish, but *a* voyou (*a* real rogue) were I not to declare at the outset my endless and bottomless gratitude, a gratitude that can never measure up, I am fully aware, to what is being given to me here.

But in thinking that the debt has no limits, and that if thanks there are I will never be able to give them, it would really be on my part, let me say it again, a bit "roguish" to silence my emotion before you all, as well as before all those who will have welcomed me in this chateau in the course of the last four decades [*décennies*], since 1959, and already, yes, in the course of four *décades.*[9]

More than four decades, therefore, and four *décades*, without mentioning the more than four others in which I have participated ("Genesis and Structure" in 1959, upon the invitation of Maurice de Gandillac, whom I am so pleased to see here, "Nietzsche," "Ponge," "Lyotard," "Genet," "Cixous"—there's the sum total).

More than four decades and more than double four *décades*—that's an entire adult life. The wheel [*roue*] turns, the merry-go-round [*la ronde*] and the revolution of anniversaries and birthdays. Beyond gratitude or recognition, and thus beyond cognition and knowledge, I would be unable to explain the good fortune of this miracle, and especially to translate it here for our English-speaking friends, who have no word to mark the difference between *décennie* and *décade*: they say "decade" for *décennie* as well as for *décade*. For me at Cerisy that would thus amount to "*four decades and more than four decades.*" In French the word *décade* for *décennie* is a bad turn, a bad turn of phrase, one that some of our dictionaries denounce as an "anglicism" to be avoided.[10] I imagine that some across the Channel or the Atlantic still hesitate to sign up for a *décade* at Cerisy, fearing that they will have to stay here, to speak here, and, especially, to listen here to some rogue who will go on nonstop for ten years. That is because such a distinction is Greek to them and they are losing their Greek and Latin: *décade*, let them be assured, meant in the Greek calendars and right up until the day of the French Revolution, only ten days, not ten years. Nor, as you might be fearing today, ten hours.

As for the itinerary of the word *voyou*, which I just ventured in its risky translation between English and French, it touches on some of the important political issues to which I would like to devote the end of this session. From "rogue state" to "Etat voyou" it is a question of nothing less than the reason of the strongest, a question of right and of law, of the force of law, in short, of order, world order, worldwide order, and its future, of the meaning or direction of the world [*sens du monde*], as Jean-Luc

Nancy would say, or, at least, more modestly, of the meaning of the words *world* [*monde*] and *worldwide*, of "globalization" or *mondialisation.*[11]

All this should pass through the eye of a needle; that is the *hubris* or mad wager of the metonymy to which I am entrusting the economy of this discourse. This eye, this "eye of the needle," would thus be the narrow, tight passage, the straits, the tiny aperture through which the word *voyou* has recently come to translate, transpose, and transcribe the war strategy directed against the "axis of evil" and so-called international terrorism by means of the American denunciation of *rogue states*, a phrase that has quite recently come to be translated by the Parisian syntagma "Etat voyou." That will be, later on, one of my references and points of departure.

Hoping not to give in, out of a certain modesty, to the emotion of the moment, I would first like to express my fervent thanks to my hosts here at Cerisy, to you, dear Edith Heurgon, to Catherine Peyrou, to your colleagues and associates present here with you, Catherine de Gandillac and Philippe Kister, and to all those who are no longer here but still come back to welcome us in spirit.

I also want to recognize those who, whether from nearby or afar, directly or indirectly, have for so long inspired what we might risk calling the politics or ethics of this unique counterinstitution. For so long, I say, because we will be celebrating in a few weeks everything that Cerisy throughout its half century of existence will have meant for a century [*siècle*] of intellectual life, each letter of the word S.I.E.C.L.E. becoming from now on, as we have learned, part of the acronym for an extraordinary adventure: *Sociabilités intellectuelles: Echanges, Coopérations, Lieux, Extensions.*[12]

My heartfelt thanks also go to the participants, organizers, and initiators of these four *décades*, beginning with Marie-Louise Mallet. After Jean-Luc Nancy and Philippe Lacoue-Labarthe in 1980, Marie-Louise—in her turn—will have done so much for us, for yet a third time. With the keen ingenuity we have all come to know, she will have used yet one more time her art, her knowledge, and her tact, as we can all attest, to soften the signs of authority, to erase them in such a sovereign fashion that none of them show, to render them through an impeccable virtuosity all of a sudden invisible. Without any orders ever being given, everything is ordered by the magic and magisterial wand of a great conductor who seems content to accompany, or indeed to follow, the interpretation or arrangement that she will have, in truth, as we all well know, secretly and for so long orchestrated.

To all of you here I must say that any words of welcome or hospitality would be too modest to name an offering that gives me more than I could ever have. For you give me here much more than I can have or make my own. I receive more than I can or ought to receive.

How is this possible? How can one accept—to say nothing of give back, know, acknowledge—something of which one is not even capable? How can one accept something one will never be able to receive, something that must thus remain unacceptable, unreceivable?

This thought of the excessive gift, of the impossible thanks, or of the aneconomic transaction, is not so foreign, in the end, to the set of questions that brings us together for this *décade*. Yet you should know that this gift goes straight to my heart. It goes to the heart of what I hold dear, to the heart of what makes me hold on, there where the work of thought and of writing still holds fast within me, still has a hold on me, still holds me to life or keeps me alive, and it is why I hold so fast to speaking from the heart, from the bottom of my heart.

I insist here on "holds me to *life* [*vie*] or keeps me *alive*" because the old word *vie* perhaps remains the enigma of the political around which we endlessly turn. What holds me here in life holds first of all in friendship. By the grace of a friendship of thought, of a friendship itself to be thought. In fidelity. And this fidelity, always trembling, risky, would be faithful not only to what is called the past but, perhaps, if such a thing is possible, to what remains to come and has as yet neither date nor figure.

I would like to believe this, and I will even go so far as to dream that fidelity, contrary to what we often tend to believe, is first of all a fidelity to . . . to come. Fidelity to come, to the to-come, to the future. Is this possible?

Let me thus venture here, and sign as a sign of gratitude, a sort of oath in the form of an obscure aphorism—still unreadable because yet again untranslatable, in the silent displacement of its syntax and its accents. The oath would go like this: *oui, il y a de l'amitié à penser*; yes, there is *friendship to (be) thought*.

I just likened this phrase to an oath. If you try to follow, within this untranslatable French, the regular displacement of the accents on this body in motion, on the animated or animal body of this phrase ("*yes, there is—* friendship to [be] thought"; "yes, there is *friendship—to be thought*"; "yes, there is—friendship *to thought*"), you will perhaps see the meaning move along the phrase like the rings of a snake.

This oath [*serment*] in fact risks looking like a snake [*serpent*]. At once threat and promise, a threat and a chance not to be missed, for it is not clear that the snake is simply, as a certain reading of Genesis would try to make us believe, a figure of the forces of evil, *along the axis of evil*.[13] Only a certain poetics can inflect differently a dominant interpretation—whether of the Bible or of any other canonical text.

In the course of an extraordinary scene of hospitality in D. H. Lawrence's poem "Snake" the figure of the snake is reinterpreted precisely along these lines. Deep within the voice of the poet, it is no doubt a woman who says "I" in order to call for its return: "And I wished he would come back, my snake." This return would resemble the returning or *revenance* of the one who had come as a peaceful guest ("he had come like a guest in quiet")—and it is in fact not only of life but of peace or hospitality that I too would like to speak.[14] This return would also be the returning or *revenance* of a guest of peace who will have been a king without a crown, a king in exile ("Like a king in exile, uncrowned in the underworld . . . ") and, especially, a lord of life, an ultimate sovereignty of life, whose chance will have been missed ("And so, I missed my chance with one of the lords / Of life. / And I have something to expiate").[15]

It is indeed on the side of chance, that is, the side of the incalculable *perhaps*, and toward the incalculability of another thought of life, of what is living in life, that I would like to venture here under the old and yet still completely new and perhaps unthought name *democracy*.

§ 1   The Free Wheel

The turn [*le tour*], the turret or tower [*la tour*], the wheel of turns and returns: here is the motivating theme and the Prime Mover, the causes and things around which I will incessantly turn.

Returning already at the outset to what will have taken place, irreversibly, I must, according to the circular movement of a future anterior, of a, dare I say, bygone [*révolu*], annulled future, alert you right away, having scarcely begun, still on the threshold, that I will have had to give in to the injunction of a preliminary question. A double question, in fact, and this was not fortuitous.

This double question (at the same time semantic and historical, by turns semantic and historical) will have won out over me [*aura eu raison de moi*], and I will have had to cede to its force no less than to its law. Its reason [*raison*], the reason of the strongest, will have been that of the greatest force.

Having just said "at the same time semantic and historical, by turns semantic and historical," saying thus by turns "at the same time" and "by turns," I am marking here, right at the outset and once and for all, one time for all, a protocol that should keep watch over everything that follows. Each time I say "time [*fois*]," "at the same time," "one time out of two," "two times," "each time," "but at the same time," "sometimes," "a few times," "another time," "in another time," I am introducing a reference to the turn and the return. And this is not only because of the Latin etymology of the word *fois*, namely, this strange word *vicis*, which has no nominative, only a genitive, an accusative, *vicem*, and an ablative, *vice*, each time to signify the turn, succession, alternation or alternative (it turns by being inverted, by turns, alternatively or vice versa, as in *vice versa* or the "vicious circle"). If I may be allowed, this one time, to refer to my little book *Shibboleth—For Paul Celan*, I would recall that this essay, political through and through, is first of all and especially a reflection on the date and on its return in the anniversary.[16] The work opens right from its first couple of pages on this lexicon of the *time* [*fois*], on the linguistic borders that delimit its translation and make any crossing difficult, especially with regard to "the vicissitudes of latinity, to the Spanish *vez*, to the whole syntax of *vicem, vice, vices, vicibus, vicissim, in vicem, vice versa*, and even *vicarius*, to its turns, returns, replacements, and supplantings, voltes, and revolutions." And the essay opens with the necessity of "returning more than one time," more than "*una volta*," as one says in Italian, to these vicissitudes. Each time in order to confirm a dangerous law of supplementarity or iterability that forces the impossible by forcing the replacement of the irreplaceable. What took place will take place another time today, although in a completely different way, even if I do not signal or underscore it each time.

A double question, therefore, *at the same time* semantic and historical, *by turns* semantic and historical. What is this question, divided or multiplied by two?

At the moment of confiding it to you, I am myself torn or split in two.

On the one hand, this double question would require us to inflect otherwise the very word *question*. It would impose itself at the very beginning of the game, and that is why I spoke without delay of an injunction and of the greatest force, of a force that will have won out over everything, and first of all over me, in the figure of a violent question, the question in the sense of an inquisitional torture where one is not only put *in* question but is put *to the* question.

On the other hand, this double question has returned to torment me. It has made a return, turning around me, turning and returning, turning around me and turning me upside down, upsetting me, as if I were locked up in a tower unable to get around, unable to perceive or conceive the workings or turnings of a circular machine that does not work or turn just right [*qui ne tourne pas rond*].

For if I say that I am confiding to you this double question, that I am sharing this confidence with you, it is because the turn taken, imposed, or contorted by this bifid and perfidious question torments me and never stopped torturing me as I was preparing for this *décade*. As you know, torture (*torqueo, tortum, torquere*), sometimes in the form of an inquisition or inquisitional questioning, never far from some Torquemada, some grand inquisitor, is always a matter of turning, of torsion, indeed of the re-turn of some re-torsion. There is always a wheel [*roue*] in torture. Torture always puts to work an encircling violence and an insistent repetition, a relentlessness, the turn and return of a circle.

The torture of the wheel belongs to a long juridical and political history. It sets in motion not only the turning apparatus of a wheel but the quartering of the alleged criminal. The subject being punished is quartered, his bound body forming one body with the wheel, subjected to its rotation. When I speak of a double question whose torture returns, when I say that this question was at the same time and/or by turns historical and conceptual or semantic, I am describing a torturing and quartering on the wheel. There is quartering properly speaking when horses pull on the four limbs of the condemned. But there is also a sort of quartering on the wheel: it turns, returns, and draws, stretches, and tears the four limbs of the body by pulling them in two opposite directions.

This double question thus returns, a returning or haunting [*revenante*], a torturing question. It concerns not only the title chosen by Marie-Louise Mallet and myself for this *décade*. "The democracy to come" was a not so very veiled reference to an expression in which I have often, for more than a decade now, sought a sort of refuge. This strange syntagma that does not form a sentence, comprising just three words—"democracy to come"—might seem to suggest that I had wished to privilege indetermination and ambiguity. As if I had given in to the apophatic virtue of a certain negative theology that does not reveal its name, instead of beginning with a rigorous definition of what "democracy" is properly speaking and what it presently signifies. This failing would be perceptible *there where I do not know*—and especially do not even know if this is a question of knowledge—what a democracy worthy of this name might presently be or what it might mean properly speaking. And where I do not even know what the locution "worthy of this name" means, a locution that I have often used and that will one day require a long justification on my part. As if "democracy to come" meant less "democracy to come" (with everything that remains to be said about it, and which I will try little by little to clarify) than "the concept to come of democracy," a meaning perhaps not null and void but not yet arrived, not yet bygone, of the word *democracy:* a meaning in waiting, still empty or vacant, of the word or the concept of democracy. As if I had been admitting for more than ten years now, turning round a confession that I would translate like this: "In the end, if we try to return to the origin, we do not yet know what *democracy* will have meant nor what democracy is. For democracy does not present itself; it has not yet presented itself, but that will come. In the meantime let's not stop using a word whose heritage is undeniable even if its meaning is still obscured, obfuscated, reserved. Neither the word nor the thing 'democracy' is yet presentable. We do not yet know what we have inherited; we are the legatees of this Greek word and of what it assigns to us, enjoins us, bequeaths or leaves us, indeed delegates or leaves over to us. We are undeniably the heirs or legatees, the delegates, of this word, and we are saying 'we' here as the very legatees or delegates of this word that has been sent to us, addressed to us for centuries, and that we are always sending or putting off until later. There are, to be sure, claims or allegations of democracy everywhere, everywhere 'we' are; but we ourselves do not know the meaning of this legacy, the mission, emission, or commission of this word or the legitimacy of this claim or allegation. The legacy and the allegation, the legibility of the legend or inscription—I'm playing here, notice, between *legare* and *legere*—only put off until later or send off elsewhere. This sending or putting off [*renvoi*] gestures toward the past of an inheritance only by remaining to come." End of confession.

The avowal would already be a strange way of going round in circles.

But that was not exactly the origin of the double question that kept tormenting me, torturing me, and putting me to the question. The scene of torture was something else; I would compare it to being tortured on the wheel, since it too takes the form of a machine in the form of a circle, indeed a hermeneutic circle. Tied to the machine, bound hand and foot, I would turn, exposed to a round of blows. Quartered.

Even if I must put off until later, after too long a detour, the formulation of this double question, we will not be able to turn round the wheel as long as we really should, even from a simply political point of view. For I will at some point have to bring this talk to a close, despite the generous amount of time that has been set aside for it. And that I will take full advantage of—rogue that I am. Much later, we will in fact have to question all the decisive implications of this strange necessity that imposes limits on a discussion, on an exchange of words or arguments, a debate or deliberation, within the finite space and time of a democratic politics. For it is said that the essence of such a politics, in its liberal form, is to authorize or call for free discussion or indefinite deliberation, in accordance, at least, with the circular figure of the Athenian assembly in the agora or the semicircular figure of the assemblies of modern parliamentary democracy. In its very institution, and in the instant proper to it, the act of sovereignty must and can, by force, put an end in a single, indivisible stroke to the endless discussion. This act is an event, as silent as it is instantaneous, without any thickness of time, even if it seems to come by way of a shared language and even a performative language that it just as soon exceeds.

But I don't imagine it was ever possible to think and say, even if only in Greek, "democracy," before the rotation of some *wheel*. When I say "wheel," I am not yet or not necessarily referring to the technical possibility of the *wheel* but, rather, rather earlier, to the roundness of a rotating movement, the rondure of a return to self before any distinction between *physis* and *tekhnē*, *physis* and *nomos*, *physis* and *thesis*, and so on.

The invention of the wheel marks, to be sure, an enormous and decisive mutation in the history of humanity, indeed of hominization, and thus, in terms of *possibility* at least, if not in terms of the fact or the event of technical invention, in the humanity of man; and, among other things, in the history of the rights of "man," beginning with the right to recognize oneself as a man by returning to oneself in a specular, self-designating, sovereign, and autotelic fashion.

When I say "wheel," I am also not referring, or at least not yet, to the purely geometrical figure of the *circle* or the *sphere*. And yet, it is true, before all the technical forms of wheelworks, of rotary motion, of the machine called the "wheel" that turns on itself around a fixed axis, before the purely geometrical forms named *circle* and *sphere*, I still have difficulty imagining, in this super-preliminary moment, any democracy at all. It seems difficult to think the desire for or the naming of any democratic space without what is called in Latin a *rota*, that is, without rotation or rolling, without the roundness or rotating rondure of something round that turns round in circles, without the circularity, be it pretechnical, premechanical, or pregeometrical, of some automobilic and autonomic turn or, rather, return to self, toward the self and upon the self; indeed, it seems difficult to think such a desire for or naming of democratic space without the rotary motion of some quasi-circular return or rotation toward the self, toward the origin itself, toward and upon the self of the origin, whenever it is a question, for example, of sovereign self-determination, of the autonomy of the self, of the *ipse*, namely, of the one-self that gives itself its own

law, of autofinality, autotely, self-relation as being in view of the self, beginning by the self with the end of self in view—so many figures and
movements that I will call from now on, to save time and speak quickly, to
speak in round terms, *ipseity* in general. By *ipseity* I thus wish to suggest
some "I can," or at the very least the power that *gives itself* its own law, its
force of law, its self-representation, the sovereign and reappropriating gathering of self in the simultaneity of an assemblage or assembly, being together, or "living together," as we say. In order to question at the same time
and at the same stroke this possibility, we will have to put and think together [*ensemble*], at the same time (*simul*), in the same sphere of a differentiated ensemble, the very values of the ensemble, of *Versammeln*, in Latin
of assembling and resembling, of simultaneity and of the simulacrum
(*simil, similis, simulacrum,* and *simulare*), which consists precisely in making similar or semblable through the semblance or false-semblance of simulation or assimilation. *Adsimilatio* is the action of making semblable, by
real or feigned reproduction, indeed by simulation or dissimulation.

On the horizon without horizon of this semantic disturbance or turbu-
lence, the question of the democracy to come might take the following
form, among others: what is "living together?" And especially: "what is a
like, a compeer [*semblable*]," "someone similar or semblable as a human
being, a neighbor, a fellow citizen, a fellow creature, a fellow man," and so
on? Or even: must one live together only with one's like, with someone
semblable? For the sake of an economy of language, let me simply announce in a word that, from now on, each time I say *ipse, metipse,* or *ipseity,* relying at once on their accepted meaning in Latin, their meaning
within the philosophical code, and their etymology, I also wish to suggest
the self, the one-self, being properly oneself, indeed being in person (even
though the notion of "in person" risks introducing an ambiguity with regard to the semblable, the "oneself" not necessarily or originally having
the status of a person, no more than that of an I, of an intentional consciousness or a supposedly free subject). I thus wish to suggest the oneself
[*soi-même*], the "self-same [*même*]" of the "self [*soi*]" (that is, the same,
meisme, which comes from *metipse*), as well as the power, potency, sovereignty, or possibility implied in every "I can," the *pse* of *ipse* (*ipsissimus*) referring always, through a complicated set of relations, as Benveniste shows
quite well, to possession, property, and power, to the authority of the lord
or seignior, of the sovereign, and most often the host (*hospites*), the master of the house or the husband. So much so that *ipse* alone, like *autos* in

Greek, which *ipse* can actually translate (*ipse* is *autos*, and the Latin translation of "Know thyself," of *gnōthi seauton*, is in fact *cognosce te ipsum*), designates the oneself as master in the masculine: the father, husband, son, or brother, the proprietor, owner, or seignior, indeed the sovereign. Before any sovereignty of the state, of the nation-state, of the monarch, or, in democracy, of the people, ipseity names a principle of legitimate sovereignty, the accredited or recognized supremacy of a power or a force, a *kratos* or a *cracy*. That is what is implied, posed, presupposed, but also imposed in the very position, in the very self- or autopositioning, of *ipseity itself*, everywhere there is some oneself, the first, ultimate, and supreme source of every "reason of the strongest" as the right [*droit*] granted to force or the force granted to law [*droit*].

But do we really need etymology when simple analysis would show the possibility of power and possession in the mere positioning of the self as *oneself* [*soi-même*], in the mere self-positioning of the self as properly oneself? The first turn or first go-round of circularity or sphericity comes back round or links back up, so to speak, with itself, with the same, the self, and with the proper of the oneself, with what is proper to the oneself proper. The first turn does it; the first turn is all there is to it [*le premier tour, c'est tout*]. The turn, the turn around the self—and the turn is always the possibility of turning round the self, of returning to the self or turning back on the self, the possibility of turning on oneself around oneself—the turn [*tour*] turns out to be it [*tout*]. The turn makes up the whole and makes a whole with itself; it consists in totalizing, in totalizing itself, and thus in gathering itself by tending toward simultaneity; and it is thus that the turn, as a whole, is one with itself, together with itself. We are here at the same time around and at the center of the circle or the sphere where the values of ipseity are gathered together, the values of the together [*ensemble*], of the ensemble and the semblable, of simultaneity and gathering together, but also of the simulacrum, simulation, and assimilation. For let us not forget that, like the circle and the sphere, the turn (all turns [*tours*], and all turrets, all towers [*tours*], including the turret of a chateau or the turning surface of a potter's wheel [*tour*]) requires surfaces, a surface area, lines that come back round to or toward themselves according to a certain motivation, a certain mover, and a possible rotational movement, but always, simultaneously, around a center, a pivot or axle, which, even if it too ends up turning, does not change place and remains quasi immobile. Without counting—and yet while counting on—this strange necessity of the zero, the necessity of a circular annulment or zeroing out in the perfectly round zero.

(Ah, the *tour*, the wheel! Let me confide in you here how much I love this image of the potter, his art, the turns of someone who, on his wheel, makes a piece of pottery rise up like a tower by sculpting it, molding it, but without subjecting himself, or herself, to the automatic, rotating movement, by remaining as free as possible with regard to the rotation, putting his or her entire body, feet and hands alike, to work on the machine, cultivating the art of a sculptor but also that of an architect and composer who imposes on or rather grants to matter differences in height, changes in color and tone, variations in rhythm, accelerations or decelerations [*allegro* or *presto, adagio* or *lento*], in a space as sonorous in the end as a sort of musical transposition or discreet word. For as sculptor or architect, the potter in his turn is by turns poet and musician, rhetorician and political orator, perhaps even a philosopher. End of this little confidence.)

Now, democracy would be precisely this, a force (*kratos*), a force in the form of a sovereign authority (sovereign, that is, *kurios* or *kuros*, having the power to decide, to be decisive, to prevail, to have reason over or win out over [*avoir raison de*] and to give the force of law, *kuroō*), and thus the power and ipseity of the people (*dēmos*). This sovereignty is a circularity, indeed a sphericity. Sovereignty is round; it is a rounding off. This circular or spherical rotation, the turn of the re-turn upon the self, can take either the alternating form of the *by turns*, the *in turn*, the *each in turn* (we will see this in Plato and Aristotle in a moment) or else the form of an identity between the origin and the conclusion, the cause and the end or aim, the driving [*motrice*] cause and the final cause.

At the end of chapter 4 of *Democracy in America* Tocqueville himself, in describing the sovereignty of the people, speaks of this circular identification of the cause with the end. He presents this circularity as the effective fulfillment of a democracy that, up until then, had been presented only as a project, an opinion, a claim or allegation, a deferral to later, a utopia, indeed the fiction of a democracy to come. "In the United States in our day," says Tocqueville in 1835, "the principle of the sovereignty of the people has been adopted in practice in every way that imagination could suggest. It has been detached from all fictions in which it has elsewhere been carefully wrapped; it takes on every possible form that the exigencies of the case require."[17]

After having cited various cases where power remains external or superior to the social body, where, as he says, "force is divided, being at the same time within the society and outside it," Tocqueville wants to show that this division is no longer operative in American democracy. Society there acts circularly "by itself," he says, "and for itself." Circularly or by turns, the people, says Tocqueville, is "the cause and the end of all things; everything rises out of it and is absorbed back into it." Tocqueville writes, "Nothing like that is to be seen in the United States [nothing that signifies the 'division' of a 'force' that would be at the same time within society and outside it]; there society acts by itself and for itself. There are no authorities except within itself; one can hardly meet anybody who would dare to conceive, much less to suggest, seeking power elsewhere" (53). He then gives what he considers to be a demonstrative description of the organization of executive and legislative powers, before concluding the chapter with the trope of a theological figure that he believes to be conventional and purely rhetorical but whose necessity seems to me much more serious and important: "The people," he concludes, "reign over the American political world as God rules over the universe. It is the cause and the end of all things; everything rises out of it and is absorbed back into it" (53).

I had to cite Tocqueville, and particularly *Democracy in America*, without letting too much more time go by, in order to announce from afar that, at the end of a long detour, right near the end, it will perhaps become clear that democracy *in* America or, more precisely, democracy *and* America will have been my theme. This volt between "democracy *in* America" and "democracy *and* America" will give another twist to the Tocquevillian turn of phrase that turns around a circle turning around itself, as "the cause and the end of all things," where "the people reign over the American political world as God rules over the universe."

God, circle, volt, revolution, torture: I should perhaps confess that what tortures me, the question that has been putting me to the question, might just be related to what structures a particular axiomatic of a certain democracy, namely, the turn, the return to self of the circle and the sphere, and thus the ipseity of the One, the *autos* of autonomy, symmetry, homogeneity, the same, the like, the semblable or the similar, and even, finally, God, in other words everything that remains incompatible with, even clashes with, another truth of the democratic, namely, the truth of the other, heterogeneity, the heteronomic and the dissymmetric, disseminal multiplicity, the anonymous "anyone," the "no matter who," the indeterminate "each one." For the democratic God of which Tocqueville speaks, this sovereign cause of itself and end for itself, would also resemble, and this resemblance never ceases to motivate thought, pure Actuality, the *energeia* of Aristotle's Prime Mover (*to proton kinoun*). Neither moving itself nor being itself moved, the actuality of this pure energy sets everything in motion, a motion of return to self, a circular motion, Aristotle specifies, because the first motion is always cyclical. And what induces or inspires this is a desire. God, the pure actuality of the Prime Mover, is at once erogenous and thinkable. He is, so to speak, desirable (*erōmenon*), the first desirable (*to proton orekton*) as the first intelligible (*to proton noēton*) thinking itself, as thought thinking thought (*hē noēsis noēseōs noēsis*) (*Metaphysics* 12.1072a–b, 1074b).[18] Aristotle also defines this first principle, and this will be important for us, as a life (*dia-gōgē*: in his commentary on this passage, Alexander of Aphrodisias uses *zōē* for life and *zēn* for living), a kind of life, a way of leading life, comparable to the best of what we might enjoy for a brief time (*mikron kronon*) in our life (*Metaphysics* 12.1072b). It is thus a life that exceeds the life of human beings, a life lived by the Prime Mover in a constant, continuous, and unending fashion, something that is for us impossible (*adunaton*). That is why the *energeia* of this pure activity is "pleasure" (*hēdonē*), the circle of a taking pleasure in oneself [*jouissance de soi*]. The energy of God and of the Prime Mover is thus at once desired, desirable (*erōmenon, to proton orekton*), and partaking in pleasure. A taking pleasure in the self, a circular and specular autoaffection that is analogous to or in accordance with the thinking of thought (*noēsis noēseōs*). We must never dissociate the question of desire and of pleasure when we treat the political, and especially the democratic, the question of conscious or unconscious pleasure, from the calculation and the incalculable to which desire and pleasure give rise. Everything is cyclical, circular, and spherical in what the *energeia* of the Prime Mover puts in motion, the incorruptibility of substance being linked to the circular eternity of motion. If there is a circularity of what is also, in sum, a sort of eternal turn and return, it is also a finity of time. God, the Prime Mover or pure actuality, is not infinite, neither in the sense of the *apeiron*, of the without-limit, that is, without horizon, contour, or turn, without *eidos*, nor in the sense of the Hegelian bad infinite, nor even in the sense of the Kantian infinite idea, nor in the sense of the infinity of full presence. After a long historical review of the number of spheres and heavens thought to be put in motion, Aristotle concludes that "the Prime

Mover, which is immovable, is one both in formula [in *logos*] and in number [*hen ara kai logō kai arithmō to prōton kinoun akinēton on*]; and therefore so also is that which is eternally and continuously in motion [*kai to kinoumenon ara aei kai sunekhōs*]" (*Metaphysics* 12.1074a).

If, in trying to announce to you the torturing question, I have referred to Aristotle's *Metaphysics* before turning to his *Politics*, it is because the final sentence of this twelfth book proposes a political analogy. Aristotle there cites the *Iliad* (2.204). The end of book 12 (Lambda) thus seems written under, or underwritten by, the sovereign authority of Homer, of his words and his verdict, precisely there where Homer himself cites a word of sovereign authority. Present on the scene are Athena, daughter of Zeus, and an Odysseus who is compared to Zeus. The word is elliptical and thus sententious. It cites a verdict and is thus placed under the guard of a sovereign authority. What does it say? It declares, declares itself by declaring the One and the sovereignty of the One, of the One and Only [*Unique*], above and beyond the dispersion of the plural. It cautions against the government of many, against *polykoirania*. Aristotle excerpts it from a long tirade. After having reprimanded the man of the people (*dēmou andra*), warning him, "In no wise shall we Achaeans all be kings here," two lines pronounce a sententious, performative, and juristic sentence: "No good thing is a multitude of lords; let there be one lord, one king [*ouk agathon polykoiraniē. heis koiranos estō, heis basileus*]."[19]

We will have occasion to speak later, in the margins of Plato, Aristotle, and Rousseau, of One God, of the One as God or of the God who is One, who does not come to democracy or else comes only to its idea [*à son idée*].[20] Here is the whole tirade:

> "Fool [*daimoni*], sit thou still, and hearken to the words of others that are better men than thou; whereas thou art unwarlike and a weakling, neither to be counted in war nor in counsel [*boulē*: deliberative assembly]. In no wise shall we Achaeans all be kings here. No good thing is a multitude of lords; let there be one lord, one king, to whom the son of crooked-counselling Cronos hath vouchsafed the scepter and judgments, that he may take counsel for his people." (*Iliad* 2.200–206)

The reference here is to Zeus, from whom issue the kings. And Zeus is a son. There is thus a source, a stock. The defeat of the father, the putting to death of the *Urvater*, as Freud would say, parricide and regicide, are related to a certain genealogical, filial, and especially fraternalistic interpretation of democratic equality (liberty, equality, fraternity): a reading of the egalitarian contract established between rival sons and brothers, in the succession of the father, for the sharing of *kratos* in the *dēmos*. Zeus is first of all a son, a male child and a descendent who, by means of ruse (*mētis*), but also with the help of his mother, manages to escape time. He thus wins out over [*a raison de*] his father, Cronos, who himself had won out over, who himself had emasculated, his own father, Ouranos. It is by winning out over time, by putting an end to the infinite order of time, so to speak, that he asserts his sovereignty. One might take this formulation to the extreme, to the point where it touches the end of time, touches the finitude or the finity of time, touches sovereignty as the instant of a decision that, at the indivisible point of its action, puts an end to time, as well as to language (and we will see the significance of this later).

Throughout this parricidal theogony there rages a political struggle over monarchic sovereignty, the intent of Cronos being to prevent one of his sons from taking up in his stead, as Hesiod puts it, "the kingly office amongst the deathless gods."[21] Among the guardians of his son Zeus, himself a combination of ruse and force, are *Kratos* and *Bia* (*Biē*), power and violent force. This theogonic mythology of sovereignty belongs to, if it does not actually inaugurate, a long cycle of political theology that is at once paternalistic and patriarchal, and thus masculine, in the filiation father-son-brother. I would also call it ipsocentric. This political theogony or theology gets revived or taken over (despite claims to the contrary by such experts as Bodin and Hobbes, whom I cannot treat here) by a so-called modern political theology of monarchic sovereignty and even by the unavowed political theology—itself just as phallocentric, phallo-paterno-filio-fraterno-ipsocentric—of the sovereignty of the people, that is, of democratic sovereignty. The attribute "ipsocentric" intersects and links with a dash all the others (those of the phallus, of the father, of the husband, son, or brother). *Ipsocentric* could even be replaced by ipso*cratic*, were that not a pleonasm, for the idea of force (*kratos*), of power, and of mastery, is analytically included in the concept of ipseity.

In speaking here of self-moving roundness or rotation, of the trope, the turn and re-turn in general, well before any opposition between *physis* and its others (and here is the proper place for force and for the differences of force), I am not yet referring, let me repeat it, either to the purely ideal objectivity of the *geometric* circle or to the *geological* possibility of a knowledge of the roundness or sphericity of the earth, even if, in a modern sense, which would no longer be that of the Stoics or Saint Paul, the thought of a cosmopolitical democracy perhaps presupposes a theocosmogony, a cosmology, and a vision of the world determined by the spherical roundness of the globe. *Mondialisation*: globalization. The celestial vault itself used to be represented as a turning wheel. Perhaps we can later formalize, still following the figure of this wheel [*roue*], this route that turns back on itself, this additional turn or twist, this roundness of the turn and of the tower, this return to self, the law of a terrifying and suicidal autoimmunity, the wheels of suicide here engaging in a singular way a gyratory coincidence between force and law, force and justice, force and the reason of the strongest.

Even though we know so little about what "democracy" should mean, it is still necessary, through a kind of precomprehension, to know something about it. And so the hermeneutic circle turns yet again. We must already anticipate, even if only by a bit; we must move toward the horizon that limits the meaning of the word, in order to come to know better what "democracy" will have been *able* to signify, what it *ought*, in truth, to have meant. We already have some "idea" of what democracy should mean, what it *will have already meant*—and the idea, the ideal, the Greek *eidos* or the *idea* also designates the turn of a contour, the limit surrounding a visible form. Did we not have some *idea* of democracy, we would never worry about its indetermination. We would never seek to elucidate its meaning or, indeed, call for its advent.

But the wheel [*roue*] of the question is not quite there, not quite there where I felt rolled or roundly beaten [*roué*] by it, not quite the place toward which I would like to try, with you, to return.

§ 2   License and Freedom: The *Roué*

You are no doubt beginning to find this introduction a bit *rouée*. But what does this word mean, this adjective *roué*, and the related noun *rouerie*? *Littré* defines *rouerie* as an "action, trick, or turn of one who is *roué*." *Roué* thus qualifies someone or the action of someone whose ruse or resources, indeed whose craftiness or *mētis*, is deployed in a mischievous, malicious, malefic, or malevolent manner. *Rouerie* would thus deserve the *roue*, the wheel, the torture that consists in being roué, that is, in being roundly beaten, beaten to a pulp, rolled, broken on the wheel, or punished in some other way for having broken the law or gone against decent moral behavior. *Littré* also defines the roué as "a man without principle or morals. A *roué* respects nothing."

A roué is a delinquent [*dévoyé*], a kind of voyou. In the same *Littré* entry a quote from Saint-Simon opens the properly political dimension that interests us here. What is condemned under the name or epithet *roué*? "This name was given under the Regency to men without morals, partners in the dissolute life of the Duke of Orleans, thus named because they deserved to be put on the *roue*, on the wheel." And Saint-Simon clarifies: "The obscure, and for the most part blackguard company, which he [the Duke of Orleans] ordinarily frequented in his debaucheries, and which he did not scruple publicly to call his *roués*, drove away all decent people." Or again: "His suppers were always in very strange company. His mistresses, sometimes an opera girl, often Madame la Duchesse de Berry, and a dozen men whom he called his *roués*, formed the party."[22]

The debauchery of the roués thus drives away all the decent, respectable people who themselves then drive away the roués. This reference to de-

bauchery becomes a leitmotif. We mustn't forget that the original meaning of *debauchery* is worklessness, the interruption of labor, a certain un-
employment, a crisis in the job market [*embauche*] or in the right to work,
but also, as a result, the playful and the lustful, the shameless, lewd, and
dissolute, the licentious and libertine. These sexual connotations cannot
but draw or attract into their magnetic field attraction itself, the power
linked to seduction and thus to leading astray [*dévoiement*]. To "seduce"
also means "to lead astray" (*seducere*), to "lure off the straight path," "to
lead off the right track [*voie*]." If the voyou is a dévoyé, one who is led
astray, the path to becoming a voyou is never very far from a scene of seduction. Following in this vein of sexual difference, this long vein that
runs, at least virtually, throughout the whole history of democracy and its
concept, we would have to find the time to ask why voyous, if not roués,
are almost always men, and why it is no doubt possible, although much
less common, secondary, and very artificial, to put *voyou* in the feminine
(we do sometimes say *voyoute*, but it always seems forced and is never very
convincing).

The attraction that organizes the seduction and that leads astray by elic-
iting desire sometimes consists, for the man who is roué, in fanning his
tail [*faire la roue*], showing off his wares [*atouts*] and what he wears
[*atours*], pluming himself like a peacock in rut—*en rut* (although *rut*, like
rue, has no etymological relation to *roué* or to *rota*, even if the *rue*, the
street, is the privileged place of the roué, the milieu and the path [*voie*] of
voyous, the road most often traveled by rogues, the place they are most
apt to roam).

In the idea of the roué there is thus an allusion to debauchery and perversity, to the subversive disrespect for principles, norms, and good manners, for the rules and laws that govern the circle of decent, self-respecting
people, of respectable, right-thinking society. *Roué* characterizes a leading
astray [*dévoiement*] that calls for exclusion or punishment. The roué is
thus indeed a sort of voyou, in this sense, but since a whole gang of voyous lies in wait for us a little further down the road, let's put them off a bit
longer. The libertine roués of the Regency described by Saint-Simon are
the debauched members of a good, decent monarchic society on the road
[*voie*] to corruption. They thus announce in their own way the decadence
of the monarchic principle and, from afar, by way of a revolution and a
beheading, a certain democratization of sovereignty. For democracy, the
passage to democracy, *democratization*, will have always been associated

with license, with taking too many liberties [*trop-de-liberté*], with the dissoluteness of the libertine, with liberalism, indeed perversion and delinquency, with malfeasance, with failing to live according to the law, with the notion that "everything is allowed," that "anything goes."

The roué thus appears to be a voyou, at once included and excluded, excluded from within the closely policed circle of respectable society. Were I to allow myself to keep coming back to this extraordinary and untranslatable French lexicon of the *roue*, to all the turns that link the uses, semantics, and pragmatics of this word to the history of France, to its social, juridical, and political history, we would never be done making the rounds of the politics of the *roue*, of the wheel, of everything it includes and excludes. For example, the word *roue*, or more often *rouelle*, was the name given to a little red and white wheel, the ancestor of the yellow star, which Jews had to wear openly on their breasts at all times or else face severe punishment. Voltaire recalls in his "Essay on the Manners and Spirit of Nations" that "the Lateran Council ordered that they [the Jews] should carry the figure of a small wheel [*roue*] on their breasts, to distinguish them from Christians."[23]

It has always been very difficult, and for essential reasons, to distinguish rigorously between the goods and the evils of democracy (and that is why I will later speak of autoimmunity). It has always been *hard* to distinguish, with regard to free will, between the good of democratic freedom or liberty and the evil of democratic license. They are hardly different. Book 8 of the *Republic*, for example, proposes a close examination of democracy as a regime (*dēmokratian . . . skepteon*). An arraignment brings forward for judgment (*eis krisin*), in crisis, the democratic man, his character, his way of being and acting, his turns of speech and his bearing, quite literally, his turn (*tropos*) or his turns (555b). The *krisis* makes a judgment, and the critique is devastating: with democratic man comes a general abdication, a complete loss of authority, a refusal to correct by means of the law the young *akolastoi*, literally those who go unpunished, unreprimanded, who are intemperate, licentious, undisciplined, delinquent, spendthrift, one might even say somewhat anachronistically voyous and roués, "wantons," says Plato, young men "averse to toil of body and mind, and too soft to stand up against pleasure and pain, and mere idlers" (556b–c). This is already beginning to look like a real bazaar, a carnival, a liberal or, better, neoliberal or precapitalist marketplace where the governing oligarchs have an economic interest in maintaining the dissolute life of the profligate in order eventually to acquire his estate. They thus lend money on hypothec, says the *Republic*, lending against the property of these men so as to enrich themselves even further through this speculation:[24]

> And there they sit within the city, furnished with stings, that is, arms, some burdened with debt, others disfranchised, others both, hating and conspiring against the acquirers of their estates and the rest of the citizens, and eager for revolution [*neōterismou erōntes*]. . . . But these money-makers with down-bent heads, pretending not even to see them, but inserting the sting of their money into any of the remainder who do not resist, and harvesting from them in interest as it were a manifold progeny of the parent sum [their capital, which is to say, in Greek, their patrimony: *tou patros ekgonous tokous pollaplasious komizomenoi*], these money-makers [these agents, so to speak, of usurious capitalization] foster the drone and pauper element in the state [*tēi polei*]. (555d–e)

We must never forget that this portrait of the democrat associates freedom or liberty (*eleutheria*) with license (*exousia*), which is also whim, free will, freedom of choice, leisure to follow one's desires, ease, facility, the faculty or power to do as one pleases. Plato says this explicitly. Or actually he *says* that this is what *is said* about democracy. "'To begin with, are they not free [*eleutheroi*]? And is not the city chock-full of liberty [*eleutherias*] and freedom of speech? And has not every man license to do as he likes [*kai exousia en autēi poiein ho ti tis bouletai*]?' 'So it is said,' he replied [*Legetai ge dē, ephē*]" (557b). He says that this is what is said. His discourse is thus indirect; it conveys a commonly held opinion.

And this opinion has spread like a rumor, varying little throughout history. Before even determining *demo-cracy* on the basis of the minimal though enigmatic meaning of its two guiding concepts and the syntax that relates them, the people and power, *dēmos* and *kratos*—or *kratein* (which also means "to prevail," "to bring off," "to be the strongest," "to govern," "to have the force of law," "to be right [*avoir raison*]" in the sense of "getting the best of [*avoir raison de*]" with a might that makes right)— it is on the basis of freedom that we will have conceived the concept of democracy. This will be true throughout the entire history of this concept, from Plato's Greece onward. Whether as *eleutheria* or *exousia*, this freedom can of course always be understood as a mere figure, as another figure, turn, or turn of phrase for power (*kratos*). Freedom is essentially the faculty or power to do as one pleases, to decide, to choose, to determine *oneself*, to have self-determination, to be master, and first of all master of oneself (*autos, ipse*). A simple analysis of the "I can," of the "it is possible for me," of the "I have the force to" (*krateō*), reveals the predicate of freedom, the "I am free to," "I can decide." There is no freedom without ipseity and, vice versa, no ipseity without freedom—and, thus, without a certain sovereignty.

But, speaking generally and all too quickly, this implication of freedom (*eleutheria* or *exousia*) will have gone more or less unquestioned throughout the entire history of the concept of democracy, although it will have been presented, by both Plato and Aristotle, and always with some reservations, as a sort of generally held or agreed on view, a belief, an accredited opinion, a *doxa* if not a "dogma," to use again Tocqueville's word. That is what everyone has agreed to say, Plato and Aristotle seem to emphasize, on the subject of democracy. This is what we are being told: democracy is freedom. After Plato ("'So it is said,' he replied [*Legetai ge dē, ephē*]"), Aristotle in the *Politics* also shows great caution. Speaking of freedom (*eleutheria*), he describes the postulates or axioms (*ta axiōmata*) and the hypothetical principle, the presupposition (*hypothesis*), the condition that is ordinarily attributed to democracy:

> And now let us state the postulates, the ethical characters and the aims of the various forms of democracy. Now a fundamental principle [a hypothesis, in truth, something one poses beneath or presupposes: *hypo-thesis*] of the democratic form of constitution is freedom—that is what is usually asserted [*touto gar legein eiōthasin*], implying that only under this constitution [*hōs en monēi tēi politeiai*] do men participate in freedom, for *they assert* this as the aim of every democracy [*toutou gar stokhazesthai phasi pasan dēmokratian*]. (6.1.1317a–b)[25]

Aristotle insists that he too is conveying a widely held belief, a hypothesis or presupposition, one that is in circulation and has the force of law in the common opinion that accredits and puts its faith in such things. He then immediately adds the following, which I cite so as to include it without delay in the case we are building around the trope, around the circular turn, the "by turns," the "in turn" or the "each in turn," *en merei* or *kata meros*:

> But one factor of freedom is to govern and be governed in turn [*eleutherias de hen men to en merei arkhesthai kai arkhein*]; for the popular [that is, democratic] principle of justice [*to dikaion to dēmotikon*] is to have equality according to number, not worth [*kat'arithmon alla mē kat'axian*], and if this is the prin-

ciple of justice prevailing, the multitude must of necessity be sovereign [*ku-rion*] and the decision of the majority must be final and must constitute justice. . . . This then is one mark of freedom which all democrats set down as a principle [*horon*: rule, limit] of the constitution. And one is for a man to live as he likes [*hen de to zēn hōs bouletai*] . . . and from it has come the claim not to be governed, preferably not by anybody, or failing that, to govern and be governed in turns [*kata meros*]; and this is the way in which the second principle contributes to freedom founded upon equality. (1317b)

In this text, as in so many others of both Plato and Aristotle, the distinction between *bios* and *zōē*—or *zēn*—is more than tricky and precarious; in no way does it correspond to the strict opposition on which Agamben bases the quasi totality of his argument about sovereignty and the biopolitical in *Homo Sacer* (but let's leave that for another time).[26]

In other words, the turn, the re-turn, the two turns, the by turns (*en merei* or *kata meros*) is what, even before determining what *dēmos* or *kratos*, what *kratein*, means, brings together the two terms of their double hypothesis or double axiom, namely *what one says* about freedom and equality. Freedom and equality are reconcilable, so to speak, only in a turning or alternating fashion, only in alternation. The absolute freedom of a finite being (and it is of just such a finitude that we are speaking here) can be equitably shared only in the space-time of a "by turns" and thus only in a double *circulation*: on the one hand, the circulation of the circle provisionally transfers power from one to the other before returning in turn to the first, the governed becoming in his turn governing, the represented in his turn representing, and vice versa; on the other hand, the circulation of the circle, through the return of this "by turns," makes the final and supreme power come back *to itself, to the itself of self, to the same as itself.* The same circle, the circle itself, would have to ensure the returning to come but also the return—or returns—of the final power to its origin or its cause, to its for-itself.

Why insist here on what remains so acute and difficult to think in freedom (*eleutheria* or *exousia*), and thus perhaps in decision and will, in sovereignty, even before the *dēmos* and *kratos*? In a freedom without which there would be neither people nor power, neither community nor force of law?

For two reasons: the first concerns what might be called the *free wheel*, the semantic vacancy or indetermination at the very center of the concept of democracy that makes its history turn; the second concerns the history of freedom, the history of the concept of freedom, of the essence or the experience of freedom that conditions the so-called free wheel. I thus announce from afar two reasons for turning toward freedom, whether *eleutheria* or *exousia*.

First, it should be noted that if this freedom, between *eleutheria* and *exousia*, seems to characterize social and political behavior, the right and power of each to do what he or she pleases, the faculty of decision and self-determination, as well as the license to play with various possibilities, it presupposes, more radically still, more originally, a freedom of play, an opening of indetermination and indecidability *in the very concept* of democracy, in the interpretation of the democratic.

Why this freedom in the concept? Why this freedom at play in the concept, opening up within it its own space of play? Why is it, in the end, so noteworthy, so striking? I say "striking" so as to avoid having to say, as I did just above out of expedience, more radical, more originary, or more primitive than freedom or license as the ability or power to do one thing or another, a power that would thus itself be conditioned by an a priori freedom.

This freedom in the concept is all the more striking inasmuch as it takes into account, as the empty opening of a *future of the very concept* and thus of the language of democracy, an *essential historicity of democracy*, of the concept and the lexicon of democracy (the only name of a regime, or quasi regime, open to its own historical transformation, to taking up its intrinsic plasticity and its interminable self-criticizability, one might even say its interminable analysis). It is a question of that democracy always to come to which I will return a bit later.

It can thus be argued that the syntagma "democracy to come" belongs to at least one of the lines of thought coming out of the Platonic tradition. This cannot always be said without a bit of duplicity, if not some polemical bad faith, but it also cannot be said without some verisimilitude. After all, to speak of "democracy to come" might consist in being content to explore, in a perfectly analytical, descriptive, constative, politically neutral fashion, the content of a concept that has been inherited and thus claimed and taken up since at least the time of Plato's Greece. I will explain myself on this later.

But what allows me for the moment to formulate things in this way by making reference to Plato is what the *Republic* itself draws our attention to just after the passage on the democratic man and his freedoms, *eleuthe-*

ria and *exousia*. Insofar as each person in this democracy can lead the life (*bion*) he chooses, we find in this regime, this *politeia*—which, as we will see, is not quite a regime, neither a constitution nor an authentic *politeia*—all sorts of people, a greater variety than anywhere else. Whence the multicolored beauty of democracy. Plato insists as much on the beauty as on the medley of colors. Democracy *seems*—and this is its appearing, if not its appearance and its simulacrum—the most beautiful (*kallistē*), the most seductive of constitutions (*politeiōn*) (557c). Its beauty resembles that of a multi- and brightly colored (*poikilon*) garment. The seduction matters here; it provokes; it is provocative in this "milieu" of sexual difference where roués and voyous roam about. The word *poikilon*, the key or master word in this passage, comes up more than once. It means in painting as well as in the weaving of garments—and this no doubt explains the allusion to women that soon follows—"multicolored," "brightly colored," "speckled," "dappled." The same attribute defines at once the vivid colors and the diversity, a changing, variable, whimsical character, complicated, sometimes obscure, ambiguous. Like the fanning [*la roue*] of a peacock, which women find so irresistible. For this multicolored beauty, Plato notes, and this is politically significant, arouses particularly the curiosity of women and children. All those who take after women and children consider it the most beautiful. Because of the freedom and the multicoloredness of a democracy peopled by such a diversity of men, one would seek in vain a single constitution or *politeia* within it. Given over to freedom, to *exousia* this time, democracy contains all the different kinds of constitutions, of regimes or states (*panta genē politeiōn*) (557d). If one wants to found a state, all one has to do is go to a democracy to pick out the paradigm of one's choice. As in a market, there is no shortage of *paradeigmata*. This market indeed resembles a bazaar (*pantopōlion*), a fair, a *souk* where one can find whatever one wants in the way of constitutions (*politeia*).

These pages of the *Republic* are filled with the language of multiple constitutional "paradigms" and of a brightly and multicolored patchwork. Beyond all the historical mutations that will have affected the concept of democracy since then and that would have to be taken into account in the most rigorous way possible, Plato already announces that "democracy" is, in the end, neither the name of a regime nor the name of a constitution. It is not a constitutional form among others. And yet there have in fact been, in addition to the monarchic, plutocratic, and tyrannical democracies of antiquity, so many so-called modern democratic regimes, regimes that at least *present themselves as* democratic, that is, under and in the name, the always Greek name, let us never forget, of democracy: democracy at once monarchic (what is called constitutional monarchy) and parliamentary (found in a large number of European nation-states), popular democracy, direct or indirect democracy, parliamentary democracy (whether presidential or not), liberal democracy, Christian democracy, social democracy, military or authoritarian democracy, and so on.

§ 3 The Other of Democracy, the "By Turns": Alternative and Alternation

Let me put forward here in a furtive, cursive, or rather cursory—although surely not frivolous—fashion, what might be called the hypothesis or the hypothec by turns Arabic and Islamic. I say Arabic *and* in turn Islamic so as to avoid the often abusive hyphen in Arab-Islamic. But I also assert "Arabic *and* Islamic" in order to refer to the Arabic literality of the language of the Koran; and I say hypothec as well as hypothesis in order to borrow from the code of borrowing, credit, lending, and transfer but also in order to evoke obstacles, difficulties, and impediments.

What is this hypothesis or hypothec? Today in what is called the European tradition (at the same time Greco-Christian and globalatinizing) that dominates the worldwide concept of the political, where the democratic becomes coextensive with the political, where the democratic realm becomes constitutive of the political realm precisely because of the indetermination and the "freedom," the "free play," of its concept, and where the democratic, having become consubstantially political in this Greco-Christian and globalatinizing tradition, appears inseparable in the modernity following the Enlightenment from an ambiguous secularization (and secularization is always ambiguous in that it frees itself from the religious, all the while remaining marked in its very concept by it, by the theological, indeed, the ontotheological), the only and very few regimes, in the supposed modernity of this situation, that *do not present themselves* as democratic are those with a theocratic Muslim government. Not all of them, to be sure, but, let me underscore this, the only regimes that *do not fashion themselves* to be democratic, the only ones that *do not present themselves* as democratic, unless I am mistaken, are statutorily linked to the Muslim faith or creed. Saudi Arabia would be a spectacular example of this. We know all too well the strategic paradoxes of the role it plays in the geopolitics and economies of American and Western democracies. On the other side, all the nation-states fundamentally linked, if not in their constitution at least in their culture, to a Jewish faith (there's only one, Israel) or Christian faith (they are too numerous to cite here, and that itself is not insignificant), but also the majority of postcolonial nation-states with a mixed religious culture, in Africa (witness South Africa and its new constitution), in Asia (especially India and China), *present themselves* today as democracies. They call themselves in Greek, and, thus, in the prevailing international juridico-political language, "democracies." Islam, or a certain Islam, would thus be the only religious or theocratic culture that can still, in fact or in principle, inspire and declare any resistance to democracy. If it does not actually resist what might be called a real or actual democratization, one whose reality may be more or less contested, it can at least resist the democratic principle, claim, or allegation, the legacy and old name of "democracy." We will return in a moment to the *double task* such a hypothec might assign one side or the other.

If one thus takes into account the link between the democratic and the demographic, if one counts, if one calculates and does the accounts, if one wants rationally to give an account, an explanation or a reason [*rendre raison*], and if one takes into account the fact that this Islam today accounts for a large number of people in the world, then this is perhaps, in the end, the greatest, if not the only, political issue of the future, the most urgent question of what remains to come for what is still called the political. The political, which is to say, in the free play and extension, in the determined indetermination, of its meaning, in the opening up of its meaning, the democratic.

My pointed reference to urgency is meant to suggest that in the necessarily finite time of politics and thus of democracy, the democracy to come certainly does not mean the right to defer, even if it be in the name of some regulative Idea, the experience or even less the injunction of democracy. I will return to this. The to-come of democracy is also, although without presence, the hic et nunc of urgency, of the injunction as absolute urgency. Even when democracy makes one wait or makes one wait for it. And I refer here to counting and to taking account of number because the question of democracy is in many respects, if not entirely, as we have known since Plato and Aristotle, the question of calculation, of numerical calculation, of equality according to number. Along with equality (*to ison*) according to value or worth (*kat'axian*), equality according to number is one of the two kinds of equality, Aristotle reminds us (*Politics*, 5.1.1301b: *to men gar arithmō*). Hence the calculation of units, that is, what are called *voices* or *votes* [*voix*] in democracy. This is one of the reasons I placed the question of number at the heart of *Politics of Friendship*. How does one count? What should count as a unit of calculation? What is a voice or a vote? What is an indivisible and countable voice or vote? So many difficult questions—difficult and more open than ever. A question of *nomos* and thus of *nemein*, of distribution or of sharing.

Perhaps this is the moment to recall an example that would appear particularly symptomatic of the current situation we have been discussing regarding Islam and democracy, namely, what happened in postcolonial Algeria in 1992 when the state and the leading party interrupted a democratic electoral process. Try to imagine what the interruption of an election between the so-called *rounds* [*tours*] of balloting might mean for a democracy. Imagine that, in France, with the National Front threatening to pull off an electoral victory, the election was suspended after the first round, that is, between the two rounds.[27] A question always of the turn or the round, of the two turns or two rounds, of the by turns, democracy hesitates always in the alternative between two sorts of alternation: the so-called normal and democratic alternation (where the power of one party, said to be republican, replaces that of another party, said to be equally republican) and the alternation that risks giving power, *modo democratico*, to the force of a party elected by the people (and so is democratic) and yet is assumed to be nondemocratic. If there was what was called in France a few weeks ago a "democratic resurgence," it was because if Le Pen had won an electoral victory the results had every chance of being accepted as legal and legitimate. Everyone was prepared for this eventuality. Indeed, Le Pen and his followers now present themselves as respectable and irreproachable democrats. When the electoral "no" to Pinochet carried the day in Chile, one of the ambiguities of the situation was that many thought that democracy had been restored. The victors claimed that the "no" to Pinochet, that is, the "yes" to democracy, would not be appropriated by anyone and would also represent the nondemocrats who said "yes" to Pinochet. The great question of modern parliamentary and representative democracy, perhaps of all democracy, in this logic of the turn or round, of the other turn or round, of the other time and thus of the other, of the *alter* in general, is that the *alternative to* democracy can always be *represented* as a democratic *alternation*. The electoral process under way in Algeria in effect risked giving power, in accordance with perfectly legal means, to a likely majority that presented itself as essentially Islamic and Islamist and to which one attributed the intention, no doubt with good reason, of wanting to change the constitution and abolish the normal functioning of democracy or the very democratization assumed to be in progress. This event is revealing and exemplary on more than one count. Indeed, on at least three.

In the first place, one might use this "Algerian" event (the rise of an Islamism considered to be antidemocratic that will have prompted the suspension of a democratic electoral process) to illustrate the hypothesis of at least a certain Islam. And this Islam, this particular one and not Islam in general (if such a thing exists), would represent the only religious culture that would have resisted up until now a European (that is, Greco-Christian and globalatinizing) process of secularization, and thus of democratization, and thus, in the strict sense, of politicization.

The two tasks I referred to a moment ago would thus be *by turns theoretical* and *political,* at the same time or successively theoretical and political.

One of the two tasks would be of the order of theoretical or hermeneutic knowledge. It would consist in an enormous, urgent, and thorough historical study of everything that does and does not authorize, in different readings of the Koranic heritage, and in its own language, the translation of a properly democratic paradigm. But it would also be essential to study and take seriously into account (something for which I have neither the time nor the competence), beginning with the Greece of Plato and Aristotle, with the political history and discourse of Athens but also of Sparta, of Hellenism and Neoplatonism, what gets passed on, transferred, translated from Europe *by* pre- and post-Koranic Arabic, as well as by Rome. I don't know how much weight to give in this whole story to the rather troubling fact that Aristotle's *Politics,* by a curious exception, was absent in the Islamic importation, reception, translation, and mediation of Greek philosophy, particularly in Ibn Ruchd (Averroës), who incorporated into his Islamic political discourse only the *Nicomachean Ethics* or, like al-Farabi, only the theme of the philosopher king from Plato's *Republic.* This latter theme seems to have been, from the point of view of what can be called Islamic "political philosophy," a locus classicus. From what I have been able to understand, certain historians and interpreters of Islam today regard the absence of Aristotle's *Politics* in the Arab philosophical corpus as having a symptomatic, if not determining, significance, just like the privilege granted by this Muslim theologico-political philosophy to the Platonic theme of the philosopher king or absolute monarch, a privilege that goes hand in hand with the severe judgment brought against democracy.

But what is not so obvious, in a still very preliminary way, is first of all the very position of this question or this *Fragestellung*. What is not so obvious is the institution of a problematic or task of this kind for the language of the Koran or for any non-Greek or non-European culture and language (non-European meaning, first of all, non-Latin since the word *democratia* began by being purely and simply latinized, imported as such from Greek into Latin). The institution of this problematic or this immense task is at once necessary and impossible. It turns in a vicious circle. It in fact presupposes, before any further study of linguistic or political translation, that there exists in Greek a proper, stable, and univocal meaning of the democratic itself. But we are beginning to suspect that this is not the case. For it is perhaps a question here of an essence without essence that, under the same name, and through a certain concept, would have no aim. It would thus be a matter of a concept without concept. That said, this fundamental reservation should not destroy the possibility and necessity of a serious and systematic study of the *references* to democracy, of the democratic *legacy* and claim or *allegation*, whether under this name or under another assumed to be its equivalent, in the ancient, and especially recent, history of Arab nation-states, and more generally in societies of Islamic culture. From the little I know, it seems that in these Arab and/or Islamic spaces such a reference to democracy will have undergone a great deal of turmoil. Whether positive or negative, whether purely rhetorical or not (although where, one will rightly ask, does reference to democracy not entail the rhetorical abuse of a claim or allegation?), democratic or democratizing discourse will have been vexed by all sorts of contradictions in Arab or Islamic lands, and it will have given rise to all sorts of complex strategies.

What, then, would be the other task, the other responsibility? It would be explicitly political, the preceding one being so only implicitly or indirectly. For whoever, by hypothesis, considers him- or herself a friend of democracy in the world and not only in his or her own country (and we will later come to this cosmopolitical dimension of a universal democracy, perhaps even independent of the nation-state structure), the task would consist in doing everything possible to join forces with all those who, and first of all in the Islamic world, fight not only for the secularization of the political (however ambiguous this secularization remains), for the emergence of a laic subjectivity, but also for an interpretation of the Koranic heritage that privileges, from the inside as it were, the democratic virtualities that are probably not any more apparent and readable at first glance, and readable under this name, than they were in the Old and New Testaments.

In the second place, the suspension of the electoral process in Algeria would be, from almost every perspective, typical of all the assaults on democracy in the name of democracy. The Algerian government and a large part, although not a majority, of the Algerian people (as well as people outside Algeria) thought that the electoral process under way would lead democratically to the end of democracy. They thus preferred to put an end to it themselves. They decided in a sovereign fashion to suspend, at least provisionally, democracy *for its own good*, so as to take care of it, so as to immunize it against a much worse and very likely assault. By definition, the value of this strategy can never be either confirmed or confuted. For such a strategic and sovereign decision is not like a reversible laboratory experiment: it effects with no turning back the process to be analyzed. In any case the hypothesis here is that of a taking of power or, rather, of a transferring of power (*kratos*) to a people (*dēmos*) who, in its electoral majority and following democratic procedures, would not have been able to avoid the destruction of democracy itself. Hence a certain suicide of democracy. Democracy has always been suicidal, and if there is a to-come for it, it is only on the condition of thinking life otherwise, life and the force of life. That is why I insisted earlier on the fact that pure Actuality is determined by Aristotle as a life.

There is something paradigmatic in this autoimmune suicide: fascist and Nazi totalitarianisms came into power or ascended to power through formally normal and formally democratic electoral processes. Since plebs are also a form of the people or the *dēmos*, we shall leave open here all the formidable questions regarding the legitimacy or democratic legality of the plebiscite—along with the demagogy of the leader, *Führer*, or *Duce*—

as well as questions regarding the many different forms of direct or non-representative democracy, the referendum, elections with direct, universal suffrage, and so on. As for this second point, the aporia in its general form has to do with freedom itself, with the freedom at play in the concept of democracy: must a democracy leave free and in a position to exercise power those who risk mounting an assault on democratic freedoms and putting an end to democratic freedom in the name of democracy and of the majority that they might actually be able to rally round to their cause? Who, then, can take it upon him- or herself, and with what means, to speak from one side or another of this front, of democracy *itself*, of *authentic* democracy *properly speaking*, when it is precisely the concept of democracy *itself*, in its univocal and proper meaning, that is presently and forever lacking? When assured of a numerical majority, the worst enemies of democratic freedom can, by a plausible rhetorical simulacrum (and even the most fanatical Islamists do this on occasion), present themselves as staunch democrats. That is one of the many perverse and autoimmune effects of the axiomatic developed already in Plato and Aristotle. It has to do with the perversity of a double couple: on the one hand, the couple "freedom and equality" and, on the other, the couple "equality according to number and equality according to worth [*esti de ditton to ison, to men gar arithmō, to de kat'axian estin*]." For in the name of one couple, the couple made up of freedom and equality, one agrees to a law of number or to the law of numbers (equality according to number) that ends up destroying both couples: both the couple made up of the two equalities (equality according to worth and equality according to number) and the couple equality-freedom.

Third, and finally, the sending, the sending that kicks off [*coup d'envoi*] democracy, calls for a sending off [*renvoi*]. The sending [*envoi*] as emission, as a mission that puts one on the path [*voie*], the sending as legacy, is here called, already at the opening send-off [*envoi*], a sending off or re-mission [*renvoi*]. *Renvoi* as reprieve or deferral as well as exclusion, at the same time murder and suicide. By following the guiding thread of this exemplary event, we might attempt an even more powerful formalization. We have here not one but a whole series of examples of an autoimmune pervertibility of democracy: colonization and decolonization were both autoimmune experiences wherein the violent imposition of a culture and political language that were supposed to be in line with a Greco-European political ideal (a postrevolutionary, constitutional monarchy at the time of colonization, then a French—and later an Algerian—republic and democracy) ended up producing exactly the opposite of democracy (French Algeria), which then helped fuel a so-called civil war, one that was really a war for independence waged in the very name of the political ideals extolled by the colonial power. The new power *itself* then had to interrupt the democratization under way; it had to interrupt a normal electoral process in order to save a democracy threatened by the sworn enemies of democracy. To immunize itself, to protect itself against the aggressor (whether from within or without), democracy thus secreted its enemies on both sides of the front so that its only apparent options remained murder and suicide; but the murder was already turning into suicide, and the suicide, as always, let itself be translated into murder.

I tried to formalize the general law of this autoimmune process in "Faith and Knowledge," a text that initially grew out of a conversation about forgiveness and went on to speak about a "democracy to come" in relation to the secret, forgiveness, and unconditionality in general, as a concept that exceeds the juridico-political sphere and yet, from the inside and the outside, is bound up with it.[28] The formalization of this autoimmune law was there carried out around the *community* as *auto-co-immunity* (the common of community having in common the same duty or charge [*munus*] as the immune), as well as the auto-co-immunity of humanity—and particularly the autoimmune humanitarian. I could thus without much difficulty, although I will not do so here in the interest of time, inscribe the category of the autoimmune into the series of both older and more recent discourses on the *double bind* and the aporia. Although *aporia*, *double bind*, and *autoimmune process* are not exactly synonyms, what they have in common, what they are all, precisely, charged with, is, more than an internal contradiction, an indecidability, that is, an internal-external, nondialectizable antinomy that risks paralyzing and thus calls for the event of the interruptive decision.

Now, the autoimmune process we have been analyzing within democracy consists always in a renvoi, a referral or deferral, a sending or putting off. The figure of the renvoi belongs to the schema of space and time, to what I had thematized with such insistence long ago under the name *spacing* as the becoming-space of time or the becoming-time of space. The values of the trace or of the renvoi, like those of différance, are inseparable from it. Here, the democratic renvoi spaces and diffracts more than one logic and more than one semantic schema.

(a) Operating in space, the autoimmune topology always dictates that democracy be *sent off* [*renvoyer*] elsewhere, that it be excluded or rejected, expelled under the pretext of protecting it on the inside by expelling, rejecting, or sending off to the outside the domestic enemies of democracy. It can, for example, send them back home, away from the voting booths and far from public space, indeed far from the national territory, or else it can take away their freedom of movement and speech, or else interrupt the electoral process or exclude the sworn enemies of democracy from that process. Now, because of the indecidability linked to this autoimmune logic, in the kind of modern, liberal, parliamentary democracy we are familiar with, that is, one that takes the form of a nation-state (even if Schmitt refused to grant the title of democracy to liberal democracy), one will never actually be able to "prove" that there is more democracy in granting or in refusing the right to vote to immigrants, notably those who live and work in the national territory, nor that there is more or less democracy in a straight majority vote as opposed to proportional voting; both forms of voting are democratic, and yet both also protect their democratic character through exclusion, through some renvoi; for the force of the *dēmos*, the force of demo*cracy*, commits it, in the name of universal equality, to representing not only the greatest force of the greatest number, the majority of citizens considered of age, but also the weakness of the weak, minors, minorities, the poor, and all those throughout the world who call out in suffering for a legitimately infinite extension of what are called *human* rights. One electoral law is thus always at the same time more and less democratic than another; it is the force of force, a weakness of force and the force of a weakness; which means that democracy protects itself and maintains itself precisely by limiting and threatening itself. Depending on the governing syntax or grammar, the inevitable *renvoi* can signify simultaneously or by turns a sending off *of* the other through exclusion and the sending off or referral *to* the other, respect for the foreigner or for the alterity of the other. It could be shown concretely, with regard, for example, to the problems of immigration, whether with or without assimilation and integration, that these two contradictory movements of renvoi, of sending off, haunt and autoimmunize one another by turns.

(b) But since the renvoi operates in time as well, autoimmunity also calls for *putting off* [*renvoyer*] until later the elections and the advent of democracy. This double renvoi (sending off—or to—the other and putting off, adjournment) is an autoimmune necessity inscribed *right onto* [*à même*] democracy, right onto the concept of a democracy without concept, a democracy devoid of sameness and ipseity, a democracy whose concept remains free, like a disengaged clutch, *freewheeling*, in the free play of its indetermination; it is inscribed right onto this thing or this cause that, precisely under the name of democracy, is never properly what it is, never *itself*. For what is lacking in democracy is proper meaning, the very [*même*] meaning of the selfsame [*même* (*ipse*, *metipse*, *metipsissimus*, *meisme*), the it-self [*soi-même*], the selfsame, the properly selfsame of the it-self. Democracy is defined, as is the very ideal of democracy, by this lack of the proper and the selfsame. And so it is defined only by turns, by tropes, by tropism. We could multiply ad infinitum these examples, and I mean ad infinitum, since they are produced by democracy itself. By democracy itself, which is to say, I insist again, by that which from within it both affirms *and* defies the proper, the it-self, the selfsameness of the same [*même*] (from *meisme*, *metipse* in Old French, *medesimo* in Italian, *mesmo* in Portuguese, *mismo* in Spanish), and thus truth, the truth of a democracy that would correspond to the adequation or the unveiling manifestation of an essence, of the very essence of democracy, of *true* democracy, authentic democracy, democracy *itself*, according to an *idea* of democracy. What is lacking is not only, as John Caputo proposes, *The Very Idea of "à venir"* but *the very idea of democracy*.[29] a certain true idea of democratic truth. I will later try to suggest that the "democracy to come" has to do neither with the *constitutive* (with what Plato would call the paradigmatic) nor with the *regulative* (in the Kantian sense of a regulative Idea). At this point we are simply examining the implications of what Plato says when he speaks of a democratic freedom or license (something that would thus be proper to what has nothing proper to it) that would authorize every constitution or paradigm and, thus, every interpretation. Which amounts to saying, in a strictly Platonic sense, that there is no absolute paradigm, whether constitutive or constitutional, no absolutely intelligible idea, no *eidos*, no *idea* of democracy. And so, in the final analysis, no democratic ideal. For even if there were one, and wherever there would be one, this "there is" would remain aporetic, under a double or autoimmune constraint. This is not the first or the last word of some democracy to come, even if it is a necessary or obligatory word or passage, an obligation for the democracy to come.

The democracy to come: if these words still have any *meaning* (but I am not so sure they do, and I am not sure that everything can be reduced here to a question of *meaning*), it cannot be reduced to an idea or democratic

ideal in the "by turns" of the renvoi. For *renvoi* signifies putting off to
later, the reprieve [*sursis*] that remits or defers [*sursoit*] democracy until the
next resurgence [*sursaut*] or until the next turn or round; it suggests the
incompletion and essential delay, the self-inadequation of every present
and presentable democracy, in other words, the interminable adjournment of the present of democracy. (The second part of *The Other Heading*, one of the first texts in which I used the expression "democracy to
come," was entitled, back in 1989, "Call It a Day for Democracy," or
"Democracy Adjourned," so as to suggest at once the deferring of a delay,
a postponement or reprieve, but also the phenomenal day [*jour*], the lu-
minous and shining *phainesthai* of the *res republica* or the Enlightenment.)
This renvoi of democracy is thus still very much related to différance. Or
if you prefer, this democracy as the sending off of the putting off, as the
emission of remission [*envoi du renvoi*], sends us or refers us back [*renvoie*]
to différance. But not only to différance as deferral, as the turn of a detour
[*tour du détour*], as a path that is turned aside [*voie détournée*], as adjournment in the economy of the same. For what is also and at the same time
at stake—and marked by this same word in *différance*—is différance as
reference or referral [*renvoi*] to the other, that is, as the undeniable, and I
underscore *undeniable*, experience of the alterity of the other, of heterogeneity, of the singular, the not-same, the different, the dissymmetric, the
heteronomous.

I underscore *undeniable* to suggest *only deniable*, the only protective recourse being that of a send-off [*renvoi*] through denial. In both senses of
différance, then, democracy is differential; it is *différance, renvoi*, and spacing. That is why, let me repeat, the theme of spacing, the theme of the interval or the gap, of the trace as gap [*écart*], of the becoming-space of time
or the becoming-time of space, plays such an important role as early as *Of
Grammatology* and "Différance."[30]

Democracy is what it is only in the différance by which it defers itself
and differs from itself. It is what it is only by spacing itself beyond being
and even beyond ontological difference; it is (without being) equal and
proper to itself only insofar as it is inadequate and improper, at the same
time behind and ahead of itself, behind and ahead of the Sameness and
Oneness of itself; it is thus interminable in its incompletion beyond all de-
terminate forms of incompletion, beyond all the limitations in areas as
different as the right to vote (for example in its extension to women—but
starting when?—to minors—but starting at what age?—or to foreign-

ers—but which ones and on what lands?—to cite at random just a few exemplary problems from among so many other similar ones), the freedom of the press, the end of social inequalities throughout the world, the right to work, or any number of other rights. Such limitations thus involve the entire history of a right or a law (whether national or international) that is always unequal to justice, democracy seeking its place only at the unstable and unlocatable border between law and justice, that is, between the political and the ultrapolitical. That is why, once again, it is not certain that "democracy" is a political concept through and through. (I leave open here the place for an endless discussion of and with Schmitt.)

I recall this in passing, with a quick turn of hand, in an algebraic and telegraphic fashion, simply to recall that there never was in the 1980s or 1990s, as has sometimes been claimed, a *political turn* or *ethical turn* in "deconstruction," at least not as I experience it. The thinking of the political has always been a thinking of différance and the thinking of différance always a thinking *of* the political, of the contour and limits of the political, especially around the enigma or the autoimmune *double bind* of the democratic. That is not to say, indeed quite the contrary, that nothing new happens between, say, 1965 and 1990. But what happens remains without relation or resemblance to what the figure that I continue to privilege here might lead one to imagine, that is, the figure of a "turn," of a *Kehre* or turning. If a "turning" turns by "veering" round a curve or by forcing one, like wind in one's sails, to "veer" away or change tack, then the trope of turning turns poorly or turns bad, turns into the wrong image. For it diverts thought or turns it away from what remains to be thought; it ignores or runs counter to the thought of the very thing that remains to be thought. If every send-off [*renvoi*] is differantial, and if the trace is a synonym for this send-off, then there is always some trace of democracy; indeed every trace is a trace of democracy. Of democracy there could only be but a trace. It is in this sense that I will later attempt a rereading of the syntagma "democracy to come."

Let us come back for just a moment to more obvious and current examples. Since I am speaking English when I say "*the very idea of democracy,*" is there, after the Algerian example, a more visibly autoimmune process than the one seen in the aftermath of what is called "September 11" (in the United States but no doubt elsewhere as well)? To follow just one among so many other possible threads in a reflection on September

11, we see an American administration, potentially followed by others in Europe and in the rest of the world, claiming that in the war it is waging against the "axis of evil," against the enemies of freedom and the assassins of democracy throughout the world, it must restrict within its own country certain so-called democratic freedoms and the exercise of certain rights by, for example, increasing the powers of police investigations and interrogations, without anyone, any democrat, being really able to oppose such measures. One can thus do little more than regret some particular abuse in the a priori abusive use of the force by which a democracy defends itself against its enemies, justifies or defends itself, of or from itself, against its potential enemies. It must thus come to resemble these enemies, to corrupt itself and threaten itself in order to protect itself against their threats. Inversely, antithetically, so to speak, it is perhaps because the United States has a culture and a system of law that are largely democratic that it was able to open itself up and expose its greatest vulnerability to immigrants, to, for example, pilots in training, experienced and suicidal "terrorists" who, before turning against others but also against themselves the aerial bombs that they had become, and before hurling them by hurling themselves into the two World Trade Towers, were trained on the sovereign soil of the United States, under the nose of the CIA and the FBI, perhaps not without some autoimmune consent on the part of an administration with at once more and less foresight than one tends to think when it is faced with what is claimed to be a major, unforeseeable event. The "terrorists" are sometimes American citizens, and some of those of September 11 might have been; they received help in any case from American citizens; they took American airplanes, took over the controls and took to the air in American airplanes, and took off from American airports.

There are thus at least two reasons to turn here toward freedom (*eleutheria* or *exousia*). The first has to do with a certain vacancy or disengagement, the free wheel or semantic indecision at the center of *dēmokratia*. Democracy could not gather itself around the presence of an axial and univocal meaning that does not destroy itself and get carried away with itself. The second reason should orient us toward all the places of thought where the interpretation, indeed the reinterpretation, of freedom, of what "freedom" means, risks disrupting the legacy and the allegation or claim, the sending, of "democracy." Wherever freedom is no longer determined as power, mastery, or force, or even as a faculty, as a possibility of the "I can" (*Facultas, Kraft, Möglichkeit,* or *Vermögen*), the evocation and evaluation of democracy as the power of the *dēmos* begins to tremble. If one values freedom in general, before any interpretation, then one should no longer be afraid to speak without or against democracy. Is the right to speak without taking sides *for* democracy, that is, without committing oneself to it, more or less democratic? Is democracy that which assures the right to think and thus to act without it or against it? Yes or no? Although there are today, apart from the Arab and Islamic exception we spoke of earlier, fewer and fewer people in the world who dare speak against democracy (the campaign posters of Le Pen claimed allegiance to both the republic and democracy, two concepts often opposed in France in an interesting but artificial way, as if one could oppose a concern for the equality of all before universal law to the obligation to concern oneself with differences, minorities, and all sorts of identities—those of community, culture, religion, or sexuality—a huge problem that we must set aside for the moment); even though almost everybody outside a certain Arab and Islamic world at least claims a certain democratism, we would do well to recall that there are in the end rather few philosophical discourses, assuming there are any at all, in the long tradition that runs from Plato to Heidegger, that have without any reservations taken the side of democracy. In this sense democratism in philosophy is something rather rare and, in the end, very modern. And perhaps not even very philosophical. Why? This democratism was, as we know, the constant target of Nietzsche, whether because of the specific forms it took in modernity or because of its genealogy in the ethico-religious, that is, Jewish, Christian, and especially Pauline perversion that turns weakness into force. More than any other form of democracy, more than social democracy or popular democracy, a Christian democracy should be welcoming to the enemies of democracy; it should turn them the other cheek, offer hospitality, grant freedom of expression and the right to vote to antidemocrats, something in conformity with a certain hyperbolic essence, an essence more autoimmune than ever, of *democracy itself,* if "itself" there ever is, if ever there is a democracy and thus a Christian democracy worthy of this name.

§ 4   Mastery and Measure

Restricting myself here to a thinking of freedom that calls into question in a deconstructive fashion the thinking of freedom as force, mastery, faculty, and so on, I will today take up neither the example of Heidegger—of whom the least that can be said is that his profound reinterpretation of freedom did not make of him a democrat—nor the example of Levinas, who not only never gave in to a democratizing rhetoric but actually subjected or subordinated freedom in accordance with a responsibility that makes me the hostage of the other in an experience of absolute heteronomy, although without servitude. Indeed Levinas placed responsibility before and above "difficult freedom."

Let us instead consider, closer to us, the remarkable example of *The Experience of Freedom*.[31] This great book of Jean-Luc Nancy's analyzes "Freedom as Thing, Force, and Gaze." That is in fact the title of a chapter. Following the two chapters "The Space Left Free by Heidegger" and "The Free Thinking of Freedom," Nancy wishes to open the way back to a freedom that "cannot be presented as the autonomy of a subjectivity in charge of itself and of its decisions, evolving freely and in perfect independence from every obstacle" (*EF*, 66).

That's the opening sentence of chapter 7, "Sharing Freedom: Equality, Fraternity, Justice," to which I must, in a terribly unjust way, or let us say more and less unjust way, grant some privilege. More unjust because I do not have the time for a more complete, refined, and thorough reading of everything that informs, precedes, and follows this chapter and, even worse, because I cannot even do justice to the entire chapter itself. But this will also be, I hope, a bit less disloyal and unjust because it seems legitimate, indeed fair, to privilege here today in this context a chapter that names democracy and even speaks of "what is lacking today, and lacking up until now in the philosophy of democracy" (*EF*, 79).

From a historical, indeed epochal, point of view, we should first dispel a possible misunderstanding with regard to the first sentence I just cited. It speaks of a "freedom" that "cannot be presented as the autonomy of a subjectivity in charge of itself and of its decisions." So firmly stated, the reference to a "subjectivity in charge of itself" might lead us to think that what is being contested, delimited, indeed deconstructed by Nancy is the modern, Cartesian or post-Cartesian, figure of a freedom of the subject, of freedom as characteristic, faculty, power, or attribute of a subject (even though, contrary to what is often believed, Descartes never elaborated a philosophical concept of the subject and this word is not part of his vocabulary). We might thus be led to believe that what is being contested or deconstructed is this freedom as force, as mastery or sovereignty, as the sovereign power over oneself, a freedom that indeed seems presupposed by every discourse of law, politics, or democracy since the seventeenth century.

But leaving aside the word *subjectivity*, whose history I will not recount here (but which, let me repeat, not only is not Cartesian but does not even really belong to immediately post-Cartesian, Enlightenment philosophers before Kant), we would not be able to limit (and Nancy does not explicitly do so) this definition of freedom to the modern epoch of this so-called subjectivity, this definition of freedom as a faculty "in charge of itself and of its decisions," as the sovereign power to do as one pleases, in short, the power to attain "perfect independence." Plato and Aristotle, to mention just them, would have surely accepted the definition or presentation of freedom as power, mastery, and independence. That is the definition at work in Plato's *Republic* and in Aristotle's *Politics*. What Nancy calls into question is thus an entire philosophy or ontology of freedom. Never one to shrink from a challenge, he dares to call into question this *entire* political ontology of freedom, while still retaining the word, the sending [*l'envoi*] of the word, and devoting an entire book to it. I, who have always lacked his temerity, have been led by the same deconstructive questioning of the political ontology of freedom to treat this word with some caution, to use it guardedly, indeed sparingly, in a reserved, parsimonious, and circumspect manner. I've always done so with some concern, in bad conscience, or so as to give myself, from time to time and in very delimited contexts determined by the classical code, politico-democratic good conscience.

In political philosophy the dominant discourse about democracy presupposes this freedom as power, faculty, or the ability to act, the force or strength, in short, to do as one pleases, the energy of an intentional and deciding will. It is thus difficult to see, and this is what remains to be thought, how another experience of freedom might found in an immediate, continuous, and effective way what would still be called a demo*cratic* politics or a demo*cratic* political philosophy.

That is one of the reasons why Heidegger, who also tried to think the "free" of freedom otherwise, was least of all a democrat. He had no desire to be one. But this is also the reason why Nancy, whom we all suspect of having such a democratic desire, acknowledges the difficulty but articulates it, and not without hope, around a certain "up until now." Up until now, to be sure, there has been no philosophy of democracy; up until now the thinking necessary for this philosophy, namely, a certain thinking of freedom, has been "lacking," as it has been lacking for the "political" in general. No doubt. But there is the future, there is a future, and in the future the future might differentiate between, on the one hand, "democracy" (Nancy tells us it is possible that it is no longer possible to think anything under this name: he does not say that it will be impossible, but he tells us, and we must weigh his words, that it is possible that it be "no longer possible") and, on the other, the "political," for which it is perhaps possible, possibly possible, to displace the concept and continue to mobilize the name. Uncertain myself whether we can separate these two avenues of the future, namely, democracy and the political, these two regimes of the possible, of the possibly impossible and the possibly possible (and it will be on these various "possibles" that I will eventually put all the weight of my question), I would prefer to cite word for word a long passage from Nancy.

To understand more fully the first sentence of this passage, which makes reference to a "space-time of initiality" (Nancy speaks above of "an initiality of being") (*EF*, 78), we must first clarify at least one premise, that of sharing [*partage*] as spacing.[32] Earlier in *The Experience of Freedom* it is a question of determining the "who," that is, the whoever of the "*who* is free," who "*exists* free," without necessarily "*being* free" (this "who" would thus no longer be a subject or a subjectivity in charge of its will and decisions). To determine this "who," Nancy again mobilizes, but puts to work otherwise, both the Heideggerian concept of *Jemeinigkeit*, which is taken in the direction of a thinking of a singularity of the *time*, of the *each time* as *other time*, and the concept of the "ipseity of singularity." For reasons I have already stated and could develop at greater length, I would have concerns and reservations about both mineness and ipseity (which both risk saving, at least surreptitiously, the "I can" of my own freedom, of the freedom that is mine, of the freedom of the I-myself, indeed of the voluntary-conscious-intentional-deciding-I-myself, the "I can," let's just say, of classical freedom). I would thus be suspicious of both these themes, did Nancy not in fact introduce each time, in a determinative but also ruinous, autoimmune fashion, the divisibility of a sharing, that is, the interval or trace of a spacing. For what I call the autoimmune consists not only in harming or ruining oneself, indeed in destroying one's own protections, and in doing so oneself, committing suicide or threatening to do so, but, more seriously still, and through this, in threatening the I [*moi*] or the self [*soi*], the *ego* or the *autos*, ipseity itself, compromising the immunity of the *autos* itself: it consists not only in compromising oneself [*s'auto-entamer*] but in compromising the self, the *autos*—and thus ipseity. It consists not only in committing suicide but in compromising *sui*- or *self*-referentiality, the *self* or *sui*- of suicide itself. Autoimmunity is more or less suicidal, but, more seriously still, it threatens always to rob suicide itself of its meaning and supposed integrity.

But returning to Nancy's gesture: even when he insists on holding on to the value of ipseity, indeed of solipsism, he acknowledges the share of, or the part played by, an essential sharing, at once partition and participation, something possible only on the basis of an irreducible spacing. Spacing, he says, is the "general 'form' . . . of existence" (*EF*, 145). He even speaks of the withdrawal of an aseity of being, of the being itself by itself of being in the sharing of ipseity:

> [I]n solitude and even in solipsism—at least understood as a *sola ipsa* of singularity—ipseity is constituted by and as sharing. This means that *the ipseity of singularity has as its essence the withdrawal of the aseity of being*. Also, the being of its "self" [the quotation marks around "self" tell the whole story about the difficulty of sustaining any "self" at all] is what remains "self" when nothing comes back to itself. (*EF*, 70)

End or interruption of the circle, a caesura of the turn in the return to self, even when the self "remains self." Even when the self remains self, its aseity and its ipseity withdraw. This sharing of freedom is spacing: "freedom is the discrete play of the interval, offering the space of play wherein the 'each time' takes place: the possibility of an irreducible singularity occurring . . . that is already free in the sense that it occurs in the free space and spacing of time where the singular *one time* is only possible. . . . Freedom is that which spaces and singularizes" (*EF*, 68). "[T]he space of existences is their spacing" (*EF*, 69). "Freedom . . . throws the subject into the space of the sharing of being. Freedom is the specific logic of the access to the self outside of itself in a spacing, each time singular, of being. . . . 'Spacing space' would mean keeping it as space and as the sharing of being, in order *indefinitely to share the sharing* of singularities" (*EF*, 70–71). "Free space is opened" (*EF*, 74).

Having recalled this essential premise, namely, sharing as *spacing* (or, as I would say, as space-time, the becoming-space of time or becoming-time of space), I can now cite in a more intelligible way the passage concerning what is lacking "up until now" in the philosophy of democracy and what distinguishes the "democratic" from the "political" as the possibly impossible or the possibly possible. The democratic is possibly impossible, and the political possibly possible. The passage opens with a reference to birth, to the beginning and the initiality that make free:

> It is the simultaneous breaking into the interior of the individual and of the community, which opens the specific space-time of initiality. What is lacking today [and we must give all the force and chance of an enigma to this *today*: where and when is today, the day of today, for the lack in question? This today, as you will see and hear, will let itself be determined by a just as enigmatic "up until now," one that, like the today, presupposes that we have already begun to go beyond this "up until now," so that the today is already yesterday], and lacking up until now in the philosophy of democracy, is the thought of this initiality, before or beyond the safeguarding of freedoms considered to be established freedoms (from nature or by right). It is possible that for this reason it may no longer even be possible, in the future, to think in terms of "democracy," and it is possible that this also signifies a general displacement of "the political," a word we have provisionally mobilized here: perhaps a liberation of the political itself. All things considered, what is lacking is a thinking of the freedom that is not established, but that *takes itself* in the act of its beginning and its recommencement. This remains for us to consider, perhaps beyond our entire political tradition—and yet in some ways the direction of this imperative has already been thought by at least one part of the revolutionary tradition. (*EF*, 78–79)

We see here a subtle play between the "today" and the "up until now," the improbable space of what remains to be thought even though it will have already begun to be thought, perhaps, possibly, even if it has been impossible up until now, and thought not by the revolution but by "at least one part of the revolutionary tradition." What is a tradition? A revolution? A revolutionary tradition? At least one part of a revolutionary tradition? In any case, a revolutionary tradition, which is not limited to any particular revolution, is already enormous and difficult to *measure*.

Indeed it is precisely the question of measure that marks the greatest difficulty, the aporicity, in fact, whether acknowledged or not, of this chapter—and precisely in relation to democracy. This difficulty is hardly an objection on my part to Nancy; it is, so to speak, part of the thing or the cause itself, part of the same impossibility of the thing, and the same could be said for the wonderful ambiguity of the word *partage*, sharing, with all its explosive consequences. The difficulty arises when one must determine politically, indeed democratically (although one could just as well say here juridically and ethically), the spacing of a presubjective or precratic freedom, one that is all the more unconditional, immense, immeasurable [*démesurée*], incommensurable, incalculable, unappropriable insofar as it "can in no way," as says Nancy, "take the form of a property" (*EF*, 70) and actually consists, Nancy repeats, outdoing himself with each formulation, in exceeding all measure. It is the incommensurable itself. "Freedom *measures itself against nothing*," he emphasizes; or again, "Freedom: to measure oneself against the nothing" (*EF*, 71). The whole difficulty will be located in the injunction of the sharing, in the injunction to share the incommensurable in a just, equitable, equal, and measured fashion. In this difficulty, which I believe to be more difficult than a difficulty, I find all the traits of the impossible itself. Nancy will give to this sharing of the incommensurable, and I will want to return to this over and over, a name that is to my eyes somewhat suspect: *fraternity*. He writes, at the end of a line of thought that I will return to in a moment: "Fraternity is equality in the sharing of the incommensurable" (*EF*, 72).

There is nothing new in what I call here the difficulty encountered by Nancy, and what I thus prefer to name the impossible, the impossible wager, the impossible sending or missive, the impossible mission, the impossible as the only possibility and as the condition of possibility. It is the persistence, the ineluctable return, in truth, of a sort of aporia or, if you prefer, of an antinomy at the heart of every -nomy, that is, at the source of every autoimmune process. This antinomy at the heart of the democratic has long been recognized. It is classical and canonical; it is the one between freedom and equality—that constitutive and diabolical couple of democracy. I would translate this into my own language by saying that equality tends to introduce measure and calculation (and thus conditionality) whereas freedom is by essence unconditional, indivisible, heterogeneous to calculation and to measure. Aristotle had already recognized this when, even before distinguishing between equality according to number, that is, numerical equality, and equality according to worth, and thus according to proportion or *logos* (*kat'axian de to tōi logōi*), he had formulated what looks to me like the very aporia of democracy, or more precisely, of the *dēmos* itself (*Politics* 1301b, 32–33). How is the people, the *dēmos* itself, born? In the passage I am about to cite, on the birth of the *dēmos*, the translation says somewhat abusively "democracy" there where Aristotle says only *dēmos*. It is found in book 5 of the *Politics*. Here is a commonly cited translation: "Thus democracy [here, the *dēmos*] arose [*egeneto*: was born] from men's thinking that if they are equal in any respect they are equal absolutely [*oiesthai haplōs isous einai*] (for they suppose that because they are all alike free [*hoti gar eleutheroi pantes homoiōs*] they are equal absolutely)" (1301a, 29–31).

The turns of this single sentence are nothing short of vertiginous. First, the birth of the *dēmos* is related to a belief, an imagining, a presumption or presupposition, a hasty evaluation, a "supposes that" that accredits or gives credit—and there is no democracy without credit, indeed without an act of faith: because they are equal in one respect, says Aristotle, they believe, they imagine themselves (*oiesthai*), they represent themselves as being equal absolutely. There is thus confusion with regard to equality; and then, because they are alike (*homoiōs*) free, they believe, they think, they judge (*nomizousin*), they presume that they are equal absolutely. The double passage to absolute equality is each time the result of a belief, of credit, of an evaluation or a presumption, indeed of a speculation that Aristotle obviously considers unjustified. But what is most ominous about this birth of the *dēmos* is not the contradiction, the antimony or simple aporia, if I can put it this way, between two terms that are in fact two laws: freedom and equality. Nor is it the tension between two equalities (numerical equality and equality according to worth or proportion [*logos*]). It is that equality is not always an opposing or rival term *beside, facing,* or *around* freedom, like a calculable measure (according to number or according to *logos*) beside, facing, or around an incommensurable, incalculable, and universal freedom. Not at all. As soon as everyone (or anyone—and we will return later to this question of the anyone) is equally (*homoiōs*) free, equality becomes an integral part of freedom and is thus no longer calculable. This equality in freedom no longer has anything to do with numerical equality or equality according to worth, proportion or *logos*. It is itself an incalculable and incommensurable equality; it is the unconditional condition of freedom, its sharing, if you will. And the antinomy is not simply born of a presumption or poised *between* equality and freedom. It is already inherent to the very concept of isonomy, which includes within itself several unequal kinds of equality: the two calculable equalities (numerical or according to worth or a proportional *logos*), of course, but also the incalculable equality in a freedom that is alike for all. Moreover, the two calculable equalities lend themselves to and call for calculation only for living beings who are also assumed to be free, that is, equally endowed with freedoms, who are, incommensurably, incalculably, unconditionally equal in their freedom.

It is this aporia that is being perpetuated still "today," "up until now," but without being acknowledged as such, if not in formulations that are themselves aporetic, at least in what Nancy tells us of equality and the sharing of freedom.

Keeping within the limits that must constrain my reading of Nancy, particularly those of time, I would assign two places, so to speak, if not two paths, to this aporia. Let me call them two *situations*. In the first I can only subscribe and share: or at least, I would join Nancy in what remains nonetheless a terrible difficulty to endure, an unsolvable difficulty, one that I will not dissimulate, or at least will dissimulate less than he does. I give it the name aporia, with all the negative and affirmative consequences that might ensue, the aporia being the condition of possibility and impossibility of responsibility. Nancy would not, I believe, speak of aporia, even if his formulations actually resemble, at least to my eyes, what I call aporia. In the second situation, and I will explain myself on this later, I will be less inclined to subscribe and to share, even though my reservations are not strictly speaking objections and might look like a mere quibbling over terms, indeed a brotherly spat, as an irenist might say, since it touches on the brother and on the question of fraternity. One of the many reasons I am wary of the brother, and particularly of whatever pacifying connotations might be heard in the expression "brotherly spat," is that there is no worse war than that between enemy brothers. There is never any war, and never any danger for the democracy to come, except where there are brothers. More precisely: not where *there are brothers* (there will always be brothers, that's not what's wrong, there's no wrong in that), but where the fraternity of brothers *dictates the law*, where a *political dictatorship* of fraternocracy comes to be imposed.

First situation. For this aporia that I endure, and endure without silencing it, so close to Nancy, who does not name it as such, I would find for the sake of economy in the paragraph I am about to read two *markers*. What they have in common—and that is why I call them markers—is that they both signify or inscribe a certain problem in silence, silencing it thus by saying it, denying it by admitting it. These markers are first of all parentheses (sentences that, so to speak, place the whole difficulty into parentheses), and then quotation marks (three words whose meaning is suspended between quotation marks because they are inadequate, inadequate to themselves and to their standard meaning, words that Nancy uses less than he mentions, and so uses without using, disavowing them, denying them, refusing to accredit them at the very moment he is nonetheless still giving them some credit). Here is the paragraph in question. I will emphasize by turns the parentheses and the quotation marks, the latter in fact appearing two out of three times in a sentence within parentheses. It is still a question—and in equal measures—of the spacing of space and of the sharing, a question of the equality of singularities. Nancy writes:

> Ontological sharing, or the singularity of being, opens the space that only freedom is able, not to "fill," but properly to space. "Spacing space" would mean keeping it as space and as the sharing of being, in order *indefinitely to share the sharing* of singularities.
>
> This is also why, as the *logos* of sharing [I assume that *logos* refers at once to the "onto*logical* sharing" mentioned above and to *logos* in the sense of *nomos*, distribution and proportionality, in the sense that Aristotle says "*logō*" (*tō logō*) for equality according to proportion], freedom is immediately linked to equality, or, better still, it is immediately *equal to equality*. Equality does not consist in a commensurability of subjects in relation to some unit of measure. It is the equality of singularities in the incommensurability of freedom [and here is the parenthesis, with its protestation in the form of an eloquent denial] (which does not impede the necessity of having a technical measure of equality, and consequently also of justice, which actually makes possible, under given conditions, access to the incommensurable). [This parenthesis thus reintroduces,

to say it all too briefly, determination, the technical, measure, conditionality, and, let's not dissimulate it, the political and the democratic themselves, where the unconditional and unlimited incommensurability of freedom, now rethought, had made them both, at the very least, indeterminable.] For its part, this incommensurability does not mean that each individual possesses an unlimited right to exercise his will [and here is the second parenthesis, quotation marks included] (moreover, if "each" designates the individual, how could such a right be constructed in relation to the singularities that divide the individual himself and in accordance with which he exists? One would first need to learn how to think the "each" on the basis of the series or networks of singular "each times"). Nor does this incommensurability mean that freedom is measured only against itself, as if "it" [quotation marks again] could provide a measure, a standard of freedom. Rather, it means that freedom *measures itself against nothing*: it "measures" itself against existence's transcending in nothing and "for nothing." Freedom: to measure oneself against the nothing. (*EF*, 70–71)

The colon here replaces the *is*; it suspends the ontological copula of the *is*. It bears the becoming-substantive of "nothing," the passage from "in nothing" and "for nothing" to "measur[ing] oneself against the nothing," a formulation that will be taken up again in the following paragraph. This substantivization of the "nothing" avoids, if not nothingness, at least a certain heroism in the confrontation with nothingness as plenitude. But it does not avoid the self, the oneself, in "measuring oneself." We again find, in a very subtle form, to be sure, all the problems of the "self" and of ipseity that have been dogging us from the beginning. Here is what follows:

Measuring oneself against the nothing does not mean heroically affronting or ecstatically confronting an abyss which is conceived of as the *plenitude* of nothingness and which would seal itself around the sinking of the subject of heroism or of ecstasy. Measuring oneself against the nothing is *measuring oneself* absolutely, or measuring oneself against the very "measure" of "measuring oneself": placing the "self" in the position [*en mesure de*] of taking the measure of its existence. [Everything is going to be collapsed into this position, this ipsocratic self-positioning that consists in *putting oneself*, putting oneself in a position to (*en mesure de*) . . . , giving oneself the power to, . . . the word *mesure* in the idiom *en mesure*, " *être en mesure de*," here playing the role of a mediating schema between the measurable, the immeasurable or the incommensurable, and the *power* to measure *oneself* against the without-measure, the "oneself" of "measuring oneself" here signaling the tenacity of ipseity.] This is perhaps, and even certainly, an excess [*démesure*]. In no way and on no regis-

ter of analysis will one avoid the excess of freedom—for which heroism and
ecstasy are in fact also figures and names, but these must not obscure other examples, such as serenity, grace, forgiveness, or the surprises of language, and
others still. (*EF*, 71)

What is thus put into parentheses and between quotation marks, suspended although not necessarily denied, would indeed be the undeniabil-
ity of an aporia. I will attempt to clarify only the part of it that touches directly on the determining appearance of the "political" and, within that,
of the "democratic." For the "political" is indeed determined in this way
(and even the "juridical"—Nancy speaks of right and of justice—indeed
even the "ethical," as soon as reference is made, as it is here, to the "exer-
cising of one's will," and I am not sure that what Western philosophy
refers to under these three names can be in this case easily distinguished).[33] Politico-juridico-ethical responsibility gets determined and becomes nameable, given some degree of semantic stability, only with the
imposition of precisely that which is contained between parentheses,
namely, the technique of equality, justice in the sense of calculable right or
law, what Nancy also calls "given conditions," and especially criteria for
"negotiations" to measure this access against the incommensurable,
which, in itself and by definition, excludes all given criteria, all calculable
rules, all measure. What makes the aporia so formidable, and, it must be
said, without any calculable, decidable, or foreseeable way out, given over
once more to the paradoxes of the autoimmune, is that equality is not
equal to itself. It is, as I suggested earlier, inadequate to itself, at the same
time opportunity or chance and threat, threat as chance: autoimmune.
Like the search for a calculable unit of measure, equality is not simply
some necessary evil or stopgap measure; it is also the chance to neutralize
all sorts of differences of force, of properties (natural and otherwise) and
hegemonies, so as to gain access precisely to the *whoever* or the *no matter
who* of singularity in its very immeasurability. Calculable measure also
gives access to the incalculable and the incommensurable, an access that
remains itself necessarily undecided between the calculable and the incalculable—and that is the aporia of the political and of democracy. But, by
the same token, by effacing the difference of singularity through calculation, by no longer counting on it, measure risks putting an end to singularity itself, to its quality or its nonquantifiable intensity. And yet the concept of measurable equality is not opposed to the immeasurable. That is

why Nancy is right to speak of "the equality of singularities in the incommensurability of freedom."

We must, however, acknowledge here *three necessities* that are hardly compatible.

(a) This "technique," this "technical measure of equality," is not some accident or fall, some mishap or misfortune for the incalculable or the incommensurable (and I insist here on "technique" because the politico-juridico-ethical, as we understand it, presupposes such a calculating technique, a seriality or circularity that is not simply secondary or auxiliary). This technique is also the chance for the incommensurable; *it is what gives access to it.* A chance given by the political, the juridical, the ethical and their invention, wherever it takes place.

(b) This chance is always given as an autoimmune threat. For calculating technique obviously destroys or neutralizes the incommensurable singularity to which it gives effective access.

(c) By definition, there is no given criterion, no assured rule, no incontestable unit of calculation, no trustworthy and natural mediating schema to regulate this calculation of the incalculable and this common or universal measure of the incommensurable. I say "common or universal" because we will soon have to ask ourselves the following, right along with the question of the brother: in politics, and even in law (and herein lies all the urgency of the question of international law and rogue states toward which I am headed), does this measure of the immeasurable, this democratic equality, end at citizenship, and thus at the borders of the nation-state? Or must we extend it to the whole world of singularities, to the whole world of humans assumed to be like me, my compeers [*mes semblables*]—or else, even further, to all nonhuman living beings, or again, even beyond that, to all the nonliving, to their memory, spectral or otherwise, to their to-come or to their indifference with regard to what we think we can identify, in an always precipitous, dogmatic, and obscure way, as the life or the living present of living [*la vivance*] in general? For in what I am calling the first situation of aporia, the one where I share or even exacerbate in my own way the possible-impossible that Nancy understands as the measure of the immeasurable or as the immeasurability of measure, the reference to the unit of calculation, that is, this "each" left in quotation marks, is all the more intractable and nonnegotiable (and thus is only to be negotiated with, endlessly, without any knowledge or assurance) insofar as freedom is not, in the language and thought of Nancy, and in the book entitled *The Experience of Freedom*, simply the attribute of an *ego*. Freedom is not to be understood simply as the "I can" of a free will, the power of a voluntary subject, of a subject assumed to be in charge, to be *master* [*maître*], one or countable, and thus measurable (and I'm almost tempted to write *maître* here, for good measure, that is, *mètre*, just measure, *metron*, a measure at once measuring and measurable). No, freedom is extended to everything that appears in the open. It is extended to the event of everything in the world—and first of all in the "there is" of the world—that comes to presence, including whatever comes in the free form of nonhuman living being and of the "thing" in general, whether living or not. One can refer here to what Nancy says of freedom as "force" and as "force of the thing" as such, indeed of "transcendental force" as "material actuality" (*EF*, 102). The whole question of "demo*cracy*" might be configured around this transcendental force: how far is democracy to be extended, the *people* of demo*cracy*, and the "each 'one'" of democracy? To the dead, to animals, to trees and rocks? This beyond of the living as a kind of freedom is evoked by Nancy in a most striking way when he asks himself in a parenthesis: "Who would dare simply to appreciate in this way the free force of the cadaver before its murderer?" (*EF*, 103). He does not say whether the "cadaver" is human, even though it seems implied, or else, as we say, "animal." One might ask about this, assuming again that we can still rely on this limit between the living and the nonliving in general. Leaving this huge question open, let me return for the time being to what makes the each or the "each 'one'" of singularity so difficult to determine, as well as the "by turns" or the "each in turn" in relation to equality and to its unit of calculation in the supposedly human order of the ethico-juridico-political. If freedom is no longer the attribute of a subject, of a mastery [*maîtrise*] or a measure [*métrique*], the unit of calculation can no longer be the civil identity of a citizen with a patronym, nor the equality of one person to another, nor the equality of one *ego* to other equal *egos*, nor even, in case one wanted to hold on to the grammatical and ontological power of saying "I," the equality of one conscious, voluntary, and intentional I to another. A whole series of questions here arises. What is to be done with what is called the unconscious, and thus with the spaced divisibility, the hierarchized multiplicity, and the conflict of forces it imposes on sovereign identity? How many voices, how many votes [*voix*], for an unconscious? How are they to be counted? What can a bygone psychoanalysis or one that is still to come tell us about democracy?

Is there any democracy in the psychic system? And in psychoanalytic institutions? Who votes, what is a vote, or a voice, in the psychic and political system? In the state, in international institutions, including those of psychoanalysis? The superego? The ego? The subconscious? The ideal ego? The ideal of the ego? The primary process, or its representatives? How are the votes to be counted? On what unit of measure and on what technique should we rely in order to calculate? What is the law of this measure? Where are we to find the metronome? How are we to rethink a psychic and yet non-egological metronomy of democracy, with its alternations and its "by turns"?

I can do little more than simply situate these questions, which would no doubt all have to be put to the test of the autoimmune. What psychoanalysts call more or less complacently the unconscious remains, it seems to me, one of the privileged sources, one of the vitally mortal and mortally vital reserves or resources, for this implacable law of the self-destructive conservation of the "subject" or of egological ipseity. To put it a bit sententiously in the interest of time, without autoimmunity there would be neither psychoanalysis nor what psychoanalysis calls the "unconscious." Not to mention, therefore, the "death drive," the cruelty of "primary sadism and masochism"—or even what we just as complacently call "consciousness."

§ 5 Liberty, Equality, Fraternity, or, How Not to Speak in Mottos

I come now to the second situation, at a place in Nancy's text where, as I announced earlier, I will be less inclined to subscribe and to share. My reservations will not be, I insist without denegation, objections in the strict sense. They might look instead like a terminological dispute, indeed a fraternal squabble over the issue of fraternity. This second situation is closely associated with the first since it is a question of determining and naming community, the common, the sharing of the incommensurable freedom or equality of each and every one. Nancy proposes calling it "fraternity."

The word appears regularly in at least five different contexts throughout *The Experience of Freedom*.[34] The first, and the one that concerns me here, appears to be the most explicit and developed. I believe it to be more faithful, more just, and more helpful to read yet another entire paragraph. It immediately follows the one I just analyzed. I will underscore, right in the middle of it, a certain "if it must be said" ("It is also fraternity, *if it must be said* that fraternity . . . "). Concerning this "if it must be said," I do not know if it must be said to betray a condition, a scruple, a hesitation, a commendable circumspection, or a half-conceded denegation. In any case, I seem to detect within it the noticeable concern of a question, "Must it be said?" to which Nancy would have apparently answered, already long ago, "Yes, it must be said"—and I, for a long time now, "No." Here is the paragraph:

> Essentially, this excess or immeasurability of freedom, as the very measure of existence, is common. It is of the essence of a measure—and therefore of an immeasurable—to be common. The community shares freedom's immeasurability. [I must admit that I here have trouble following the "therefore": that

measure would be by essence common is clear, but why would it "therefore" be of the essence of an *im*measurable to be common? What justifies this "therefore"? How does one share and make common an immeasurable? Wouldn't immeasurability be symmetrically opposed to, coupled with and dependent on, measure, indeed common measure? But I continue.] Because this immeasurability consists in nothing other than the fact or gesture of measuring itself against nothing, against the nothing, the community's sharing is itself the common (im)measurability [*(dé)mesure*] of freedom. [Here again I do not understand the connection and this parenthetical ("im"), as if im-measurability were still a measure, a simple modality or negative modification of measure; for I myself would tend to think of immeasurability as heterogeneous to all measure rather than as a simple negative measure or negation of measure. Undaunted, Nancy will draw the consequences of this logic, which I have difficulty following, by following up with a first "thus."] Thus, it has a common measure, but not in the sense of a given measure to which everything is referred: it is common in the sense that it is the excess or immeasurability of the sharing of existence. It is the essence of equality and relation. It is also fraternity, if it must be said that fraternity [I interrupt again for a moment the quotation: I must say that, from one reading to the next, this turn of phrase "if it must be said" seems to me more and more bizarre, subjected, in truth, to a strange contortion in philosophy, inflected by a circumvolution for which I know no other example and to which I would want to devote an entire book. In any case, he is going to tell us what must be said, and with authority, all the while asking if what must be said must be said, and while politely, almost apologetically, setting as a condition that he be authorized to say something that is not self-evident but that will end up being affirmed, conditionally, because in the end it must be that what must be said must indeed be said, especially since it has already been said, and he is going to repeat it, even though he is in fact vaguely aware that perhaps it should not be said, except in order to clarify a few things that are not any more self-evident, namely, about the kind of fraternity that is to be discussed. Let me return to the quotation:] It is also fraternity, if it must be said that fraternity, aside from every sentimental connotation (but not aside from the possibilities of passion it conceals, from hatred to glory by way of honor, love, competition for excellence, etc.), is not the relation of those united by a same family but the relation of those whose *Father*, or common substance, *has disappeared*, delivering them to their freedom and to the equality of this freedom. Such are, in Freud, the sons of the inhuman Father of the horde: becoming brothers in the *sharing* of his *dismembered* body. Fraternity is equality in the sharing of the incommensurable. (*EF*, 71–72)

I cannot return here to what I tried in *Politics of Friendship* to deconstruct, namely, the Greek, Abrahamic, Jewish, but especially Christian and Islamic privileging of the figure of the brother in ethics, law, and politics, and particularly in a certain democratic model. In fraternalism or brotherhoods, in the confraternal or fraternizing community, what is privileged is at once the masculine authority of the brother (who is also a son, a husband, a father), genealogy, family, birth, autochthony, and the nation. And any time the literality of these implications has been denied, for example, by claiming that one was speaking not of the natural and biological family (as if the family was ever purely natural and biological) or that the figure of the brother was merely a symbolic and spiritual figure, it was never explained why one wished to hold on to and privilege this figure rather than that of the sister, the female cousin, the daughter, the wife or the stranger, or the figure of anyone or whoever. I shall not return to this line of argumentation, to the examples and the numerous texts where I have tried to justify this deconstruction, including within the psychoanalytic institution, and even within the works of Blanchot and Levinas. I also recalled in passing—and it is, perhaps, precisely a deconstruction of Christianity that is at work here—that if the revolutionaries of 1789 long hesitated to include the word *fraternity* in the republican motto, a word that appears neither in the Declaration of Human Rights nor in the Constitution of 1793 nor in the Charter of 1830, but only in an addendum to the Constitution of 1791, it is because of its strongly Christian connotations. There are countless indications of this, as I tried to show in *Politics of Friendship*. Mona Ozouf says that this "kinship between Christianity and the Revolution explains why fraternity emerged alongside liberty and equality, completing what was perceived as another trinity."[35]

One thus has to ask oneself, one has to ask Nancy, why he is so keen on keeping the word *fraternity* in order to say equality in the sharing of the incommensurable, "if it must be said," as he says, that fraternity is to be understood "aside from every sentimental connotation," and "if it must be said" that fraternity is not a familial relation, not "the relation of those united by a same family."

So why retain the word *fraternity* rather than another? Nancy's answer, at once Freudian and Christian, is one that we would have difficulty understanding as nonfamilial; it concerns the figure not of a mother, wife, daughter, or sister, outside, it might be said, "the relation of those united by a same family," but a "*disappeared* Father," a father defined as "common substance" (an expression that appeared at the beginning of the chapter and a definition whose connotations, at least, are profoundly Christian, if not trinitarian), a father who, in fact, has disappeared in the course of being put to death by men, by his sons, who, as in a eucharistic transubstantiation, share among themselves the body of the father, in memory of him. Let me reread this sentence, at once Christian and Freudian, situated somewhere between the Gospels and *Totem and Taboo,* the religion of the son and thus of brothers succeeding, as Freud would say, the religion of the father, succeeding but also renewing it: "Such are, in Freud, the sons of the inhuman Father of the horde: becoming brothers in the *sharing* of his *dismembered* body. Fraternity is equality in the sharing of the incommensurable." That is why Nancy will add a few pages later, as if "fraternity" caused him to have some doubt or suspicion regarding the "sharing": "Freedom (equality, fraternity, justice)" (*EF,* 77), the trinity of these three concepts determining and, in short, sharing freedom between them.

I will not add anything new to what I tried to demonstrate in *Politics of Friendship* concerning this notion of fraternity as the equitable sharing of the remains of the father, of a common substance that has disappeared and is consumed, after the dismemberment ("brothers in the *sharing* of his *dismembered* body")—a dismemberment that, once again, like a quartering combined with a circular reappropriation of the so-called common substance, in mourning and in memory, comes to resemble a cross on a wheel. What, then, is the only noncritical concern that I would like to formulate here, in an incisive, distinctive, and, I hope, productive way within the context of this *décade* and on the subject of democracy?

I insist on this being a noncritical concern because, after all, Nancy can always say: "It's not me, it's not me who is saying this, I am simply recounting, simply telling a story, a history, the one that we tell ourselves and that has gained currency and credit in our culture and inherited language (the language of everyday culture, of religions, of psychoanalysis, and so on); I am analyzing what this history says, what this concept implies, the history and concept of freedom and equality as fraternity, the father who has disappeared, and so on." I too often find myself saying: "You see, I am first of all analyzing the content and implications of a *received* concept, interpretation, or narrative, one to which I myself do not necessarily subscribe." But, of course, this is always, in my case, so as to ask myself at the end of the day whether it is receivable, acceptable, and where and why it would be unacceptable. My noncritical concern thus remains somewhat

colored by the hypothesis that Nancy *would like to believe* in the fraternity
of this received narrative. I too, in fact, would like to believe in it; or rather,
there is someone in me who would like to believe it; but another, another
who no longer resembles me like a brother, simply cannot bring himself to
believe it, another who even believes, on reflection, and with experience,
that it would be better not to believe it, not only but especially when it
comes to politics. Perhaps in the discussion to follow I might be able to
elaborate on a series of values most often associated with that of the
brother: the values of the neighbor [*prochain*] (in the Christian sense), the
fellow, the compeer or the like [*semblable*] (the enormous question of the
like: I tried to argue in my seminar this year that pure ethics, if there is any,
begins with the respectable dignity of the other as the absolute *unlike*, recognized as nonrecognizable, indeed as unrecognizable, beyond all knowledge, all cognition and all recognition: far from being the beginning of
pure ethics, the neighbor as like or as resembling, as looking like, spells the
end or the ruin of such an ethics, if there is any. Some might then be
tempted to say, for we must at least grant the hypothesis, that this is actually the border between pure ethics and the political, a political that would
begin by choosing and preferring the like, knowledge, cognition and recognition, technique and calculating law, all of which require knowing and
recognizing the like and the same as units of measure). This, as I was saying, is the series of values most often associated with the brother: the values of the neighbor (in the Christian sense), the like, and finally, in the last
analysis, bringing together the values of the neighbor and the like, the values of man, of the rights of the humanity of man: the brother is always a
human brother. Let us not forget this overwhelming and thus terribly
blinding fact: the brother of which one speaks is always a man. Nancy literally says, in fact, that with the disappearance of the "common substance,"
with the disappearance of the "in-human" father, of the "father disappeared," dismembered and shared, *brothers as men* are born, equal and
alike. The humanity of man is born as fraternity. The father is not necessarily human, but the sons and thus the brothers are.[36]

My concern here stems not simply from my regret that Nancy did not
put more quotation marks, in either letter or in spirit, around the word
fraternity. Nor that he did not show himself to be more circumspect about
the affinity, indeed the line of filiation, between this genealogism and the
theme of "ontological generosity" that comes up so regularly in his book.
Nor that he risks over-Christianizing the wonderful concept of "sharing"

at the very heart of his thought. No, I am simply concerned that when it comes to politics and democracy this fraternalism might follow at least the temptation of a genealogical descent back to autochthony, to the nation, if not actually to nature, in any case, to birth, to *naissance*. I would wish to put this crucial word from the same family, this word *naissance*, before any other, before nature and before nation. I say *naissance* but not necessarily, despite the temptation, the "nativity" of the son of God the Father and a Virgin Mary. The theme of birth is not in and of itself worrisome or something to be suspicious of. The experience of birth, with all it implies, does indeed call for a singular thought—singular first of all because it does not reduce birth to either genesis or creation or beginning or origin. And I believe that Nancy is attentive to these distinctions. Similarly, the theme of filiation or genealogy is not itself something to be suspicious of. But these two themes become "critical," they call for a critical and deconstructive deciphering, when their intersection becomes political, when a particular model, figure, or hegemony—for example, the paternal, fraternal, or maternal—ends up getting politicized. The same goes for all the problems, both old and new, that use this notion of birth to forge relations between, on the one hand, democracy, wherever it is linked (and that is almost everywhere) to the nation-state, to nation-state sovereignty, to autochthony, to the right to citizenship *by birth* (whether as blood right or land right, itself always a birth right), and, on the other hand, cosmopolitanism and its beyond, the future of international law, the lines of division between so-called legitimate states and bastard or "rogue" states, and so on—so many questions toward which this might help serve as a transition.

Now, I have put such emphasis on birth because of this undeniable fact: Nancy everywhere, but particularly in *The Experience of Freedom*, makes of birth (which must not be too quickly reduced, let me again underscore this, to nativity, or origin, or beginning, or genesis, or creation) a powerful and original, irreducible theme, connected to his discourse on the event, creation, and especially freedom. The chapter we have been reading opens with an essential equation between freedom and birth, between the act of a certain liberation and the act or certificate of birth [*acte de naissance*]. It is here that genealogy and the generousness of ontological generosity resemble and gather round one another. Here is the first page of our chapter:

Singularity consists in the "just once, this time," whose mere enunciation—similar to the infant's cry at birth, and it is necessarily *each time* a question of birth—establishes a relation at the same time that it infinitely hollows out the time and space that are supposed to be "common" around the point of enunciation. At this point, it is each time freedom that is singularly *born*. (And it is birth that *frees*.) (*EF*, 66; Nancy's emphasis)

§ 6   The Rogue That I Am

How not to speak of brothers?

In its constitutive autoimmunity, in its vocation for hospitality (with everything in the *ipse* that works over the etymology and experience of the *hospes* through the aporias of hospitality), democracy has always wanted by turns and at the same time two incompatible things: it has wanted, on the one hand, to welcome only men, and on the condition that they be citizens, brothers, and compeers [*semblables*], excluding all the others, in particular bad citizens, rogues, noncitizens, and all sorts of unlike and unrecognizable others, and, on the other hand, at the same time or by turns, it has wanted to open itself up, to offer hospitality, to all those excluded. In both cases, let us recall, and here is a problem I take up elsewhere, this hospitality remains limited and conditional. But even in this restricted space it is typical for democracy to do one or the other, sometimes one and the other, sometimes both at the same time and/or by turns. Rogues or degenerates [*les voyous ou les roués*] are sometimes brothers, citizens, compeers.

Who are they? Who are the others of brothers, the nonbrothers? What makes them separate beings, excluded or wayward, outcast or displaced, left to roam the streets [*rues*], especially those of the suburbs? (But, again, there is no etymological relationship, unfortunately, between *rue* and *roué*, although the roué, like the voyou, is defined always in relation to some street, in relation to that normal path [*voie*] that is the street [*rue*] in a city, in the urbanity and good conduct of urban life: the voyou and the roué introduce disorder into the street; they are picked out, denounced, judged, and condemned, pointed out as actual or virtual delinquents, as those accused and pursued by the civilized citizen, by the state or civil society, by decent, law-abiding citizens, by their police, sometimes by international law and its armed police who watch over the law and over morals, over politics and over politesse, over all the paths [*voies*] of circulation—all the pedestrian zones, highways, sea and air routes, information highways, e-mail, the Web, and so on.)

Between the democrat and the asocial voyou, the proximity [*voisinage*] remains ambiguous, the inseparability troubling, despite some essential differences. This stems from at least two reasons.

First of all, in French, a French difficult to translate (and we will get to what the recent French expression "Etat voyou" attempts to translate), *voyou* remains a *popular* expression in all senses of the term. This word *voyou*, which I am following [*que je suis*] here, is fairly recent: 1830 is the date of the conquest of Algeria under Charles X (and I don't quite know what to make of the fact that when I was born this word was but a century old). The noun *voyou* can become an attribute or an adjective—always a very qualifying adjective, most often pejorative and accusatory. It is never a neutral attribute, the object of an observation. Rather, it casts a normative, indeed performative, evaluation, a disdainful or threatening insult, an appellation that initiates an inquiry and prepares a prosecution before the law. It is an appellation that looks already like a virtual interpellation. When speaking of a voyou, one is calling to order; one has begun to denounce a suspect, to announce an interpellation, indeed an arrest, a convocation, a summons, a bringing in for questioning: the voyou must appear before the law.

The voyou is always the other, always being pointed out by the respectable, right-thinking bourgeois, the representative of moral or juridical order. The voyou is always a second or third person, always designated in the second or third person. Even if one says *I*, for example, "I am after [*je suis*] and am following after [*poursuis*] a voyou," no one will say, in principle, "I am [*je suis*], *ego sum*, a voyou." The word not only has a popular origin and use but is intended to designate someone who, by social pedigree or by manners, belongs to what is most common or popular in the people. The *dēmos* is thus never very far away when one speaks of a voyou. Nor is democracy far from voyoucracy [*voyoucratie*]. Democracy is perhaps something else, as we will see, but before *voyouterie* (a word coined, it seems, by the Goncourts in 1884—which is to say just yesterday), the bourgeois Flaubert had invented the word *voyoucratie* back in 1865. It was a way of designating, or actually of questioning and denouncing before the law, an organized force, not yet the quasi state of a mafia but a sort of occult or marginal power, the delinquent counterpower of a secret society or conspiracy, the counterinstitution of a clandestine brotherhood that brings together outlaws and the wayward [*dévoyés*]. But of course, if a voyoucracy resembles a secret but popular society, democracy, for its part, cannot be a clandestine community, even if it is just as popular and just as much a thing of the people as a voyoucracy. A democracy must be public and phenomenal through and through, something of the Enlightenment. But since it must also recognize, in the name of democracy, the right to the secret, things again get complicated. It will be difficult to do away with every dream of a democracy to come as a secret society, as a society of the secret. Shared, to be sure, but like any secret in the end. . . .

The word *voyou* has an essential relation with the *voie*, the way, with the urban roadways [*voirie*], the roadways of the city or the *polis*, and thus with the street [*rue*], the waywardness [*dévoiement*] of the voyou consisting in making ill use of the street, in corrupting the street or loitering in the streets, in "roaming the streets," as we say in a strangely transitive formulation. This transitivity is in fact never very far from the one that leads to "walking the streets." In the wake of Baudelaire, Benjamin, or Aragon, all this would be part of another portrait of "modern life," of the modern city in the urban and capitalistic landscape of industrial civilization from the nineteenth century to the present. Today the voyou sometimes roams the roadways [*voies*] and highways [*voiries*] in a car [*voiture*], that is, when he or she is not stealing it or setting it on fire. Voyous might also, on an international scale, and this gets us right into the problematic of rogue states, be involved in drug trafficking, in parasiting, or actually subverting, as terrorists in training, the pathways [*voies*] of normal communication, whether of airplanes, the telephone, e-mail, or the Web. In a word, of cyberspace. (In "The University Without Conditions" I try to treat this question of democracy in cyberspace, the question of what has been called *cyberdemocracy*.)

The voyou is at once unoccupied, if not unemployed, and actively occupied with occupying the streets, either by "roaming the streets" doing nothing, loitering, or by doing what is not supposed to be done, that is, according to established norms, laws, and the police. The voyou does what is not supposed to be done in the streets and on all the other byways, which the voyoucracy actually has the power to make less viable or trustworthy.

Voyoucracy is a corrupt and corrupting power of the street, an illegal and outlaw power that brings together into a voyoucratic regime, and thus into an organized and more or less clandestine form, into a virtual state, all those who represent a principle of disorder—a principle not of anarchic chaos but of structured disorder, so to speak, of plotting and conspiracy, of premeditated offensiveness or offenses against public order. Indeed, of terrorism, it will be said—whether national or international. Voyoucracy is a principle of disorder, to be sure, a threat against public order; but, as a *cracy*, it represents something more than a collection of individual or individualistic voyous. It is the principle of disorder as a sort of substitute order (a bit like a secret society, a religious order, a sect or brotherhood, a kind of Freemasonry). This will become significant for us when we reach the limits, within a historically determined space and time, of an *epoch* of Etats voyous or rogue states. The *voyoucracy* already constitutes, even institutes, a sort of counterpower or countercitizenship. It is what is called a *milieu*. This milieu, this environment, this world unto itself, gathers into a network all the people of the crime world or underworld, all the singular voyous, all individuals of questionable morals and dubious character whom decent, law-abiding people would like to combat and exclude under a series of more or less synonymous names: big man, bad boy, player, hence something of a seducer—the libidinal connotation remaining ineffaceable in the accusation "voyou"—rascal, hellion, good-for-nothing, ruffian, villain, crook, thug, gangster, shyster [*canaille*] (in Spanish, *canalla* translates "rogue"[37] in rogue state, *Etat voyou*), scoundrel, miscreant, hoodlum, hooligan, *frape* (a feminine noun, written with one or two *p*'s, that names a thief—the force of the voyoucracy being the force of *frappes*, the force of thugs who strike blows); one would also say today *banger* [*loulou*], *gang-banger* [*loubard*], sometimes even outside the inner city, in the suburbs, the suburban punk [*loubard des banlieues*].

The popular origin of the word *voyou*, its origin in the rabble, is also *Parisian*. This provenance has been confirmed. Auguste Barbier says in his *Iambes* (*La Cuve*, "The Vat"): "The Parisian race is that of the pale *voyou* of stunted growth."[38] Nerval: "This accent of Parisian *voyous* that sounds like a rattle."[39] Indeed, the voyou is someone who rattles, who shakes things up, who agitates.

An urban and, thus, political origin. The voyou milieu is first of all the municipality, the polis, the city, indeed the capital city. And when one speaks of voyous, the police are never very far away. In Paris the term dis-

criminates between the various neighborhoods of Paris (bourgeois or popular arrondissements), and then between Paris intra muros and the suburbs. Between the two, there are the city limits, the old city walls or forti-
fications, the favorite stomping ground of all voyous. Indeed it is generally
thought that there are more voyous in the suburbs. The question of a democratic politics of the city must thus always begin with the very serious
question: "What is a suburb?," which is to say, "What is a voyou?" "Under what conditions is a voyoucracy possible?"

Just a couple more words for whoever is following the voyou, the interpellation *voyou*, even if no one is ever able to declare or to confess, "I am
a voyou."

First, this word remains generally, as it was originally, a masculine noun
or adjective. *Voyoute* is extremely rare, artificial, and forced. In any case,
the sexual connotations remain at work; although the woman who is
called a *voyoute* is not a bad boy [*mauvais garçon*]—even if she leads a bad
life [*mauvaise vie*] and is a bit tomboyish [*garçonne*]—she dares to declare
herself just as free and master of her own life as a man. A *voyoute* is a liberated woman who, especially during the Belle Epoque, or after World
War I, would wear her hair like a boy and would do as she pleased with
her body and her language. She is man enough to give herself the air of a
liberated feminist. We would have to draw all the consequences of the
supposed masculinity of this being-voyou. The voyou is always a part of
mankind, always human, of our kind, and almost always a man, if not actually a ladies' man. From a political point of view, the representatives of
order, the forces of bourgeois or moral order, try to present as voyous all
rebels, agitators, and insurgents, indeed all revolutionaries, regardless of
whether they come from bad neighborhoods or from the suburbs,
whether they erect barricades, as in 1848, 1870, or 1968, or commit acts of
vandalism, crime, organized crime, or terrorism. This is as true for the revolutions of the left as for those of the right. Fascism, Nazism, populism,
today's movements of the far right also often recruit from among a popu-
lation that might easily be described as a voyoucracy. Criteria are often
lacking in this area, which is also a *zone*, that is, a belt, for distinguishing
between voyoucracy and the people as plebeians, between democratic
election, referendum, and plebiscite. Demagogues sometimes denounce
voyous, but they also often appeal to them, in the popular style of populism, always at the indecidable limit between the demagogic and the democratic. Moreover, if the *voyou-cracy* represents a sort of competing

power, a challenge to the power of the state, a criminal and transgressive countersovereignty, we have here all the makings of a counterconcept of sovereignty such as we might find in Bataille. Beyond mastery, beyond the Hegelian concept and state, beyond or contrary to the classical notion of sovereignty, the sovereignty of which Bataille speaks cultivates evil and sexual as well as poetic transgression. The voyou who aspires to sovereignty is not just a sexual delinquent but someone whose language and ways of speaking, whose offenses against proper speech and against the "good word," are to be condemned. One begins acting like a voyou as soon as one begins uttering "profanities."

The voyou can also be one of those "great criminals [*grosse Verbrecher*]" who, as Benjamin tells us in "Critique of Violence," fascinates because he defies the state, that is, the institution that, in representing the law, secures and maintains for itself a monopoly on violence.[40] The "great criminal" voyou thus rises up, in an insurrection of countersovereignty, to the level or height of the sovereign state; he becomes a counterstate to rival the sovereignty of the legal or putatively legitimate state, which is in a position of monopoly and hegemony.

We will observe a homologous structure later when we speak of so-called Etats voyous, states denounced, confronted, and repressed by the police of supposedly legitimate states, those that respect an international law that they have the power to control—for example, in the modern and complex formation of a heterogeneous but oftentimes closely knit and tightly bound grouping like the United States, the United Nations, and the Security Council, even NATO (to which one might add for good measure alliances and coalitions like the G8, the IMF, and so on).

Second, we called these men a moment ago outlaws. Now, on the way [*voie*] to the question of the animal that, in English, a *rogue* also is, I would like to note an interesting, even if suspect, etymology of the word *voyou*. For the word *voyou* is itself a suspect word and the voyou himself a suspect character. Shady, questionable, of dubious character [*mauvais aloi*], which is to say of suspicious origin [*mauvais alliage*] (as is said of bad or counterfeit money, illegal money that passes for genuine). It is always a question of a suspicious or mixed origin, of *alliage* and alliance, of, this time, some "alligation" (*alligare*).[41] In 1860, not long after the first appearance of the word (which is also to say just after the appearance of the thing, the voyou-thing, the voyou being inseparable from the work of appellation, interpretation, and interpellation), the provenance of this new lexicon became a subject of inquiry. In the *Revue de l'instruction publique*, Charles Nisard thought he could disqualify the derivation that would put us back on the way [*voie*] to the way [*voie*]. *Voyou* would not come from *voie*, like *dévoyé*, or *dévoiement*, but, by alteration or deviation, from *voirou*, which was used in place of *loup-garou*. *Voyou* would in fact mean "loup-garou," "werewolf." Not much credit is given to this hypothesis and, I am tempted to think, for good reason. But such a conjecture is interesting. Its semantic logic seems in fact to follow on the pragmatic meaning conveyed by the gesture of interpellation, the insult or the denunciation, the exclamation "Voyou!" that follows upon meeting someone who, like the loup-garou (*werewolf, Werwolf, garulphus, lupo mannaro* in Italian) acts as an outlaw. I will not develop this point any further here, however important it might be, so as not to tire a number of friends present here who did me the honor of attending with such assiduity my seminar this year on "The Beast and the Sovereign." Packed full of wolves from the four corners of the world, the seminar was in large part a *lycology* and a *genelycology*, a genealogical theory of the wolf (*lycos*), of all the figures of the wolf and werewolf in the problematic of sovereignty. It just so happens that the word *loup-garou* in Rousseau's *Confessions* has sometimes been translated into English not as *werewolf* but as *outlaw*. We will see a bit later that *outlaw* is a synonym often used by the American administration along with or in place of *rogue* in the expression "rogue state." The terms *pariah state* and *outlaw nation* are also sometimes used.

When I proposed a title for this session today, even before my seminar had begun, "the reason of the strongest" was an allusion to the first line of La Fontaine's fable "The Wolf and the Lamb." In that seminar I ended up devoting a great deal of time and attention to the fabulous in general and to this fable in particular, to its structure and historico-political context, to its dedication to the Dauphin, and more generally still to lycology. I thus really must resist going down the same path here. But as a tiny addendum, and so as to situate the question of the voyou, and more precisely of the Etat voyou, let me simply note this: in the logic of the La Fontaine fable, there is, from three different points of view, no place for a voyou. There is no place from the point of view of (1) La Fontaine or the fabulist signatory who says, "The strong are always best at proving they're right [*La raison du plus fort est toujours la meilleure*] / Witness the case we're now going to cite," of (2) the wolf, the fabulous character who develops the argumentation in four easy steps,[42] but, also, of (3) the lamb, who suffers the consequences of all this. The wolf is not, in principle, a voyou, since he represents the sovereign force that gives law and gives itself the right [*le droit*] to . . . , who reasons about and declares what is right [*donne raison*], who gives reasons for why he is right [*se donne raison*], and who wins out over [*a raison de*] the reasons of the lamb. The lamb is not a voyou, of course, and voyous are not innocent lambs.

Where then has he gone, the voyou I am taking after [*suis*] here?

§ 7 God, What More Do I Have to Say? In What Language to Come?

Out of what you would no doubt want to characterize as a certain roguishness [*rouerie*] on my part, I have not yet told you what was, in fact, the double "preliminary question" that, simultaneously, at the same time or by turns, has been torturing me ever since I began to prepare for this *décade*.

Here, finally, is the first question: can one and/or must one speak democratically of democracy? To speak democratically of democracy, to speak on the subject *of democracy* in an intelligible, univocal, and *sensible* fashion, would mean making oneself understood by *anyone* who can hear this word or the sentences formed with this word, since, as Austin has said and I constantly repeat, only a sentence, not a word, has meaning. But when I say, let me repeat it, "To speak democratically of democracy, to speak on the subject *of democracy* in an intelligible, univocal, and *sensible* fashion, would mean making oneself understood by *anyone* who can hear this word or the sentences formed with this word," I am already multiplying the protocols and conditions. When one says "to make oneself understood by anyone who *can* hear," the word *can* can point, at the same time or by turns, toward the possibility of a power, capacity, or force, a *kratos* or *kratein*, but also toward the possibility of a right, of a legitimate or legitimated authorization by law (*nomos*) or justice (*dikē*), by an authorized force or legitimate power. "Anyone must be able to understand, in democracy, the univocal meaning of the word and the concept democracy": this seems to imply that *anybody* or *anyone can* or *may*, or *should be able to*, or *should have the right to*, or *ought to*, and so on.[43] I have just spoken Greek, French, and English; but in German, to take only this among so many other possible examples, the word *Gewalt* and the lexicon of *wal-*

ten point us toward force as violence, toward the violence of power but also toward authority and legitimate power, toward government, reign, commandment, law, and order. Yet all these meanings are not equivalent. Possible confusions thus await us at every turn. Between power as force and power as right or law, between law and justice, between *kratos* and *nomos* or *kratos* and *dikē*, between what is in fact [*le fait*] and what is in principle [*le droit*], between the constative, the prescriptive, the normative, and the performative, a whole panoply of differences and nuances unfolds and then folds back in on itself, differences and nuances that, in democracy, should be clarified and made intelligible if anyone is ever to be able to have access to the meaning of *democracy*.

All this is not for tomorrow. When I seemed to imply that it was necessary already to live in a democracy in order for anyone not just to have access to the clear and univocal meaning of this word whose semantic range is so overdetermined (and all the more so, as we have confirmed, inasmuch as it oscillates between an excess and a lack or default of meaning, inasmuch as it is excessive, so to speak, by default), but in order for anyone to be able to debate and continuously discuss it, this seemed already rather circular and contradictory: what meaning can be given to this right to discuss freely the meaning of a word, and to do so in the name of a name that is at the very least supposed to entail the right of anyone to determine and continuously discuss the meaning of the word in question? Especially when the right thus implied entails the right to self-critique—another form of autoimmunity—as an essential, original, constitutive, and specific possibility of the democratic, indeed as its very historicity, an intrinsic historicity that it shares with no other regime?

If what is thus required and postulated, beyond the concepts of force, power, right, law, and justice, is that this be accessible, through so many often unworkable translations, and in more than one language, then reference to the Greek language, which seems to enjoy a unique and undeniable privilege, can bring us no reassurance. First of all because, as we have seen, democracy is, already in Greek, a concept that is inadequate to itself, a word hollowed out at its center by a vertiginous semantic abyss that compromises all translations and opens onto all kinds of autoimmune ambivalences and antinomies. Next, because we cannot really be assured of any continuity in the philological, semantic, or etymological filiation running through the history of the political and all the mutations that have affected for more than twenty-five centuries, in Europe and outside Europe, the paradigm without paradigm of some Greek or Athenian democracy. To speak democratically of democracy, it would be necessary, through some circular performativity and through the political violence of some enforcing rhetoric, some force of law, to impose a meaning on the word *democratic* and thus produce a consensus that one pretends, by fiction, to be established and accepted—or at the very least possible and necessary: on the horizon.

A second preliminary question has been torturing me. It may look like a kind of regret for having used and abused the expression "democracy to come." And especially, through this use and abuse, for having repeated, while feigning innovation, a truism. As if all I had been saying were: "You know, the perfect democracy, a full and living democracy, does not exist; not only has it never existed, not only does it not presently exist, but, indefinitely deferred, it will always remain to come, it will never be present in the present, will never present itself, will never come, will remain always to come, like the impossible itself." Had I said or meant only that, wouldn't I have been simply reproducing, even plagiarizing, the classical discourses of political philosophy? For example that of *On the Social Contract*, where it is not by chance that a particular formulation resembles the one I just evoked as a plausible but, to my eyes, unacceptable reading of the syntagma "democracy to come"? As we know, Rousseau still thinks he can take the term *democracy* in what he calls its "strict sense." Referring to this strict sense, which we have seen to be the first mirage, he draws this conclusion in the chapter of *On the Social Contract* entitled "On Democracy": "Taking the term in the strict sense, a true democracy has never existed and never will."[44]

What should we take from this argument in anticipation of what is to follow?

First of all, that such a democracy would be "contrary to the natural order." Rousseau places his trust in the concept of a natural order and in the calculation of forces it seems to entail. It would be contrary to the "natural order" for the greater number to govern and the smaller to be governed. Next, what in the past has deprived, and in the future will continue to deprive, democracy of any existence, that is, of any presence and self-presentation as such, is the impossibility of counting on the inhuman virtues of man (namely, and I am here citing Rousseau's words, virtue, vigilance, courage, constancy, and force—force being one of these qualities). Now, if these qualities are lacking in human beings, if they are inhuman and, in truth, divine, this lack is due less to a given deficiency of human nature than to the excessive demands placed on anyone by a government that, more than any other in the world, "tends so forcefully and continuously to change its form." Whence the permanent risk of "civil war" and "internal agitations." "[No government] tends so forcefully and continuously to change its form": in this revival of the Platonic philosopheme concerning the plasticity of democracy, Rousseau names (and in two different places) force, the force that forces the form, the force that forces a change in form, and then, right after, the force required of the citizen to remain a democrat despite this unpresentability.

The absence of a proper form, of an *eidos*, of an appropriate paradigm, of a definitive turn, of a proper meaning or essence and, at the same time, the obligation to have *only* turns, rounds, tropes, strophes of itself: that is what makes democracy unpresentable in existence. But this unpresentability responds and corresponds to the force of this democratic weakness. For at the very moment Rousseau seems to despair of any democracy ever being presently possible, existent and presentable, he speaks at once of necessity and obligation (translated by the word *ought* in the passage I am about to read), an "it is necessary," an "it is necessary" to maintain, by force of force, a fidelity to what he nonetheless calls the democratic "constitution," the survival of democratic desire, the resurgence of a preference that prefers the risks, dangers, and perils of freedom to the slumbering quietism of servitude. Freedom is necessary; there ought to be a desire for freedom even where there is none, even where there will never be any. That is force regardless of forms. *If* [*si*] democracy does not exist and *if* [*si*] it is true that, amorphous or polymorphous, it never will exist, is it not necessary to continue, and with all one's heart, to force oneself to achieve it? Well, *yes* [*si*], it is necessary; one must, one ought, one cannot not strive toward it with all one's force.

Woven into the grammar of this "ought," this "it is necessary" that expresses the constraint and obligation just as much as the resignation of the "it is necessary to resign oneself to there not being any," is the conditional grammar of an "if there were": if there were a people of gods, then that would be democracy. In reading these final lines of "On Democracy" one must not forget that this chapter is part of a whole discourse that treats in very classical fashion the forms of government. That is a fundamental limitation because it remains to be seen, in a completely preliminary way, whether *democracy* (especially in "democracy to come") ought to name only a constitution or form of government. Rousseau thus advances the following, between the "it is necessary," the "ought," and the "if": "It is under this constitution that the citizen *ought* [my emphasis] to arm himself with force and constancy, and to say *each day* [my emphasis] of his life from the bottom of his heart what a virtuous Palatine said in the Diet of Poland: *Malo periculosam libertatem quam quietum servitium* [I prefer to have liberty fraught with danger than servitude in peace]" (*SC*, 56).

Let's not simply shrug off these words: such a preference is played out in the heart (that is to say, in secret and off the public stage, where what is at stake in this danger is often nothing less than life itself, between life and death). It is indeed a question of the essence of man as well as of chance or fortune, of the last chance [*échéance*] or misfortune of his future. Rousseau begins a new paragraph to conclude, after the "ought," with a double *si*, which I here underscore, *si* and *si*, *if* and *so*: "*If* [*si*] there were a people of gods, it would govern itself democratically. *So* [*si*] perfect a government is not suited to men." Two times *si* and one plural: "*If* [*si*] there were a people of gods . . . " and "*So* [*si*] perfect a government . . . ," two *si*'s, a conjunction of conjecture and an adverb of intensity or comparison (so, so much, to such an extent), in actuality a superlative comparison (so perfect, so perfectly perfect, so absolutely perfect, more than perfect). The plurality that then affects the word *gods*, the dissemination by which it is literally taken into account (the gods, yes, but how many, and will they be as equal as they are free?), this *more than one* [*plus d'un*] announces democracy, or at least some democracy beyond government and democratic sovereignty. This "more than one" affects God with divisibility precisely there where sovereignty, that is, force, *cracy*, does not suffer division, where the force of the One God [*Dieu unique*], single and sovereign, God as the power of political sovereignty, will have been called single, one and indivisible, by all those who have analyzed sovereignty, from Plato and Aristotle to Bodin, Hobbes, and Rousseau.

These latter three in fact used the very word *indivisible* to qualify the essence of sovereignty or sovereign government. As for Plato and Aristotle, each time they treated democracy as a government, and thus as a political regime, as a paradigm or constitution, each time they named God, it was always by attributing to him an exceptional and indivisible unicity. This political turn toward or salutation [*salut*] of the One God signs, by turns, the *Politikos* and the *Politikon*, that is, the *Statesman* of Plato

(303a–b) and the *Politics* of Aristotle (3.1283b.8, 13–15). This happens each time in the context of the question of number, the question of the multitude or of the masses—and thus of democracy. In the *Statesman*, *monarkhia* is the best of the six constitutions when it is not only constitutional but bound by written laws; it is the worst and most unbearable when it is anomic, that is, when the sovereign is above the laws, as Plato puts it (a trait that is, one might say with Schmitt, what is proper to the sovereign, notably, his ability to dictate the law, to grant or not grant pardons above the law and to give himself the right to suspend rights and law; although it is also true that this right must be written into a constitution). As for democracy, a government of number, of the greatest number, it is exactly the opposite, for it is weak, asthenic (*asthenēs*). It has little power (*dynamis*) to effect either good or bad because of a polyarchic multiplicity that disperses command. It is thus the opposite of monarchy: when democracy is subject to constitutional laws, it is the worst regime, the last in which one would wish to live (*zēn*); but it is the best when the laws are broken. When the written constitution is not respected, one is better off in a democracy than anywhere else. Since all six constitutions or regimes are but semblances of constitutions that imitate the one, single constitution, that is, that of the one, the single and unique one who has knowledge and *tekhnē*, competence (*tēn tou henos meta tekhnēs arkhontes politeian*), they must do everything to respect the letter of the laws and the customs of the country (301a). For this model constitution, this unique constitution of the one and unique, the seventh or the first, the absolutely sovereign one whose *arkhē* (as principiel or princely command) has at its disposal *tekhnē* (technoscientific competence, knowledge, philosophy as knowledge and as know-how), this constitution that all the others, mere semblances, are trying to imitate, this exceptional constitution of the one and only, must ultimately be set aside. Even if it comes to be inscribed in alternation, in a "by turns," its unity or its unicity does not belong to a numerical series, for it is like a god among men (*hoion theon ex anthrōpōn*) (303b). One is reminded of the ideal city described at the end of book 7 of the *Republic*: it is governed by philosophers trained in dialectic, men and women, as Plato notes and underscores. This same passage of the *Republic* also prescribes the "by turns": these governors or governesses who will have seen the Good in itself, the good itself (*to agathon auto*), and who will use it as a paradigm for the city, turn out to be more than one, to be sure, but *each time* one. Each *one* will have power alone: "each in turn [*en merei*]" (540b).

All this is of the order of the possible, of the nonimpossible. This each in turn of the one and only, this inalterable alternation, is not negatively impossible. It is necessary to insist on this in thinking of the future, of a to-come that would be neither a chimera nor a regulative Idea nor a negative and simply impossible impossibility. This politics of philosophers, says Plato, is not a utopia or a dream. More precisely, it is not a wish, a pious promise, or a "prayer [*eukhē*]" (540d). It is a possibility. These are difficult things (*khalepa*), to be sure, but possible, accessible, practicable (*dunata*).

When Aristotle's *Politikon*, his *Politics*, takes up the formulation of Plato's *Politikos*, namely, "like a god among men [*hosper gar theon en anthrōpois*]" (1284a.11), it is again with regard to number. If there is one or more than one, but not enough to constitute an entire city of incomparable, incommensurable virtue and political ability, unequal to that of other cities, then this one or this "just more than one" will not be a mere part (*meros*, and this is also the word for *turn*, *by turns*, *each in turn* [*en merei*], *alternation*), this *one* or *just more* will not belong, like the part of a whole, to what it governs. Such a one would not be a fraction of a whole, or an arithmetic unit in a calculable series. We would thus do such a man wrong, we would do him an injustice (*adikēsontai*), were we simply to grant him rights. Equal rights, calculable right or law, and proportional isonomy would thus all betray justice (*dikē*). For or against such beings who are like a god among men, there is no law, no *nomos*. There is no law for them or against them, but there is the law, and they are themselves, in their very ipseity, the law (*autoi gar eisi nomos*). And that's where the fable of sovereignty returns, along with the reason of the strongest to which this text alludes. "They are themselves a law," says Aristotle, who adds: "Indeed a man would be ridiculous if he tried to legislate for them, for probably they would say what in the story of Antisthenes the lions said when the hares made speeches in the assembly and demanded that all should have equality" (1284a.14–17).[45]

The democracy to come, will this be a god to come? Or more than one? Will this be the name to come of a god or of democracy? Utopia? Prayer? Pious wish? Oath? Or something else altogether?

While waiting—and what we have been talking about here is precisely what *waiting* means—can one speak democratically of democracy in this chateau?

§ 8 The Last of the Rogue States: The "Democracy to Come," Opening in Two Turns

I have already played a great deal with this verbal thing "voyou," this idiom of recent or modern French invention (dating back only to the nineteenth century, to the beginning, therefore, of an urban society entering the age of industrial capitalism), an idiom of popular origin and barely French but also, in spite of or actually because of all this, an untranslatable, or barely translatable, incrimination, a sort of French interjection or exclamation, "Voyou!" which, I neglected to say, can be turned with the right intonation into something tender, affectionate, maternal (when I was little, my maternal grandmother would sometimes say, pretending to be angry with me, "Voyou, va!" [You little rascal!]). I have played a great deal with this word, which, while remaining untranslatable, nonetheless becomes in the expression "Etat voyou" a more than recent translation, almost still brand new, barely used, approximate, *franglaise*, of the Anglo-American "rogue state"—that so very singular indictment that I discovered for the first time in my own language a little more than a year ago, and doubly associated with the state, when it was announced after a Cabinet meeting that the president and the prime minister at the time, in spite of their "*cohabitation*," that is, in spite of belonging to different political parties, had agreed on the development of a nuclear weapon aimed at combating or deterring what the statement read on the steps of the Elysée Presidential Palace called "Etats voyous." I have thus spoken a great deal of this word *voyou* (for the word itself is a voyou of language), of what has recently become and, such is my hypothesis, will remain for only a short time still, a useful slogan or rallying cry for the coalition of what are called Western democracies. In this word *voyou* I have thus let appear by turns the noun and the attribute or adjective, a nominal adjective some-times attached to a "who" and sometimes accorded to a "what," for exam-ple, "Etat voyou." For in the French idiom, someone can do something that is "voyou" without actually being *a* voyou. And, in beginning, I said successively, you may recall, using the word *voyou* four different times, sometimes as a noun, sometimes as an adjective qualifying someone or something of someone: "It would no doubt be on my part, dare I say it, a bit *voyou*, a bit roguish, if not *roué*, were I not to begin here by declaring, yet one more time, my gratitude" (*voyou* here qualifies something, an atti-tude). I then added: "I would thus be, you might think, not only voyou, or roguish, but *a* voyou (*a* real rogue), were I not to declare at the outset my endless and bottomless gratitude." (This time, after the attribute of a subject, of a *who*, the substantive *un voyou*, "a rogue," referred to the sub-ject, a "who.")

The attribute "voyou" can thus sometimes be applied to a subject that is not substantially, that is, through and through, or naturally, *a* voyou, *a* rogue. The quality "voyou" is always precisely an attribution, the predicate or *categoria* and, thus, the accusation leveled not against something nat-ural but against an institution. It is an interpretation, an assignation, and, in truth, always a denunciation, a complaint or an accusation, a charge, an evaluation, and a verdict. As such it announces, prepares, and begins to justify some sanction. The Etat voyou must be punished, contained, ren-dered harmless, reduced to a harmless state, if need be by the force of law [*droit*] and the right [*droit*] of force.

I am drawing attention to this idiomatic distinction between the adjec-tive and the noun in order already to help us think about the fact that in this French expression of very recent date, "Etat voyou," which, as un-translatable as it is, as I said, will have been but an approximate transla-tion of the Anglo-American *rogue state*, we do not know exactly how *voyou* should be heard or understood. We do not know whether it should be, as a substantive, linked by a hyphen to the substantive state, thereby indicating that some state is substantially a voyou and thus would deserve to disappear as a nonconstitutional state or state of nonlaw, or whether *voyou* is an attribute, the quality temporarily attributed out of some strate-gic motivation by certain states to some other state that, from some point of view or in some context, during a limited period of time, would be ex-hibiting voyou behavior, appearing not to respect the mandates of inter-national law, the prevailing rules and the force of law of international de-

ontology, such as the so-called legitimate and law-abiding states interpret
them in accordance with their own interests. These are the states that have
at their disposal the greatest force and are prepared to call these Etats voyous to order and bring them back to reason, if need be by armed inter-
vention—whether punitive or preemptive.

Here is where the problem of Etats voyous that I announced in the beginning forms a real knot. To understand this knot—I am not saying to
undo it—I will follow *three threads* of very unequal length, unequal for
reasons of economy and because I do not wish to try your patience.

The *first thread*, the longest, although still little more than a quick connection, would be the one that links the question of what we have called
the "democracy to come," of what this syntagma might mean, to the current situation: states accuse other states of being Etats voyous or rogue
states. They intend to draw the conclusion, the armed conclusion, of this,
namely, to use force to confront them in the name of a presumed right
and the reason of the strongest, according to modes that we no longer
know, in principle and in all rigor, how to qualify, and that, according to
my hypothesis, are and will remain forever foreign to every accredited
qualification and every acceptable conceptual distinction: army as opposed to police, engaged in war (civil war, national war, or partisan war)
or in peacekeeping operations, or else in state terrorism.

Every "democracy to come," whatever meaning or credit we attribute
to this expression, will have to treat this problem and its urgency. It is
only in post-Kantian modernity that the problematic, and first of all the
definition, of democracy comes to be rooted in the turbulent terrain of
relations between states, in questions of war and peace. As at the end of
On the Social Contract, questions of foreign policy, of war and peace,
were still excluded, marginalized or deferred in the treatment of the concept and stakes of democracy. This democracy remained and still remains
a model of intranational and intrastate political organization within the
city. Despite some appearances, it is not certain that things have
changed. Whether we follow the guiding thread of a post-Kantian political thought of cosmopolitanism or that of the international law that
governed throughout the twentieth century such institutions as the
League of Nations, the United Nations, the International Criminal
Court, and so on, the democratic model (equality and freedom of sovereign state subjects, majority rule, and so on) sometimes seems to become

or tends to become "in spirit" the norm of this politics of international law. But this appearance is deceptive, and the question of a universal, international, interstate, and especially trans-state democratization remains an utterly obscure question of the future. It is one of the possible horizons of the expression "democracy to come." The democratic paradigm does not govern the tradition of Kant's treatise *Perpetual Peace*, which it would be necessary to read here closely, with its concept of a "world republic [*Weltrepublik*],"[46] which is not a democracy, and its distinction between a "treaty of peace [*Friedensvertrag, pactum pacis*]" and a "league of peace [*Friedensbund, foedus pacificum*]" (*PP*, 18), this latter alone being capable of assuring a perpetual peace in a federation of free, which is to say, sovereign, states. All this, we must never forget, is in the context of Kant's claim that the "majesty of the people," that is to say, the sovereignty of the people, is an "absurd expression [*Volksmajestät ist ein ungereimter Ausdruck*]" (*PP*, 16). *Majestas* has always been a synonym of *sovereignty*.[47] Only a state can be or have a sovereign. A league of peoples (*Völkerbund*) cannot become a state of peoples (*Völkerstaat*) or be joined into a single state. As for democracy in the interstate or trans-state relations, law, and institutions of today, the least that can be said is that it remains entirely to come. It is thus the place of which we must speak: not necessarily *from* this place or *in view of* this place but on the subject of the possibility or impossibility of such a place.

In saying that this place (possible, impossible, or unlocatable but not necessarily utopic) constitutes *the* place or *proper* place with any chance of giving some weight or scope to the expression "democracy to come," I should in all honesty commit myself, although I will not be able to do so today, to a patient analysis of all the contexts and inflections that have marked this sort of motto that is not even a sentence ("democracy to come"): for I have most often used it, always in passing, with as much stubborn determination as indeterminate hesitation—at once calculated and culpable—in a strange mixture of lightness and gravity, in a casual and cursory, indeed somewhat irresponsible, way, with a somewhat sententious and aphoristic reserve that leaves seriously in reserve an excessive responsibility.

Each time, the context and the inflection have differed, to be sure, beginning with what was probably, although I am not certain, the first occurrence, in 1989–90 in *Du droit à la philosophie*. *Democracy* was there defined as a "philosophical concept" and something that "*remains* still to come."[48] The same year, in the conference that then became *Force of Law*, in the course of analyzing in a more *or* less, more *and* less, deconstructive fashion the already autodeconstructive discourse of Benjamin in his revolutionary critique of parliamentary government and liberal democracy, I noted that, from Benjamin's point of view, "democracy would be a degeneration of law, of the violence, the authority and the power of law," and that "there is not yet any democracy worthy of this name. Democracy *remains* to come: to engender or to regenerate."[49]

The feeling of aporetic difficulty affects not only some supposedly endless approach of democracy *itself*, of the democratic thing, if one can still say this (and precisely on account of the autoimmunity of the same and the proper). This aporia-affect affects the very use of the word *democracy* in the syntagma "democracy to come." That is what I tried to suggest in *Sauf le nom* (1993) with regard to the meaning of *sans* in the apophatic discourse of so-called negative theology, indeed of a khōra or a spacing before any determination and any possible reappropriation by a theologico-political history or revelation, and even before a negative theology, which is always fundamentally related to some historical, and especially Christian, revelation. The democracy to come would be like the khōra of the political. Taking the *example* of "democracy" (but we shall encounter with the example of democracy the paradox of the example), one of the voices of this text (which is a polylogue) explains what the locution "democracy to come" should above all not mean, namely, a regulative Idea in the Kantian sense, but also what it *remained*, and could not but remain [*demeurer*], namely, the inheritance of a promise: "The difficulty of the 'without [*sans*]' spreads into what is still called politics, morals, or law, which are just as threatened as promised by apophasis."[50]

It is thus indeed already a question of autoimmunity, of a *double bind* of threat and chance, not alternatively or by turns promise and/or threat but threat *in* the promise itself. And here is the example, which is certainly not fortuitous:

> Take the example of democracy, of the idea of democracy, of democracy to come (neither the Idea in the Kantian sense, nor the current, limited, and determined concept of democracy, but democracy as the inheritance of a promise). Its path passes perhaps today in the world through (across) the aporias of negative theology.

The other voice then protests: "How can a path pass through aporias?"

Once a response has been given to this question, the voice again protests, recalling that this possibility seems just as well impossible, and then adds:

> So difficult in any case that this passage through aporia seems first of all (perhaps) reserved as a secret for a few. This esoterism seems strange for a democracy, even for this democracy to come that you define no more than apophasis defines God. Its to-come would be jealously thought, watched over, hardly taught by a few. Very suspect. (*ON*, 83)

This voice was trying to insinuate that this was not the most democratic language, that is, the most commendable, in which to recommend democracy. An advocate for democracy should have learned to speak to the people, to speak democratically of democracy.

To this suspicion the other voice responds by appealing to a double injunction, one that very much resembles the autoimmune contradiction or counterindication of which we have been speaking today, as well as the properly democratic paradox of the exemplary "anyone" or "no matter who":

> Understand me, it's a matter of maintaining a double injunction. Two concurrent desires divide apophatic theology, at the edge of nondesire, around the gulf and chaos of the Khōra: the desire to be inclusive of all, thus understood by all (community, *koinē*), and the desire to keep or entrust the secret within the very strict limits of those who hear/understand it *right*, as secret, and are then capable or worthy of keeping it. The secret, no more than democracy or the secret of democracy, must not, besides, cannot, be entrusted to the inheritance of no matter whom. Again the paradox of the example: the no-matter-who (any example sample) must also give the *good* example. (*ON*, 83–84)

Reference is thus made each time to the regulative Idea in the Kantian sense, to which I would not want the idea of a democracy to come to be reduced.

Yet the regulative Idea remains, for lack of anything better, if we can say "lack of anything better" with regard to a regulative Idea, a last resort. Although such a last resort or final recourse risks becoming an alibi, it retains a certain dignity. I cannot swear that I will not one day give in to it.

My reservations with regard to the regulative Idea would be, in brief, of *three sorts*. Some of them concern, first of all, the very loose way in which this notion of a regulative Idea is currently used, outside its strictly Kantian determination. In such cases the regulative Idea remains in the order of the *possible*, an ideal possible that is infinitely deferred. It partakes of what would still fall, at the end of an infinite history, into the realm of the possible, of what is virtual or potential, of what is within the power of someone, some "I can," to reach, in theory, and in a form that is not wholly freed from all teleological ends.

To this I would oppose, in the first place, all the figures I place under the title of the *im-possible*, of what must remain (in a nonnegative fashion) foreign to the order of my possibilities, to the order of the "I can," ipseity, the theoretical, the descriptive, the constative, and the performative (inasmuch as this latter still implies a power for some "I" guaranteed by conventions that neutralize the pure eventfulness of the event, and inasmuch as the eventfulness of the to-come exceeds this sphere of the performative). It is a question here, as with the coming of any event worthy of this name, of an unforeseeable coming of the other, of a heteronomy, of a law come from the other, of a responsibility and decision of the other—of the other in me, an other greater and older than I am. It is thus a question of separating democracy and autonomy, something that is, I concede, more than difficult, indeed im-possible. It is more im-possible, and yet necessary, to separate sovereignty and unconditionality, law and justice, as I proposed in "The University Without Condition" (2001).

This im-possible is not privative. It is not the inaccessible, and it is not what I can indefinitely defer: it announces itself; it precedes me, swoops down upon and seizes me *here and now* in a nonvirtualizable way, in actuality and not potentiality. It comes upon me from on high, in the form of an injunction that does not simply wait on the horizon, that I do not see coming, that never leaves me in peace and never lets me put it off until later. Such an urgency cannot be *idealized* any more than the other as other can. This im-possible is thus not a (regulative) *idea* or *ideal*. It is what is most undeniably *real*. And sensible. Like the other. Like the irreducible and nonappropriable différance of the other.

In the second place, then, the responsibility of what remains to be decided or done (in actuality) cannot consist in following, applying, or carrying out a norm or rule. Wherever I have at my disposal a determinable rule, I know what must be done, and as soon as such knowledge dictates the law, action follows knowledge as a calculable consequence: one *knows* what path to take, one no longer hesitates. The decision then no longer decides anything but is made in advance and is thus in advance annulled. It is simply deployed, without delay, presently, with the automatism attributed to machines. There is no longer any place for justice or responsibility (whether juridical, political, or ethical).

Finally, in the third place, if we come back this time to the strict meaning Kant gave to the *regulative* use of ideas (as opposed to their *constitutive* use), we would, in all rigor, in order to say anything on this subject and, especially, in order to appropriate such terms, have to subscribe to the entire Kantian architectonic and critique, something I cannot seriously undertake or even commit myself to doing here. We would have to begin by asking about what Kant calls "those differences in the interest of reason [*ein verschiedenes Interesse der Vernunft*],"[51] the *imaginary* (the *focus imaginarius*, that point toward which all the lines directing the rules of understanding—which is not reason—tend and converge and thus indefinitely *approximate*), the necessary *illusion*, which need not necessarily deceive us, the figure of an approach or approximation (*zu nähern*) that tends indefinitely toward rules of universality, and especially the indispensable use of the *as if* (*als ob*).[52] I cannot treat this here, but I thought it necessary at least to note, in principle, how circumspect I would be to appropriate in any rigorous way this idea of a "regulative Idea." Let us not forget, since we have been talking so much about the world and the worldwide [*mondialisation*], that the very idea of *world* remains a *regulative Idea* for Kant.[53] It is the second of the regulative Ideas, between two others that remain, so to speak, two forms of sovereignty: the ipseity of the "myself" (*Ich selbst*), as soul or as thinking nature, and the ipseity of God.

Those are some of the reasons why I, without ever giving up on reason and on a certain "interest of reason," hesitate to use the expression "regulative Idea" when speaking of a to-come or of democracy to come. In *The Other Heading* (1991) I explicitly set aside the "status of the regulative Idea in the Kantian sense" and insisted at once on the absolute and unconditional urgency of the *here and now* that does not wait and on the structure of the promise, a promise that is kept in memory, that is handed down [*léguée*], inherited, claimed and taken up [*alléguée*]. Here is how the "to-come" was there defined: "not something that is certain to happen tomorrow, not the democracy (national or international, state or trans-state) of the *future*, but a democracy that must have the structure of a promise—*and thus the memory of that which carries the future, the to-come, here and now.*"[54]

All of this was written in the context of a series of aporias and antinomies to which I cannot return here.

I should, it seems to me, clarify a bit better here what still remains enveloped in these gestures, which will become more frequent and somewhat differently inflected in subsequent references to the "democracy to come." I shall do this rather quickly around *five foci*.

1. The expression "democracy to come" does indeed translate or call for a militant and interminable political critique. A weapon aimed at the enemies of democracy, it protests against all naïveté and every political abuse, every rhetoric that would present as a present or existing democracy, as a de facto democracy, what remains inadequate to the democratic demand, whether nearby or far away, at home or somewhere else in the world, anywhere that a discourse on human rights and on democracy remains little more than an obscene alibi so long as it tolerates the terrible plight of so many millions of human beings suffering from malnutrition, disease, and humiliation, grossly deprived not only of bread and water but of equality or freedom, dispossessed of the rights of all, of everyone, of anyone. (This "anyone" comes before any other metaphysical determination as subject, human person, or consciousness, before any juridical determination as compeer, compatriot, kin, brother, neighbor, fellow religious follower, or fellow citizen. Paulhan says somewhere, and I am here paraphrasing, that to think democracy is to think the "first to happen by" [*le premier venu*]: anyone, no matter who, at the permeable limit between "who" and "what," the living being, the cadaver, and the ghost. The first to happen by: is that not the best way to translate "the first to come"?)

The "to-come" not only points to the promise but suggests that democracy will never exist, in the sense of a present existence: not because it will be deferred but because it will always remain aporetic in its structure (force *without* force, incalculable singularity *and* calculable equality, commensurability *and* incommensurability, heteronomy *and* autonomy, indivisible sovereignty *and* divisible or shared sovereignty, an empty name, a despairing messianicity or a messianicity in despair, and so on).

But, beyond this active and interminable critique, the expression "democracy to come" takes into account the absolute and intrinsic historicity of the only system that welcomes in itself, in its very concept, that

expression of autoimmunity called the right to self-critique and perfectibility. Democracy is the only system, the only constitutional paradigm, in which, in principle, one has or assumes the right to criticize
everything publicly, including the idea of democracy, its concept, its history, and its name. Including the idea of the constitutional paradigm and
the absolute authority of law. It is thus the only paradigm that is universalizable, whence its chance and its fragility. But in order for this historicity—unique among all political systems—to be complete, it must be freed
not only from the Idea in the Kantian sense but from all teleology, all
onto-theo-teleology.

2. This implies another thinking of the event (unique, unforeseeable,
without horizon, un-masterable by any ipseity or any conventional and
thus consensual performativity), which is marked in a "to-come" that, beyond the future (since the democratic demand does not wait), names the
coming of *who* comes or of *what* comes to pass, namely, the newly arrived
whose irruption should not and cannot be limited by any conditional hospitality on the borders of a policed nation-state.

3. This naturally presupposes, and that is what is most difficult, most
inconceivable, an extension of the democratic beyond nation-state sovereignty, beyond citizenship. This would come about through the creation
of an international juridico-political space that, without doing away with
every reference to sovereignty, never stops innovating and inventing new
distributions and forms of sharing, new divisions of sovereignty. (I refer to
inventing here because the to-come gestures not only toward the coming
of the other but toward invention—invention not of the event but
through the event.) The discourse concerning the New International in
Specters of Marx (1993) tried to point in this direction. The renewed declaration of human rights (and not the "rights of man and the citizen") at
the end of World War II remains an essential democratic reference for the
institutions of international law, especially the United Nations. This reference is thus in virtual contradiction with the principle of nation-state
sovereignty, which there remains also intact. It is by democratic reference
to the Universal Declaration of Human Rights that one tries, most often
to no avail, to impose limits on the sovereignty of nation-states. One example of this, among so many others, would be the laborious creation of
an International Criminal Court.

The Declaration of Human Rights is not, however, opposed to, and so does not limit, the sovereignty of the nation-state in the way a principle of nonsovereignty would oppose a principle of sovereignty. No, it is one sovereignty set against another. Human rights pose and presuppose the human being (who is equal, free, self-determined) as sovereign. The Declaration of Human Rights declares *another* sovereignty; it thus reveals the autoimmunity of sovereignty in general.

4. In *Specters of Marx* the expression "democracy to come" is inextricably linked to justice. It is the *ergo* or the *igitur*, the *thus* between "democracy to come and justice": "For the democracy to come and thus for justice," as a verbless phrase puts it in *Specters of Marx.*[55]

This gesture inscribes the necessity of the democracy to come not only into the axiomatic of the messianicity without messianism, the spectrality or hauntology, that this book develops, but into the singular distinction between law and justice (heterogeneous but inseparable). This distinction was first developed in *Force of Law* and was further elaborated in *Specters of Marx* in the course of a discussion of the Heideggerian interpretation of *dikē* as gathering, adjoining, and harmony. Contesting that interpretation, I proposed aligning justice with disjointure, with being *out of joint*, with the interruption of relation, with unbinding, with the infinite secret of the other. All this can indeed seem to threaten a community-oriented or communitarian concept of democratic justice. This discussion, which I cannot reconstitute here, plays a discreet but decisive role throughout the book. It could orient us toward the question of the future: why are there so few democrat philosophers (if there have been any at all), from Plato to Heidegger? Why does Heidegger remain, in this regard as well, still Platonic?

This conjunction of democracy *and* justice is also one of the themes of *Politics of Friendship*, which, a year later, explicitly says—still without a verb—"With regard to democracy *and* with regard to justice,"[56] linking the thought of the to-come of the event to the irreducible "perhaps," questioning this name democracy by recalling what the *Menexenus* said of the regime under which the Athenians had lived most of the time, "a form of government which receives various names, according to the fancies of men, and is sometimes called democracy (*dēmokratia*), but is really an aristocracy or government of the best which has the approval of the many" (*PF*, 95).

It is here that a certain question gets developed, more explicitly in *Pol-*

itics of Friendship than anywhere else: the *question of the name*, of what is happening "today" "in the name of democracy." I must be content to signal, so as then to put a bit finer point on it, the place that then, in the course of a deconstructive critique of Schmitt's conceptuality (notably around the concepts of decision and war—whether war between nation-states, civil war, or so-called partisan war), opens onto a whole series of questions surrounding the "democracy to come." I ask:

> If, between the name on the one hand, the concept and the thing on the other, the play of a gap offers room for *rhetorical* [I emphasize this word for reasons that will become apparent in a moment] effects which are also political strategies, what are the lessons that we can draw today? Is it still *in the name of democracy* that one will attempt to criticize such and such a determination of democracy or aristo-democracy? Or, more radically—closer, precisely, to its fundamental *radicality* (where, for example, it is *rooted* in the security of an autochthonous foundation, in the stock or in the genius of filiation)—is it still in the name of democracy, of a democracy to come, that one will attempt to deconstruct a concept, all the predicates associated with the massively dominant concept of democracy, that in whose heritage one inevitably meets again the law of birth, the natural or "national" law, the law of homophilia or of autochthony, civic equality (isonomy) founded on equality of birth (isogony) as the condition of the calculation of approbation and, therefore, the aristocracy of virtue and wisdom, and so forth?
>
> What remains or still resists in the deconstructed (or deconstructible) concept of democracy which guides us endlessly? Which *orders* us not only to *engage* [I here underscore *orders* and *engage*, which I will return to in a moment] a deconstruction but to keep the old name? And to deconstruct further in the name of a *democracy* to come? That is to say, further, which *enjoins* [my emphasis] us still to inherit from what—forgotten, repressed, misunderstood, or unthought in the "old" concept and throughout its history—would still be on the watch, giving off signs or symptoms of a stance of survival coming through all the old and tired features? (*PF,* 103–4; see also *PF,* 305–6)

This did not thus exclude the possibility, even the right, of perhaps one day abandoning the inheritance or heritage of the name, of changing names. But always in the name of the name, thereby betraying the heritage *in the name of* the heritage.

> Saying that to keep this Greek name, *democracy,* is an affair of context, of rhetoric or of strategy, even of polemics, reaffirming that this name will last as long as it has to but not much longer, saying that things are speeding up remarkably in these fast times, is not necessarily giving in to the opportunism or

cynicism of the antidemocrat who is not showing his cards. Completely to the contrary: one keeps this indefinite right to the question, to criticism, to deconstruction (guaranteed rights, in principle, in any democracy: no deconstruction without democracy, no democracy without deconstruction). One keeps this right strategically to mark what is no longer a strategic affair: the limit between the conditional (the edges of the context and of the concept enclosing the effective practice of democracy and nourishing it in land and blood) and the unconditional, which, from the outset, will have inscribed a self-deconstructive force [I could have in fact said "autoimmune" force] in the very motif of democracy, the possibility and the duty for democracy itself to de-limit itself. Democracy is the *autos* [I would today say the *ipse* or ipseity] of deconstructive self-delimitation. Delimitation not only in the name of a regulative Idea and an indefinite perfectibility but every time in the singular urgency of a *here and now*. (*PF*, 105)

5. In speaking of an unconditional injunction or of a singular urgency, in invoking a *here and now* that does not await an indefinitely remote future assigned by some regulative Idea, one is not necessarily pointing to the future of a democracy that is going to come or that must come or even a democracy that *is* the future. One is especially not speaking about some real imminence, even if a certain imminence is inscribed in the strange concept of "democracy to come." One is not saying what is going to happen or what is already in the process of happening, as Tocqueville did when he spoke of being "constantly preoccupied by a single thought," a thought at once realistic and optimistic, as he was writing *Democracy in America*. Tocqueville *announced*, in effect, in the preface to the twelfth edition of the book, "the approaching irresistible and universal spread of democracy throughout the world" (*DA*, lxxxvii). This was an *announcement*. Tocqueville was announcing not simply the imminent future but, in the present, the present: "A great democratic revolution is taking place in our midst" (*DA*, 3), he says in his introduction.

As for "democracy to come," it actually announces nothing. But then what are these three words doing? What is the modal status of this syntagma that names, in general, the "democracy to come" without forming a sentence, especially not a proposition of the sort "democracy *is* to come." If I happen to have written that it "remains" to come, this remaining [*restance*], as always in my texts, at least since *Glas*, this democracy in waiting or as remaining [*en restance*], pending [*en souffrance*], withdraws from its ontological dependence. It does not constitute the modification of an "is," of an ontological copula marking the present of essence or existence, indeed of substantial or subjective substance.

Now, I would wish to claim that the question of the obscure status or mode of this phrase without a verb is *already* political and that it is, moreover, *the* question *of* democracy. For "democracy to come" can hesitate endlessly, oscillate indecidably and forever, between two possibilities: it can, on the one hand, correspond to the neutral, constative analysis of a concept. (In this case I would simply be describing, observing, limiting myself to analyzing, as a responsible philosopher and logician of language, as a semanticist, what the concept of democracy implies, namely, everything we have just spoken about: the semantic void at the heart of the concept, its rather ordinary insignificance or its disseminal spacing, memory, promise, the event to come, messianicity that at once interrupts and accomplishes intrinsic historicity, perfectibility, the right to autoimmune self-critique, and an indefinite number of aporias. This would amount to saying: if you want to know what you are saying when you use this inherited word *democracy*, you need to know that these things are inscribed or prescribed within it; for my part, I am simply describing this prescription in a neutral fashion. I am *mentioning* the word *democracy* as much as *using* it.) But, on the other hand, no longer satisfied to remain at the level of a neutral, constative conceptual analysis, "democracy to come" can also inscribe a performative and attempt to win conviction by suggesting support or adherence, an "and yet it is necessary to believe it," "I believe in it, I promise, I am in on the promise and in messianic waiting, I am taking action or am at least enduring, now you do the same," and so on. The *to* of the "to come" wavers between imperative injunction (call or performative) and the patient *perhaps* of messianicity (nonperformative exposure to what comes, to what can always not come or has already come).

Wavering between the two, the *to* can also, at the same time or by turns, let the two *to*'s be heard. These two possibilities or two modalities of discourse, these two postures, can alternate; they can be addressed to you by turns, or else they can haunt one another, parasite one another in the same instant, each becoming by turns the alibi of the other. In saying this myself right now, in cautioning you that I can by turns or simultaneously play on the two turns or turns of phrase, I withdraw into the secret of irony, be it irony in general or the particular rhetorical figure called irony. But here is yet one more turn, and it is political: is it not also democracy that gives the right to irony in the public space? Yes, for democracy opens public space, the publicity of public space, by granting the right to a change of tone (*Wechsel der Töne*), to irony as well as to fiction, the simulacrum, the secret, literature, and so on. And, thus, to a certain nonpublic public within the public, to a *res publica*, a republic where the difference between the public and the nonpublic remains an indecidable limit. There is something of a democratic republic as soon as this right is exercised. This indecidability is, like freedom itself, granted by democracy, and it constitutes, I continue to believe, the only radical possibility of deciding and of making come about (performatively), or rather of letting come about (metaperformatively), and thus of thinking *what* comes about or happens and *who* happens by, the arriving of whoever arrives. It thus already opens, for whomever, an experience of freedom, however ambiguous and disquieting, threatened and threatening, it might remain in its "perhaps," with a necessarily excessive responsibility of which no one may be absolved.

With these references to right or law and justice, I am already beginning to pull on my *second* guiding thread, the one I will cut shortest. It concerns the connection between law and justice, these two heterogeneous yet inseparable concepts, but also, and especially, the connection between law, justice, and force, particularly in relation to the international and transnational stakes inscribed-prescribed, preinscribed, paradoxically, in the syntagma "democracy to come." As for law, justice, and force, as for knowing whether the reason of the strongest is always best, I ask your permission to make *as if*, through an economical fiction, we had already agreed on the necessity of this reinterpretation or reactivation of an enormous traditional problematic with the question of rogue states in view. This problematic—always open, abyssal, chaotic—runs from at least Plato (for example, from Callicles' discourse in the *Gorgias* or Thrasymachus's in the *Republic*, both of which maintain that the just or the right [*dikē, dikaion*] is on the side of or in the interest of the strongest), to Machiavelli, Hobbes, and the Pascal of that well-known and vertiginous thought that has been so often and so well discussed (by Louis Marin and Geoffrey Bennington in particular): "Justice-might . . . being unable to make what is just strong, we have made what is strong just,"[57] to the La Fontaine of "The Wolf and the Lamb" (a couple that goes back to at least Plato and one that I submitted to an interminable analysis in my seminar this year), to the Rousseau of *On the Social Contract* ("On the Right of the Strongest: The strongest is never strong enough to be master all the time, unless he transforms force into right . . . " [*SC,* 19]), and especially, and I insist on this, to a certain Kant, whose definition of strict right (*das stricte Recht*), whose doctrine of right proper (*eigentliche Rechtslehre*), implies in the very concept of right the faculty or the possibility of reciprocal constraint or coercion (*wechselseitigen Zwanges*), and thus the possibility of force, of a reason of the strongest in accordance with universal laws and consistent with the freedom of all.[58] This simple definition is meant to be pure and a priori. It entails at once the democratic (the freedom of everyone), universality, the international, and cosmopolitical law, beyond the nation-state (universal laws). It prescribes or authorizes the legal and legitimate recourse to force (the a priori necessity of constraint), that is, some sovereignty, even if it is not of the state.

We now have available to us, after this interminable detour, all the necessary elements to approach the knot we spoke of earlier and so finally address, by following our *third thread,* what I will provisionally call the epoch of rogue states.

If the expression "rogue state" appears rather recent, the word *rogue,* as an adjective or substantive, has inhabited the English language and haunted its literature longer than the word *voyou* has the French language and its literature. In use since the middle of the sixteenth century, it refers in everyday language, in the language of the law, and in great works of literature, already in Spenser and often in Shakespeare, to beggars and homeless vagabonds of various kinds but also, and for this same reason, to all sorts of riffraff, villains, and unprincipled outlaws ("a dishonest, unprincipled person," says the *Oxford English Dictionary,* "a rascal"). From there the meaning gets extended, in Shakespeare as well as in Darwin, to all nonhuman living beings, that is, to plants and animals whose behavior appears deviant or perverse. Any wild animal can be called rogue but especially those, such as *rogue elephants,* that behave like ravaging outlaws, violating the customs and conventions, the customary practices, of *their own* community. A horse can be called rogue when it stops acting as it is supposed to, as it is expected to, for example as a race horse or a trained hunting horse. A distinguishing sign is thus affixed to it, a badge or hood, to mark its status as rogue. This last point marks the point rather well; indeed it brands it, for the qualification *rogue* calls for a marking or brand-

ing classification that sets something apart. A mark of infamy discrimi-
nates by means of a first banishing or exclusion that then leads to a bringing before the law. It is somewhat analogous to the wheel, forerunner of
the yellow star, I spoke of earlier. Something similar can be heard in the
German word *Schurke,* which is used to translate *rogue* in the expression
"rogue state," and which also means "rascal," "scoundrel," "crook," "thief,"
"villain," and so on.

But whereas *voyou, Schurke, canalla* are used to speak only of human
outlaws, the English *rogue* can be extended to plants and, especially, animals, as we just noted. This will be one of the reasons it has recently held
such a privileged position in American political rhetoric, as we will show
in a moment. As an article in the *Chronicle of Higher Education* notes, "in
the animal kingdom, a rogue is defined as a creature that is born different.
It is incapable of mingling with the herd, it keeps to itself, and it can attack at any time, without warning."[59]

§ 9 (No) More Rogue States

In American diplomatic and geopolitical discourse the expression or figure of speech "rogue state" as a denunciation appears to have gained currency only after the so-called end of the so-called Cold War. During the 1960s it was rarely used, and used only to refer to the *internal* politics of regimes that were not very democratic and did not respect what is called the state of law or the constitutional state. It was only in the 1980s, and especially after 1990, after the collapse of the communist bloc, that the qualifying expression "rogue state" left the sphere of domestic politics, of internal nondemocracy, if you will. In a movement that accelerated during the Clinton administration by reference to what was already being called international terrorism, the term was extended to international behavior and to supposed failings with regard to either the spirit or the letter of international law, a law that claims to be fundamentally democratic.

The hypothesis that I would like to put before you today in order to conclude is that if we have been speaking of rogue states for a relatively short time now, and in a recurrent way only since the so-called end of the so-called Cold War, the time is soon coming when we will no longer speak of them. I will try to explain why. Following this hypothesis, I thus propose to speak of an "epoch of rogue states" by asking not only if there are rogue states but particularly what the phrase *plus d'Etats voyous*, "(no) more rogue states," might mean, that is, *more than we think, more than one or soon no more at all [plus qu'on ne pense, plus d'un ou bientôt plus du tout]*.

There are many signs, statements, and statistics that attest to the fact that it was between 1997 and 2000 under Clinton, and first of all in the speeches of Clinton himself and those of his top advisers (particularly

Madeleine Albright), that the literal denunciation of "rogue states" became more and more pronounced. The phrase appeared during this time with the greatest frequency, sometimes replaced by two or three synonyms, *outcast, outlaw nation,* or *pariah state.* Ronald Reagan had preferred the term *outlaw,* and George Bush tended to speak of *renegade regimes.* After 2000, just before and just after September 11, people began taking an interest in a systematic and public way in this discourse and in the American strategy for dealing with rogue states. A couple of recent works make this abundantly clear, most notably Noam Chomsky's scathing indictment, *Rogue States: The Rule of Force in World Affairs,* published in 2000, that is, before September 11, 2001 (an event to which Chomsky has since devoted another book, a collection of interviews entitled *9-11,* which develops the same line of thought).[60] *Rogue States* lays out an unimpeachable case, supported by extensive, overwhelming, although in general not widely publicized or utilized information, against American foreign policy. The crux of the argument, in a word, is that the most *roguish* of rogue states are those that circulate and make use of a concept like "rogue state," with the language, rhetoric, juridical discourse, and strategico-military consequences we all know. The first and most violent of rogue states are those that have ignored and continue to violate the very international law they claim to champion, the law in whose name they speak and in whose name they go to war against so-called rogue states each time their interests so dictate. The name of these states? The United States.

We know, in fact, just how a rogue state is identified by Robert S. Litwak (whom Chomsky does not cite). Director of the Division of International Studies at the Woodrow Wilson International Center for Scholars, Litwak, who was part of the Clinton team and served on the National Security Council staff, has recently published a book entitled *Rogue States and U.S. Foreign Policy.*[61] Knowing, then, whereof he speaks, Litwak defines the rogue state in this way: A rogue state is basically whomever the United States says it is.[62] Litwak is responding indirectly to a question posed by certain journalists and university experts: does the discourse concerning rogue states reflect a reality or is it purely rhetorical? As one of them formulated the issue: "As the United States gets closer and closer to spending $60 billion on a missile-defense system designed to fend off attacks from 'rogue states,' I would like to get a bit clearer on what a rogue state is."[63]

The most perverse, most violent, most destructive of rogue states would thus be, first and foremost, the United States, and sometimes its allies. The body of information gathered to support these charges is impressive. Another, even more virulent, book argues in a similar vein, William Blum's *Rogue State*.[64] Written by a former employee of the State Department, this book was originally published just before September 11 (although it now includes a new preface written in the aftermath of 9-11) and has recently appeared in a French translation.

The first regime to be treated as a rogue was Noriega's regime in Panama. An exemplary example: the American administration leveled this accusation only when the threats of revolution in Central America were beginning to die down, that is, after the CIA, Carter, Reagan, and Bush had consistently and continuously supported Noriega, even though he acted in complete defiance of the state of law or the constitutional state, torturing and massacring dissidents and strikers, participating in drug trafficking, and arming the contras of Nicaragua. To take just one more typical and more recent example, Saddam Hussein's Iraq was declared by Washington and London during the crisis of 1998 to be a "rogue state" and an "outlaw nation." In this new situation Saddam Hussein was himself sometimes called, and with all the animal connotations I noted earlier, the "beast of Baghdad," after having been, like Noriega, a long-standing ally and valuable economic partner. The beast is not simply an animal but the very incarnation of evil, of the satanic, the diabolical, the demonic— a beast of the Apocalypse. Before Iraq, Libya had been considered by the Reagan administration to be a rogue state, although I don't believe that the word itself was ever used. Libya, Iraq, and Sudan were bombed for being rogue states and, in the last two instances, with a violence and cruelty that fall nowise short of those associated with what is called "September 11." But the list is endless (Cuba, Nicaragua, North Korea, Iran, and so on). For reasons that would be interesting to study, India and Pakistan, despite their reckless postures with regard to nuclear disarmament, particularly in 1998, have never figured among rogue states in the eyes of the United States (although India did everything it could at the United Nations to have Pakistan condemned as a rogue state).

From the point of view of international law two principal characteristics seem to define, for our purposes here, the juridical situation that serves as the stage for playing out the script for all these operations. That stage is the United Nations and its Security Council. Two laws articulate together, although in an aporetic way and by turns, a democratic principle and a principle of sovereignty.

First, the decisions of the General Assembly, regardless of whether they end up being respected, are made democratically, after deliberation, and they must be passed by a majority of the representatives of the member states elected by the assembly, member states that are each sovereign at home. In addition to a constitutive reference to the Declaration of Human Rights, which is democratic in spirit and essence, the Charter of the United Nations institutes a legislative model along the lines of a democratic Parliament, even if the representatives are not elected by the state that delegates them, although every candidate state is elected and accepted by the assembly after meeting certain conditions. As we know, in the wake of the decolonization of the past few decades, Western states allied to the United States or to Israel can no longer count on a majority in the General Assembly, except in cases where something called, precisely, "international terrorism"—and even then!—threatens the sovereignty of *all* states. This lack of an established majority for the United States and its allies (for what are called "Western democracies") has no doubt become, with the end of the Cold War, the setting and stage for this rhetoric of rogue states.

But since the democratic sovereignty of the United Nations General Assembly is powerless, since it has at its disposal no executive and coercive force of its own, and thus no effective or even juridical sovereignty (for, as Kant would say, there is no right without force), it is the Security Council, with its veto power, that has the power to make binding or enforceable decisions, that wields all the force of effective sovereignty. And this will continue to be the case right up until the day a radically new situation rectifies this monstrosity. To put it in the most cut-and-dried terms, I would say that the fate of the democracy to come, in its relation to world order, depends on what will become of this strange and supposedly all-powerful institution called the Security Council.

To understand the role and composition of the council, we must recall a bit of history: the United Nations was instituted in 1945, at the end of the Second World War—and with the intention of preventing a third—by the victors who were and remain the only *permanent* members of the Security Council (the United States, the United Kingdom, the USSR [now Russia], a group then expanded to include France and China). The other members of the council—first eleven, then fifteen—are not permanent but are elected to serve for a period of two years by the General Assembly, making their power all the more limited. The only permanent members of the council are thus those states that were and remain (in the precarious, critical, and ever-changing situation we are examining) great world powers in possession of nuclear weapons. This is a diktat or dictatorship that no universal law can in principle justify. One of the mechanisms used to render ineffective and inconsequential the decisions democratically deliberated on and agreed to by the United Nations is the sovereign veto of the Security Council. The three countries that have made the most use of that veto, in numerous situations where the vote of the United Nations did not seem to them to serve their interests, are, in order, the United States, the United Kingdom, and France. The Charter of the United Nations, a "solemn treaty" recognized as the foundation of international law and world order, in effect states that the Security Council shall determine everything that threatens or interrupts peace, every act of aggression, and it shall make recommendations or decide on measures to be taken in accordance with articles 41 and 42. These two articles provide for different kinds of recourse or sanction: preferably without the use of armed force but with such force if need be. (Yet we must never forget that neither the United Nations as a whole nor the Security Council has an effective force of its own; their operations thus have to be entrusted to one or many nation-states. It is thus not hard to see how everything gets played out in the appropriation and exercise of this power by one or another member of the Security Council.)

Then comes the exception, as if to confirm that the exception is always what determines or decides sovereignty or, inversely, to paraphrase or parody Schmitt, that the sovereign is the one who determines the exception and decides with regard to the exception. The only exception in the Charter of the United Nations is article 51. It recognizes the individual or collective right to defend oneself against an armed attack "until the Security Council has taken the measures necessary to maintain international peace and security." This is the only exception to the recommendation made to all states not to resort to force. As we know, and as countless examples since the founding of the United Nations have shown, this clause of the charter gave the two permanent members of the Security Council, states that were then called superpowers, that is, the United States and the USSR, a decisive supremacy right up to the end of the Cold War over UN policy—at least with regard to the fundamental mission of maintaining international peace and security (for the United Nations has a whole host of other missions that I cannot take into account here).

This exception marks several things, one just as fundamental as the next; first, since "the reason of the strongest is always best," the de facto situation, the relations of force (military, economic, technoscientific, and so on) and the differences of force end up determining through their intrinsic effectiveness a world law that, in the aftermath of a world war, is in the hands of certain sovereign states that are more powerful (or really superpowerful) than other sovereign states. The reason of the strongest not only determines the actual policy of that international institution but, well before that, already determined the conceptual architecture of the charter itself, the law that governs, in its fundamental principles and in its practical rules, the development of this institution. It organizes and implements for use by the United Nations—precisely so that it itself may then use the United Nations—all the concepts, ideas (constitutive or regulative), and requisite Western political theorems, beginning with *democracy* and *sovereignty*. Those of democracy: the law of majority rule, the counting of votes in the General Assembly, the election of the secretary general, and so on. Those of sovereignty: the sovereignty of each state but also, so that the sovereignty of the United Nations might be effective, the acknowledgment, in what is always an arbitrary, unjustifiable, silent, and unavowable manner, of the supremacy of the permanent members of the Security Council and, chief among them, the two superpowers.

As always, these two principles, democracy and sovereignty, are at the same time, but also by turns, inseparable and in contradiction with one another. For democracy to be effective, for it to give rise to a system of law that can carry the day, which is to say, for it to give rise to an effective power, the *cracy* of the *dēmos*—of the world *dēmos* in this case—is required. What is required is thus a sovereignty, a force that is stronger than all the other forces in the world. But if the constitution of this force is, in principle, supposed to represent and protect this world democracy, it in fact betrays and threatens it from the very outset, in an autoimmune fashion, and in a way that is, as I said above, just as silent as it is unavowable. Silent and unavowable like sovereignty itself. Unavowable silence, denegation: that is the always unapparent essence of sovereignty. The unavowable in community is also a sovereignty that cannot but posit itself and impose itself in silence, in the unsaid. Even if it multiplies discourses to the point of an endless repetition of the theory of law or of every political rhetoric, sovereignty itself (if there is one and if it is pure) always keeps quiet in the very ipseity of the moment proper to it, a moment that is but the stigmatic point of an indivisible instant. A pure sovereignty is indivisible or it is not at all, as all the theoreticians of sovereignty have rightly recognized, and that is what links it to the decisionist exceptionality spoken of by Schmitt. This indivisibility excludes it in principle from being shared, from time and from language. From time, from the temporalization that it infinitely contracts, and, thus, paradoxically, from history. In a certain way, then, sovereignty is ahistorical; it is the contract contracted with a history that retracts in the instantaneous event of the deciding exception, an event that is without any temporal or historical thickness. As a result, sovereignty withdraws from language, which always introduces a sharing that universalizes. As soon as I speak to the other, I submit to the law of giving reason(s), I share a virtually universalizable medium, I divide my authority, even in the most performative language, which always requires another language in order to lay claim to some convention. The paradox, which is always the same, is that sovereignty is incompatible with universality even though it is called for by every concept of international, and thus universal or universalizable, and thus democratic, law. There is no sovereignty without force, without the force of the strongest, whose reason—the reason of the strongest—is to win out over [*avoir raison de*] everything.

Now, if sovereign force is silent, it is not for lack of speaking—it might go on speaking endlessly—but for lack of meaning. That is why I said earlier, "The democracy to come: if these words still have any *meaning* (but I am not so sure they do, and I am not sure that everything can be reduced here to a question of *meaning*)." To confer sense or meaning on sovereignty, to justify it, to find a reason for it, is already to compromise its deciding exceptionality, to subject it to rules, to a code of law, to some general law, to concepts. It is thus to divide it, to subject it to partitioning, to participation, to being shared. It is to take into account the part played by sovereignty. And to take that part or share into account is to turn sovereignty against itself, to compromise its immunity. This happens as soon as one speaks of it in order to give it or find in it some sense or meaning. But since this happens all the time, pure sovereignty does not exist; it is always in the process of positing itself by refuting itself, by denying or disavowing itself; it is always in the process of autoimmunizing itself, of betraying itself by betraying the democracy that nonetheless can never do without it.

Universal democracy, beyond the nation-state and beyond citizenship, calls in fact for a supersovereignty that cannot but betray it. The abuse of power, for example that of the Security Council or of certain superpowers that sit on it permanently, is an abuse from the very beginning, well before any particular, secondary abuse. Abuse of power is constitutive of sovereignty itself.[65]

What does this mean for rogue states? Well, that those states that are able or are in a state to denounce or accuse some "rogue state" of violating the law, of failing to live up to the law, of being guilty of some perversion or deviation, those states that claim to uphold international law and that take the initiative of war, of police or peacekeeping operations because they have the force to do so, these states, namely, the United States and its allied states in these actions, are themselves, as sovereign, the first rogue states. This is true even before any evidence is gathered to make a case against them, however useful and enlightening such a case may be, as is evidenced, for example, in the works of Chomsky and Blum entitled *Rogue States*.[66] It is not a criticism of these courageous works to wish for a more fully developed political thought within them, especially with regard to the history, structure, and "logic" of the concept of sovereignty. This "logic" would make it clear that, a priori, the states that are able or are in a state to make war on rogue states are themselves, in their most legitimate sovereignty, rogue states abusing their power. As soon as there is sovereignty, there is abuse of power and a rogue state. Abuse is the law of use; it is the law itself, the "logic" of a sovereignty that can reign only by not sharing. More precisely, since it never succeeds in doing this except in a critical, precarious, and unstable fashion, sovereignty can only *tend*, for a limited time, to reign without sharing. It can only tend toward imperial hegemony. To make use of the time is already an abuse—and this is true as well for the rogue that I therefore am. There are thus only rogue states. Potentially or actually. The state is voyou, a rogue, roguish. There are always (no) more rogue states than one thinks. *Plus d'Etats voyous*, how are we to hear this? (No) more rogue states: how are we to read this?

Apparently, at the end of this long excursion, one would be tempted to answer "yes" to the question posed in the title of this talk: "The reason of the strongest (are there rogue states?)." Yes, yes there are, but always more than one thinks and says. That would be a first reversal or turnabout.

But here is the last turnabout or about-face, the very last, the last turn of a volte-face, of a revolution or *revolving door*.[67] In what does it consist? The first temptation, which I will resist, since it is just a bit too easy even if it is legitimate, is to think that when all states are rogue states, when voyoucracy constitutes the very *cracy* of state sovereignty, when there are only rogues, then there are *no more rogues.* When there are always more rogues than one says and leads others to believe, then there are no more rogues. But beyond the in some sense intrinsic necessity of rendering useless the meaning and range of the word *rogue,* as soon as the more there are the less there are, as soon as "*plus de voyous,*" "*plus d'Etats voyous,*" (no) more rogues, (no) more rogue states, signifies two so very contradictory things, there is another necessity to do away with this appellation and circumscribe its epoch, to delimit the frequent, recurrent, and compulsive recourse that the United States and certain of its allies have had to it.

Here, then, is my hypothesis: on the one hand, this epoch began at the end of the so-called Cold War, a time when two highly militarized superpowers, founding and permanent members of the Security Council, thought they could maintain order in the world through a balance of nuclear and interstate terror; on the other hand, even if one continues now and then to make use of this locution, its end has been, if not exactly announced, theatrically or media-theatrically confirmed on September 11 (a date that is indispensable here for referring economically to an event to which no concept corresponds, and for good reason, an event constituted, in fact, in a structural way, as a *public* and *political* event—and thus beyond all the tragedies of the victims for whom we cannot but have a limitless compassion—by a powerful media-theatricalization calculated on both sides). Along with the two towers of the World Trade Center, what has *visibly* collapsed is the entire apparatus (logical, semantic, rhetorical, juridical, political) that made the ultimately so reassuring denunciation of rogue states so useful and significant. Soon after the collapse of the Soviet Union ("collapse" because this is one of the premises, one of the first turns [*tours*], of the collapse of the two towers [*tours*]), as early as 1993, Clinton, after coming to power, in effect inaugurated the politics of retaliation and sanction against rogue states by declaring in an address to the United Nations that his country would make use whenever it deemed it appropriate of article 51, that is, of the article of exception, and that the United States would act "multilaterally when possible, but unilaterally when necessary." This declaration was reiterated and confirmed on more than one occasion, both by Madeleine Albright, when she was ambassador to the United Nations, and by Secretary of Defense William Cohen. Cohen, in fact, announced that to combat rogue states the United States was ready to intervene militarily in a unilateral way (and thus without the prior accord of the United Nations or the Security Council) each time its vital interests were at stake; and by vital interests he meant "ensuring uninhibited access to key markets, energy supplies, and strategic resources," along with anything that might be considered a vital interest by a "domestic jurisdiction."[68] It would thus be enough for the Americans, from within the United States and without consulting anyone, to deem that their "vital interests" give them reason, good reason, to attack, destabilize, or destroy any state whose politics run contrary to those interests. To justify this sovereign unilaterality, this nonsharing of sovereignty, this violation of that supposedly democratic and widely accepted institution called the United Nations, to give reason to this reason of the strongest and show that might was indeed right, it was thus necessary to declare that the state deemed an aggressor or a threat was acting as a rogue state. As Litwak argued, a rogue state is whomever the United States says it is. And this occurred at the very moment that the United States, announcing that it would act unilaterally, was basically behaving like rogue states do. Rogue states, United States, which, on September 11, was officially authorized by the United Nations to act as such, that is, to take all measures deemed necessary to protect itself anywhere in the world against so-called international terrorism.

But what happened or, more exactly, what was signaled, made explicit, confirmed on September 11? Beyond everything that has already been said, more or less legitimately, and to which I will not return here, what became clear on that day, a day that was not as unforeseeable as has been claimed?[69] This overwhelming and all-too-obvious fact: after the Cold War, the absolute threat no longer took a state form. If such a threat had been held in check by two state superpowers in a balance of terror during the Cold War, the spread of nuclear capabilities outside the United States and its allies could no longer be controlled by any state. However much one may try to contain the effects of September 11, there are many clear indications that if there was a trauma on that day, in the United States and throughout the world, it consisted not, as is too often believed of trauma in general, in an effect, in a wound produced by what had effectively already happened, what had just actually happened, and risked being repeated one more time, but in the undeniable fear or apprehension of a threat that is *worse* and still *to come*. The trauma remains traumatizing and incurable because it comes from the future. For the virtual can also traumatize. Trauma takes place when one is wounded by a wound that has not yet taken place, in an effective fashion, in a way other than by the sign of its announcement. Its temporalization proceeds from the to-come. And the future, the to-come, is here not only the virtual fall of other towers or similar structures, or else the possibility of a bacteriological, chemical, or "cyber" attack—although these can never be ruled out. The worst to come is a nuclear attack that threatens to destroy the state apparatus of the United States, that is, of a democratic state whose hegemony is as obvious as it is precarious, in crisis, a state assumed to be the guarantor, the sole and ultimate guardian, of world order for all legitimate, sovereign states. This virtual nuclear attack does not exclude others and may in fact be accompanied by chemical, bacteriological, or cyber attacks. Such attacks were in fact envisioned very early on, indeed already with the appearance of the term *rogue state*. But, at the time, they were identified as originating from within certain states and thus from within organized, stable, identifiable, localizable, territorialized powers, nonsuicidal powers, or so it was assumed, that would be susceptible to certain dissuasive tactics. In 1998 House Speaker Newt Gingrich put it well when he said that the USSR had been reassuring inasmuch as its power, exercised in a bureaucratic and collective, and thus nonsuicidal, fashion, was open to dissuasion. He added that this was unfortunately no longer the case for two or three regimes in the world. He should have gone on to say that it is in fact no longer even a question of states or regimes, of state organizations linked to a nation or a territory.

As I myself saw when I was in New York less than a month after September 11, certain members of Congress wasted little time to announce on television that the appropriate technical measures had been taken to ensure that an attack on the White House would not destroy in a few seconds the apparatus of the state and everything that represents the constitutional state. Never again will the president, vice president, and all members of Congress come together in the same place at the same time, as would happen, for example, during the president's State of the Union Address. This absolute threat was still contained during the days of the Cold War by the strategies of game theory. It can no longer be contained when it comes neither from an already constituted state nor even from a potential state that might be treated as a rogue state. Such a situation rendered futile or ineffective all the rhetorical resources (not to mention military resources) spent on justifying the word *war* and the thesis that the "war against international terrorism" had to target particular states that give financial backing or logistical support or provide a safe haven for terrorism, states that, as is said in the United States, "sponsor" or "harbor" terrorists. All these efforts to identify "terrorist" states or rogue states are "rationalizations" aimed at denying not so much some absolute anxiety but the panic or terror before the fact that the absolute threat no longer comes from or is under the control of some state or some identifiable state form. It was thus necessary to dissimulate through this identificatory projection, to dissimulate first of all *from oneself*, the fact that nuclear arms or weapons of mass destruction are potentially produced and accessible in places that no longer have anything to do with a state. Not even a rogue state. The same efforts, the same posturing, the same "rationalizations" and denegations all come to naught as they desperately attempt to identify rogue states or as they try to ensure the survival of concepts as moribund as those of war (as it was once understood by European law) and terrorism. From now on it will no longer be a question of inter-national war in the classical sense, since no nation-state has actually declared war or entered into war as a nation-state against the United States; nor will it be a question of civil war, since no nation-state is present as such; nor will it even be a question of "partisan war" (in the unique sense Schmitt gives to this concept), since it is no longer a matter of resisting territorial occupation, of waging a revolutionary war or a war of independence so as to liberate a colonized state and found another. For the same reasons, the concept of terrorism will be considered without pertinence, having always been associated with "revolutionary wars," "wars of independence," or "partisan wars," wars where the state was always at stake, always on the horizon, and always the battleground.

There are thus no longer anything but rogue states, and there are no longer any rogue states. The concept will have reached its limit and the end—more terrifying than ever—of its epoch. This end was always close, indeed, already from the beginning. To all the more or less conceptual indications I have mentioned, we must add the following, which represents a symptom of another order. The very officials who, under Clinton, most accelerated and intensified this rhetorical strategy, who most abused or exploited the demonizing expression "rogue state," are the very ones who, in the end, on June 19, 2000, publicly declared their decision to give up at least the term. Madeleine Albright made it known that the State Department no longer considered it an appropriate term and that, henceforth, it would use the more neutral and moderate expression "states of concern."

How is one in all seriousness to translate into French the phrase "states of concern"? Perhaps by "*états préoccupants*"—that is, states that give us reason to be concerned, but also states with which we must be seriously concerned, and with which we must concern ourselves, in order to treat their case appropriately. Their "case," in the medical or legal sense. In fact, and this was noted, dropping the term *rogue state* signaled a real crisis for the missile-defense system and its budget. Even if Bush has occasionally brought the expression back, it has nonetheless fallen, probably forever, into desuetude. That is, in any case, my hypothesis, and I have tried to justify the ultimate reason for it—as well as the ground without ground. For the word *voyou* was sent, sent from and back down into the depths; its sending has a history and, like the word *rogue*, it is not eternal.

And yet *voyou* and *rogue* will outlive for a time the *Etats voyous* and the *rogue states* that they will have in truth preceded.

§ 10 Sending

To end without ending when the end is near, since it seems always necessary to hasten the end, here, finally, is the *envoi*, the sending.

Yet one more time, *envoi* is the word.

"Democracy to come": one will have been able to hear in this a response to the sending of the sender. In being sent back or sent off as soon as it is sent, the send back [*renvoi*] affecting differantially and leaving intact no originary sending, everything beginning by sending back or by responding, it will have been necessary to take note of what time, and thus history, must be lacking, unless history is made up of this time that is lacking and that is necessary. Time must always be lacking for democracy because democracy does not wait and yet makes one wait for it. It waits for nothing and loses everything for waiting.

"*It is necessary, for the democracy to come, that it give the time there is not*": we have perhaps experienced this in three different ways that amount to the same.

First, insofar as this interminable session must, through an act of decision, come to an end, just like any finite economy, any deliberative discussion, any exchange in a parliamentary semicircle or in the philosophical agora of a democratic regime.

Next, I tried to persuade you that the democratic injunction does not consist in putting off until later or in letting itself be governed, reassured, pacified, or consoled by some ideal or regulative Idea. It is signaled in the urgency and imminence of an *à-venir*, a to-come, the *à* of the à-venir, the *to* of the to-come, inflecting or turning into an injunction as well as into messianic waiting the *a* of a différance in disjunction.

Finally, and especially, however one understands *cratic* sovereignty, it has appeared as a stigmatic indivisibility that always contracts duration into the timeless instant of the exceptional decision. Sovereignty neither gives nor gives itself the time; it does not take time. Here is where the cruel autoimmunity with which sovereignty is affected begins, the autoimmunity with which sovereignty at once sovereignly affects and cruelly infects itself. Autoimmunity is always, in the same time without duration, cruelty itself, the autoinfection of all autoaffection. It is not some particular thing that is affected in autoimmunity but the self, the *ipse*, the *autos* that finds itself infected. As soon as it needs heteronomy, the event, time and the other.

In these three ways, on these three tracks, a certain annulment of time is announced. It is signaled, dated, like the yearly turn or anniversary return of the year [*année*], like the revolution or the volt of the ring [*anneau*], in the *trivium* of the *il faut*, the "it is necessary," in which we need to hear at once *défaut*, that is, default, fault, or failing; *faillir*, meaning to fail at something or fail to do something; *faillite*, that is, failure, collapse, or bankruptcy; and *défaillance*, meaning a failing or weakness: "time is needed [*il faut le temps*]"; "it is necessary, for democracy, that it give the time there is not."

Why did I think it necessary in order to formalize this strange and paradoxical revolution to privilege today something that might look like a generalization, without any *external* limit, of a biological or physiological model, namely, autoimmunity? It is not, you might well imagine, out of some excessive biologistic or geneticist proclivity on my part.

On the one hand, I began by noting that the circular or rotary movement of the self's return to itself and against itself, in the encounter with itself and countering of itself, would take place, as I understand it, before the separation of *physis* from its others, such as *tekhnē*, *nomos*, and *thesis*. What applies here to *physis*, to *phuein*, applies also to life, understood before any opposition between life (*bios* or *zōē*) and its others (spirit, culture, the symbolic, the specter, or death). In this sense, if autoimmunity is *physio*logical, *bio*logical, or *zoo*logical, it precedes or anticipates all these oppositions. My questions concerning "political" autoimmunity thus concerned precisely the relationship between the *politikon*, *physis*, and *bios* or *zōē*, life-death.

On the other hand, by speaking in just this way of autoimmunity, I specifically wanted to consider all these processes of, so to speak, normal or normative perversion quite apart from the authority of representative consciousness, of the I, the self, and ipseity. This was also the only way, it seemed to me, of taking into account within politics what psychoanalysis once called the unconscious.

In preparing for this lecture, I often asked myself whether everything that seems to me to link the democracy to come to the specter, or to the coming back or *revenance* of a messianicity without messianism, might not lead back or be reducible to some unavowed theologism. Not to the One God of the Abrahamic religions, and not to the One God in the political and monarchic figure spoken of by Plato in the *Statesman* and Aristotle in the *Politics*, and not even to the plural gods who are the citizens of that impossible democracy evoked by Rousseau when he longs for a "people of gods" who, if they existed, would govern democratically.

No, but on account of the to-come, I asked myself whether this did not resemble what someone in whom we have never suspected the slightest hint of democratism said one day of the god who alone could still save (*retten*) us: "Only a god can save us [*Nur noch ein Gott kann uns retten*]."[70] I think I know just about everything that has been said or could be said about this declaration, along with everything else in the *Der Spiegel* interview, everything about what is revealed there and what is kept silent. I think I know rather well the program, the irony, the politics, and the caustic responses to which such a provocation might give rise. Trust me on this. My intention is not for the moment to enter into the debate or take sides. Even if I might share certain well-known reservations, my objective today is rather different. Let me begin, then, with this undeniable fact: there is always the risk—for this is also the effect of the so-called freedom of what is called the democratic press—that this sententious phrase ("Only a god can save us") might be considered in isolation from an enormous network of related propositions, analyses, and meditations in Heidegger. Particularly those where this god, the one who might save us, would no longer owe anything to the god of the religions of the Book, and especially not to the Christianization of the world. Heidegger says "a god," not the One God (as the Bible or the Koran, Plato, and Aristotle, and so many others in essence do). Nor does he speak in the plural, as does *On the Social Contract*, of "a people of gods." A god is neither the One God nor gods. What interests me first here is this difference in number: neither the One God nor gods, neither the One God of the Bible nor the God or gods of the philosophers and of ontotheology. This "a god" is also apparently not the "last god" of the *Beiträge*, the one who, in fact, "is not the end but the other beginning of immeasurable possibilities for our history [*Der letzte Gott ist nicht das Ende, sondern der andere Anfang unermesslicher Möglichkeiten unserer Geschichte*]." Or again, as Heidegger says, emphasizing "last [*letzte*]," "The *last* god is not an end but rather . . . [*Der letzte Gott ist kein Ende, sondern . . .*].''[71]

Were I able to avoid having to give such an excessively elliptical lecture, I would have started back out from this point in the other direction. I would have done it in the form of an about-face or "half-turn [*demi-tour*]," a figure I have yet to mention. I would have done it so as to measure this figure of the half-turn against the dimension of *dimension*, that is, of *measure* (since, as we have seen, the relationship between the commensurable and the incommensurable is what is at stake in democracy) or, more precisely still, against the *dimension of the half-measure*. I would have done it not only to try to think, in the wake of Heidegger, what *last* means in the expression "der letzte Gott" but in order to reconstitute several problematic connections.

First of all, the link, in the *Der Spiegel* interview (which dates from 1966 but was not published, I remind you, until 1976, after Heidegger's death), between this enigmatic proposition and the references to democracy. When Heidegger speaks of the planetary movement of modern technology, he wonders what political system might correspond to this technological age. He does not then say that it is not democracy. But neither does he say that it is democracy. He says with a cautiousness that certain people, although I am not necessarily one, might consider a bit cunning or roguish: "I am not convinced that it is democracy [*Ich bin nicht überzeugt dass es die Demokratie ist*]" (*DS*, 276).

This so very measured rhetoric is the rhetoric of the half-measure. But the half-measure reappears explicitly when the journalists of *Der Spiegel* take Heidegger at his word. They jump on the word *democracy* and ask for clarification. Like most journalists, they are first of all interested, or perhaps only interested, in what they take to be politics and the political. Like all journalists, they insist on clear, univocal, easily understandable answers on a particular subject. And they are here right to recall the ambiguity of the word *democracy*.

> "Democracy" is a catch-all word [*Sammelbegriff*] under which quite different ideas [*Vorstellungen*] can be brought together. The question is whether a transformation of this political structure is still possible. After 1945, you addressed yourself to the political aspirations of the Western world and then you spoke

also of democracy, of the political expression of the Christian worldview [*christlichen Weltanschauung*], and even of the idea of a constitutional state [*Rechtsstaatlichkeit*]—and you have labelled all these aspirations "half-measures" [*Halbheiten*]. (*DS*, 276)

Heidegger's answer assigns the journalists a task that should also be ours: "First of all, would you please tell me where I spoke about democracy and all the other things you refer to? I would in fact characterize them as half-measures because I do not see in them a genuine confrontation with the technological world [*weil ich keine wirkliche Auseinandersetzung mit der technische Welt sehe*]" (*DS*, 276).

The journalists become more and more insistent, impatient: "In your view, which of all these things you have just sketched out is the most timely?" Heidegger's answer is again measured and cautious: "That I don't see. But I do see a decisive question here. We must first clarify what you mean by 'timely,' that is, what 'time' means here. [*Das sehe ich nicht. Aber ich sehe hier eine entscheidende Frage. Zunächst wäre zu klären, was sie hier mit 'zeitgemäss' meinen, was hier 'Zeit' bedeutet.*]" (*DS*, 276).

Beginning here, it would be necessary to reread very carefully the entire interview and all the paths that lead to and from it. The one I would have liked to privilege in the context of our discussion would be at the intersection of this political question of modern technology and the entire semantic network of "saving" in the expression: "Only a god can save us [*Nur noch ein Gott kann uns retten*]." The word translated here as "save" is *retten*. The enormous question of "saving" is that of the "safe [*sauf*]," of salvation [*salut*], of soundness or health [*santé*], and security. There is no need to insist here, as I have in "Faith and Knowledge" and elsewhere, on what makes it communicate with questions of indemnity or the unscathed, the intact and untouched, the safe and sound, the immune and immunity. So much is at play or at stake here between *retten* and *heilen, das Heilen,* the Unscathed, the safe, the sound. *Das Rettende* is at the center of "Die Frage nach der Technik" (The Question Concerning Technology), which we would also have to reread here.[72] In "Bauen Wohnen Denken" (Building Dwelling Thinking [1951]), Heidegger revives the word *freedom* through the chain of words *Friede* (peace), *das Freie, das Frye, fry,* which means the free but also what is preserved, economized, spared, *saved. Freien* means to save or "preserve from harm and danger"; one might also say to "indemnify" or "immunize" (*schonen*). "*Freien bedeutet eigentlich schonen,*" says Heidegger: "*Freien* actually means to spare," "to save," "to immunize."[73] Whence the particular meaning of *retten* still known to Lessing, as Heidegger later says. *Retten* means not only to "snatch someone from a danger" but "to set something free into its own essence [*etwas in sein eigenes Wesen freilassen*]" ("BDT," 352).

We encounter here the same problematic we discussed earlier in relation to Nancy's book. As for the unscathed, the safe, salvation [*salut*] or health (*heil, heilen, heilig,* and so on), there is nothing fortuitous about the appearance of such words in the following paragraph, in a series of associations that is at once internal to this text and rearticulated throughout so many other writings of Heidegger on *retten, heilen, heilig,* and so on. I cannot reconstitute and problematize all this here as it ought to be done, that is, in a micrological way, in particular when it is a question of death for mortals, a question of power or capacity, the capacity to die death as death (*den Tod als Tod vermögen*):

> Mortals dwell in that they initiate their own essential being [*ihr eigenes Wesen*]—their being capable of death as death—into the use and practice of this capacity [*in den Brauch dieses Vermögens. Brauch* is a word, as you well know, that is difficult to translate in this context], so that there may be a good death [*damit ein guter Tod sei*]. ("BDT," 352)

It is in this way that mortals await both the divinities and salvation:

> Mortals dwell in that they await the divinities as divinities [*die Göttlichen als die Göttlichen erwarten*]. In hope they hold up to the divinities what is unhoped for [*Hoffend halten sie das Unverhoffte entgegen*]. They wait for the sign of their coming [*Sie warten der Winke ihrer Ankunft*] and do not mistake the marks of their absence [*die Zeichen ihres Fehls*]. They do not make their gods for themselves and do not worship idols [*Götzen*]. Deprived of salvation [*im Unheil*], they still await the salvation that has been withdrawn [*Im Unheil noch warten sie des entzogenen Heils*]. ("BDT," 352)

Such propositions would have to be reread in conjunction with many others. For example in *Holzwege* ("Wozu Dichter" [What Are Poets For?]): "*Unheil als Unheil spurt uns das Heile. Heiles erwinkt rufend das Heilige. Heiliges bindet das Göttliche. Göttliches nähert den Gott.*"[74] Unable to translate, or to trust wholly in the existing translations, let me paraphrase: "The nonsafe, the absence of salvation, the incurable disaster as such, puts us on the traces of, or traces for us, salvation, the sound, the safe, the unscathed, the immune. The immune gestures toward, by evoking, the safe, the sound, the sacred or the holy. This engages or binds the divine. The divine approaches the God."

What follows speaks of the risk taken by those who sing of the safe and who remain, like the poet, on the track or trace of the immune (*Spur zum Heilen*) and of the fugitive gods (*die Spur der entflohenen Götter*). Between the immune and that which threatens it or runs counter to it, between *Heil* and *Unheil*, the relation is neither one of exteriority nor one of simple opposition or contradiction. I would say the same about the relationship between immunity and autoimmunity. If to the notion of *salut* as *Retten* and *Heilen* we were to add the sense of *salut* as *Gruss* or *grüssen* (and this is not absent from Heidegger's texts, notably in relation to Hölderlin, in *Heimkunft* and *Andenken*), and if, as I have attempted and am still tempted to do elsewhere, one were to separate as irreconcilable the notion of *salut* as greeting or salutation to the other from every *salut* as salvation (in the sense of the safe, the immune, health, and security), if one were to consider the greeting or salutation of the other, of what comes, as irreducible and heterogeneous to any seeking of *salut* as salvation, you can guess into what abysses we would be drawn.

How are we, following these traces, to come back to the to-come of democracy and to this terrible axiom of autoimmunity? Although I cannot demonstrate this here, I would maintain that between these themes (the three meanings of *salut*—*retten, heilen, grüssen*—the safe, the sound, the immune, health, and security, the assurance of salvation and the salutation without assurance to the other who comes or who leaves) and the question of democracy, we would be led rather quickly not only toward what became of the Terror and the Committees of Public Safety during the French Revolution but toward everything that, today and tomorrow, is so urgent to transform in the areas of public health and security and with regard to the institutional and sovereign structure of what is called the Security Council in the war it is waging against the Terror of so-called international terrorism. If, god forbid, a god who can save us were a sovereign god, such a god would bring about, after a revolution for which we have as yet no idea, an entirely different Security Council.

To be sure, nothing is less sure than a god without sovereignty; nothing is less sure than his coming, to be sure. That is why we are talking, and what we are talking about. . . .

All that is not for tomorrow, no more than the democracy to come.

Democracy to come—fare well [*salut*]![75]

PART II

The "World" of the Enlightenment to Come
(Exception, Calculation, and Sovereignty)

Before even venturing a first word, please allow me too to pay my respects [*saluer*], from the depths of my extreme sorrow, to my friend Dominique Janicaud. For more than thirty-five years his friendship and support, the vigilance of his thought, have accompanied me. I shared so much with him. (And he in fact liked this word *share*, and precisely concerning reason; toward the end of his *Powers of the Rational*, in speaking about what he called "the future *as such*," he added after a colon: "its *partage*, its sharing.")[1] I was fortunate to share so many things with him in life and in philosophy; my respect for him grew from so many sources that I would be unable to do it justice in just a few words. Like many among you, I was so looking forward to seeing him here today, and that was no doubt one of the very good reasons for being here.

Unable to say anything more at this moment, I shall simply cite as exergues to my remarks a couple of fragments from *Powers of the Rational*: "To grasp the Incalculable within the general order of calculation: this is, here, no magical operation but the revelation of what is *eventful* in the epoch."[2] And at the end of the book, as a next-to-last word: "The incalculable is there, but we ought not exempt ourselves from counting—counting with it, though not on it—from measuring ourselves against time, always our adversary. . . . There is no need to invoke our certain death. Finitude is inscribed in the very structure of life, in the fragile destiny of the planet as well as of all other beings" (*PR*, 261).

§ 1 Teleology and Architectonic: The Neutralization of the Event

At the moment when, fearful—as I am at this very instant—of being unable to measure up to the *task* (and, yes, I said *task*) that has been at once entrusted and assigned to me, at the moment when, feeling myself so unworthy of the *honor* (and, yes, I said *honor*) that has been conferred upon me, I began to prepare myself for this exposition, for this exposing of myself, this exposing of my inadequacies in the course of a *finite* exposé (and, yes, I said *finite*)—especially in terms of time: an hour and a half, I've been told—well, at that moment, it was these very words I just emphasized and repeated (*task, honor, finitude*) that came in advance to obligate me.

These words obligated me to retain them, to recall them. They themselves asked me to be responsible for them, and to do so in a responsible way. They insisted on telling me something about the *obligation* or the *responsibility* that is here mine, as well as, I would like to assume, ours.

These words, let me repeat them, are the words *task* or *obligation* (whether finite or infinite), and thus *responsibility* (whether finite or infinite), but also *honor*. But why *honor*, you will ask?

A terribly ambiguous hypothesis came at the time, as any good *hypothesis* must, *to place itself beneath*. A hypothesis *imposed* itself *beneath* what I had just heard myself say. The idiomatic phrasing of its motto or rallying call could be squeezed into six words: "to save the honor of reason." Someone in me whispered to me: "Perhaps it would be a matter of saving the honor of reason." "Perhaps on that day, in the daylight of today, in the light of the enlightenment of this day, it would be a matter of saving the honor of reason." Perhaps it would even be necessary. *It would be a matter of* here means *it would be necessary.* Slipping in under every word, the hypothesis opened an abyss beneath each of my steps.

This abyssal hypothesis will never leave me, even if in the future I must silence it. Here, then, let me emphasize it, is its first figure, the first "if . . .": "what *if* we were called here to save the honor of reason?" Or, if you prefer the fiction of the *as if* to a hypothesis, the fiction of the *als ob* honored in philosophy, and in the name of reason itself, by Kant and others, "it would be *as if* we were called here to save the honor of reason." What if we were called to this end by those who took the initiative to organize this conference and give it its title? What if it were we who had called *ourselves, as if* we philosophers, in these times of danger or distress, these tempestuous times of loss, had to save the honor of reason, *so as to* save the honor of reason and, in the same and single, indivisible gesture, to do so in the French language, if not in the name of the French language, which is to say, in a European language of Latin, rather than Greek or German, lineage (*reor* means *I believe, I think, I calculate,* and *ratio:* reason or calculation, account and proportion)? In a Latin language, therefore, already burdened with translations, already bearing witness to an experience of translation that, as we will later see, takes upon itself the entire destiny of reason, that is, of the world universality to come? It is as if we were called on to take this responsibility here and now, the responsibility of saving the honor of reason, as philosophers of the French language, on the shores of the Mediterranean, in a city in France with a Greek name fixed by war, like the monument of a victory that consists always in winning out over [*avoir raison de*] the other, over and against the other. We would already begin to make out, at dawn, in the mist of beginnings, a shoreline and the ports of Europe. Whether armed or disarmed, the great question of reason would already begin to unfurl its sails for a geopolitical voyage across Europe and its languages, across Europe and the rest of the world. Is reason (*logos* or *ratio*) first of all a Mediterranean thing? Would it have made it safely to port, with Athens or Rome in view, so as to remain until the end of time tied to its shores? Would it have never really lifted anchor or been set adrift? Would it have never broken away, in a decisive or critical fashion, from its birthplaces, its geography, and its genealogy?

In a first moment I am tempted to trust naively in a very first hearing of this expression that came to surprise me: "to save the honor of reason."

The honor of reason—is that reason? Is honor reasonable or rational through and through? The very form of this question can be applied analogically to everything that evaluates, affirms, or prescribes reason: to prefer reason, is that rational or, and this is something else, reasonable? The value of reason, the desire for reason, the dignity of reason—are these rational? Do these have to do wholly with reason? What authorizes one to inscribe again or already under the authority of reason a particular *interest* of reason (*Interesse der Vernunft*), this interest *of* reason, this interest *in* reason, this interest *for* a reason that, as Kant reminds us, is at once practical, speculative, and architectonic, though *first of all architectonic*?[3] For Kant declares, and this will be important for what follows, "human reason is by nature architectonic."[4] That is what motivates Kant in the antinomies to privilege the moment of the thesis over against an antithesis that threatens the systemic edifice and thus disturbs the architectonic desire or interest, most often so as to take into account, antithetically, themes that should be important to us today, namely, divisibility, eventfulness, and conditionality.

If reason passes for being disinterested, in what is it still interested? Would this "interest" of reason still have to do with reason? With the rationality of a reason that is past, present, or still to come? If this architectonic vocation of reason is indeed systemic and unifying, what risks threatening it today are not only the figures of the antithesis in the antinomies of the transcendental dialectic. It is also the just as rational necessity, rational, that is, from the point of view of a history and of a development [*devenir*] of the sciences, to take into account plural rationalities. Each of these has its own ontological "region," its own necessity, style, axiomatics, institutions, community, and historicity. These plural rationalities thus resist, in the name of their very rationality, any architectonic organization. They do so through their distinct historicity, through the figures and configurations that inform them, however they might be named or interpreted by means of such categories as *paradigm, themata, episteme*, the supposed *epistemological break*, and so on; and they do so through all the differences between mathematics, the natural or life sciences, the human sciences, the social sciences or the humanities, physics as well as biology, law and political economy, politology, psychology, psychoanalysis, and literary theory, along with all the techniques and institutional communities that are inseparable from their knowledge. Such an architectonic organization would do these violence by bending their untranslatable heterogeneity, one that is without analogy, and inscribing them in the unity of a "world" that Kant spoke of as a "regulative Idea of reason," one for which the unification of the experience that totalizes it requires an "as if" (*als ob*). It is as if all the modal, rhetorical, logical, or phenomenological trajectories of the "as," the "as such," and the "as if" (phenomenality, fiction, analogy, *logos* of proportion, simulacrum and simulation, art and *tekhnē*, technique and artifact) converged on and confronted one another here so as to provoke or defy this architectonic desire, this unifying and appropriating order of reason. A reason that is essentially *analogical*. Is it not then in the name of these heterogeneous rationalities, in the name of their specificity and their future, their history, and their "enlightenment," that we must call into question the masterly and mastering authority of architectonics and thus of a certain "world," that is, the unity of the regulative Idea of the world that authorizes that world in advance? Which presupposes, therefore, a veritable genealogy of the world, of the concept of world, in the discourses concerning *mondialisation* [worldwide-ization] or, what should be something else altogether, *globalization* or *Globalisierung*.

On first hearing, the expression "to save the honor of reason" speaks not only of the respectful saving [*salut*] and honoring of reason. *Salut* is also the security, the assurance, or honorable rescue [*sauvetage*] of reason. Its indemnity or its immunity. The saving or rescue of a reason that perhaps also consists in saving, in saving itself—which is also to say, in running for safety. "To save the honor" might suggest the imminent failure, the announcement of a *loss*—where reason risks *losing* or *getting lost*, where reason is lost, for example, in madness, through some aberration or mental illness, or where consciousness, conscience, or science, that is, responsible lucidity in general, is lost, or where reason has become a lost cause. Wherever reason *gets lost*, wherever it is lost or losing, we would say to ourselves, let's save its honor. When everything seems to be breaking down or in decline, darkening or going under, in the vanishing twilight of an imminent default or failure [*d'une échéance ou d'un échec*], it would be as if reason, *this* reason that we so quickly claim to be "ours" or "human," had to choose between only two ends, two eschatologies, two ways of going aground [*échouer*]: between running aground [*échouement*] and grounding [*échouage*]. With the coast in view, in mind, and, in keeping with the maritime metaphor that interests us here, in view of or far from shore, without any assured arrival, between land and sea.

Running aground [*l'échouement*]: that is the moment when a ship, touching bottom, gets accidentally immobilized. This accident is an event: it happens, it happens because, without foreseeing it and without calculation, one will have been sent down to the bottom [*fond*]. I don't need to remind you of the proximity between many of the figures of reason and those of the bottom or the ground, the foundation, the groundwork, the principle of sufficient reason, the *principium rationis*, the *nihil est sine ratione* as *Satz vom Grund*, the *Satz vom zureichenden Grunde* of the Leibnizian theodicy and its reinterpretative repetition by Heidegger.[5] Indeed, I would have wanted, had I the time, and if the economy of a conference on reason were reasonable, to try to reread this text of Heidegger's with you, patiently, literally, paragraph by paragraph, attempting the probing and problematizing analysis that such a text seems to me to call for. We would have especially questioned its epochal periodizations, its denied teleology, its interpretation of representation in the rationalisms of the seventeenth century, its resounding silence concerning Spinoza, and so on. And I would have wanted to show how everything here gets played out at the limit between the calculable and the incalculable, there where the *Grund* opens up onto the *Abgrund*, where giving reasons [*rendre-raison*] and giving an account [*rendre-compte*]—*logon didonai* or *principium reddendae rationis*—are threatened by or drawn into the abyss, indeed by more than one abyss, including the abyss of translation between the different languages I just juxtaposed. For I did not juxtapose them so as to suggest their transparent equivalence but, on the contrary, and I want to underscore this again, so as to gesture toward a hypothetical and problematic universal translatability that is one of the fundamental stakes of reason, of what we have called, and will still call tomorrow, reason, and reason in the world.

As for *grounding* [*échouage*], this is not the same as *running aground*. Grounding is the moment when, this time intentionally, freely, deliberately, in a calculable and calculated, autonomous manner, the captain of a ship, failing to keep his heading, takes responsibility for touching bottom—and this decision too resembles an event. And yet the accident of running aground, as we said, is also an event. Between running aground and grounding, we would endure the desperate attempt to save from a disastrous shipwreck, at the worst moment of an admitted defeat, what remains honorable at the end of a battle lost for a just cause, a noble cause, the cause of reason, which we would wish to salute one last time, with the eschatological melancholy of a philosophy in mourning. When nothing more can be saved, one tries to save honor in defeat. To save honor would thus be not the salvation [*salut*] that saves but the salutation [*salut*] that simply salutes or signals a departure, at the moment of separation from the other. A philosophy in mourning, I said, either because the world would be on the verge of *losing reason*, indeed of *losing itself as world*, or else because reason itself, reason as such, would be on the verge of becoming threatening; it would be a power, it would have the power to threaten itself, to lose the meaning and humanity of the world. To lose itself all by itself, to go down on its own, to *autoimmunize* itself, as I would prefer to say in order to designate this strange illogical logic by which a living being can spontaneously destroy, in an autonomous fashion, the very thing within it that is supposed to protect it against the other, to immunize it against the aggressive intrusion of the other. Why speak in this way of *autoimmunity*? Why determine in such an ambiguous fashion the threat or the danger, the default or the failure, the running aground or the grounding, but also the salvation, the rescue, and the safeguard, health and security—so many diabolically *autoimmune* assurances, virtually capable not only of destroying themselves in suicidal fashion but of turning a certain death drive against the *autos* itself, against the ipseity that any suicide worthy of its name still presupposes? In order to situate the question of life and of the living being, of life and death, of life-death, at the heart of my remarks.

But in this first hearing of the phrase "to save the honor of reason," how are we not to recall, so as to formulate a rather overdetermined question, the important warnings Husserl issued in 1935–36, between the two so-called world wars, between two globalizations or worldwide-izations [*mondialisations*] of war? We will return to these dates later—as well as to these two concepts, that of the "world" or of the end of a world (in globalization [*mondialisation*] and in *world war*), and especially that of "war," a wholly other end of war that we are perhaps living at this very moment, an end of war, the end of the very concept of war, of the European concept, the juridical concept, of war (of every war: war between nation-states, civil war, and even what Schmitt calls "partisan war," which, whether in a form called terrorist or not, would still be fought, in the end, within the horizon of a nation-state to be combated, liberated, or founded). And we will also return to what links this juridical concept of war to the supposed sovereignty of the state, of the enemy as state or nation-state. This end of the concept of war would be anything but peace. Its stakes will appear inseparable, in fact, from the future of reason, that is, of philosophy, everywhere that the concepts of international law, nation-state sovereignty, or sovereignty in general, tremble from this same tremor that is so confusedly called "globalization [*mondialisation*]."

What would have changed for us since 1935–36, since this Husserlian call to a philosophical and European coming to awareness in the experience of a crisis of the sciences and of reason? Would we be able to repeat this call? Should we displace it? Should we contest its premises or its teleology? Or should we seek to reactivate it and found it anew? Are we going through a time that can in fact be gone through, hoping to go through it so as one day to get beyond it in the course of a *critical*, dangerous, but provisional or periodic, passage, one that we would thus have the right to call a *crisis*? And all this in the course of a long circumnavigation whose circuit or odyssey would lead us in circular fashion safely back to the shores of an origin that Husserl thought only needed to be reactivated? Perhaps we must try to think, on the contrary, something other than a crisis. Perhaps we are enduring a tremor at once more and less serious, something other, in any case, than a crisis of reason, beyond a crisis of science or of conscience, beyond a crisis of Europe, beyond a philosophical crisis that would be, to recall a title of Husserl, a *crisis of European humanity*.

Were I able to develop this question further, without however reconstituting Husserl's entire, well-known itinerary in these texts, I would do so in *five* directions, of which I will indicate here only the heading.

1. As I have done elsewhere, I have here granted to this autoimmune schema a range without limit, one that goes far beyond the circumscribed biological processes by which an organism tends to destroy, in a quasi-spontaneous and more than suicidal fashion, some organ or other, one or another of its own immunitary protections. Now, let me recall that in one of the texts of the *Crisis* (the so-called Vienna Lecture from 1935), Husserl evokes, in the name of phenomenological reason, the inevitability of a transcendental pathology.[6] As a sickness of reason. The medical model is deployed from the very outset of the lecture. Although Husserl distinguishes between "scientific medicine" and the "nature cure" (*Crisis*, 269), that is, between medicine as a science of nature (*Naturwissenschaftliche Medizin*) and a natural medicine (*Naturheilkunde*), although he distinguishes, within life, between living (*Leben*) in the physiological sense and

living in the spiritual and teleological sense, although he recalls that there is "no zoology of peoples" (*Es gibt wesensmässig keine Zoologie der Völker*) (*Crisis*, 275), he does not hesitate to say that the difference between health and sickness (*Gesundheit und Krankheit*) holds for communities, peoples, and states. With this word *health* [santé], and thus with the notion of a certain public health or historical health, it becomes a question of what *sauver* means, in one of its senses, namely, the safe, the sound, the healthy, the unscathed or the immune (*heilig*), salvation itself (*Rettung*), right up to and including the expression "to save the honor." Husserl wonders why we have never developed a "scientific medicine for nations and supranational communities." "The European nations are sick; Europe itself, it is said, is in crisis [*Die europäischen Nationen sind krank, Europa selbst ist, sagt man, in einer Krisis*]" (*Crisis*, 270).

There was already, even before the irruption in spiritual Greece of the infinite *telos* of scientific and philosophical rationality, a form of mythical and mystical speculation, a sort of "speculative knowledge" (*spekulative Wissen*), says Husserl, that aimed to serve humankind and its life in the world (*Weltleben*). Such knowledge had to immunize humans against sicknesses, distress, and even death. But beyond and following the speculation of this pretheoretical and prephilosophical knowledge, I would risk speaking, in the wake of Husserl, of a transcendental pathology and even a transcendental autoimmunity. For the Husserlian diagnosis implicates an evil that concerns the very thing that, in inaugurating a "perpetual transformation in the form of a new [type of] historicity" (*Crisis*, 277), inscribed and prescribed the spiritual telos of European humanity, namely, the infinite idea (in the Kantian sense) of an infinite task as *theoria*, as theoretical attitude, and then as philosophical *theoria*. Now, it is precisely this ideal of a "new sort of praxis" (*Crisis*, 283), namely, says Husserl, "universal scientific reason," that produces this amnesic evil called *objectivism*. Reason itself produces this evil as if by an irresistible internal secretion that is nothing other than finitude. Finitude, that is, the inevitable forgetting of the origin of subjective and historical acts. Husserl singles out objectivism and denounces it in a passage from the so-called Vienna Lecture. Rationality can become an "evil" when it is one-sided and specialized (*So kann einseitige Rationalität allerdings zum Übel werden*—"a one-sided rationality can certainly become an evil" [*Crisis*, 291]). Because of this specialization (which is, however, so necessary, each regional science having its own rationality), the infinite task of pure rationality is, to slip in a maritime metaphor that I find appropriate but that is not Husserl's here, *arraisonnée*—that is, boarded and inspected, its identity verified by a division of labor and a model of some specific knowledge or rationality. Just before speaking of this "ill" or "evil" (*Übel*), Husserl names the danger, an interior and intimate danger, an immanent danger or risk that philosophical reason *made itself run*, as if it wrongly gave itself reason—as if it wrongly considered itself right—to win out over itself [*se donnait raison d'avoir raison d'elle-même*], as if what it did were ill-suited to what it has to do, as if it did itself ill [*se faisait mal*] in winning itself over to winning out over itself, between the factual finiteness of its determined figures and the idea of its infinite task. For Husserl says he has been convinced that it is a mode of thought (*Denkweise*), that is, rational prejudices and presuppositions, that bear some of the responsibility for the sickness of Europe (*mitschuldig wäre an der europäischen Erkrankung*):

> But now this is the danger point! "Philosophy" [the danger is indeed named "philosophy" here and Husserl puts an exclamation point, a danger point, just before putting the name "philosophy" in quotation marks: *"Aber hier liegt nun der Gefahrenpunkt! "Philosophie"*—and he then picks up after a dash]—here we must certainly distinguish between philosophy as a historical fact at a given time and philosophy as idea, as the idea of an infinite task. Any philosophy that exists at a given historical time is a more or less successful attempt to realize the guiding idea of the infinity and at the same time even the totality of truths. (*Crisis*, 291)

Let us simply note in anticipation that this infinite task of philosophy as theory is, before all else, as task and as duty (*Aufgabe*), a "practical ideal," one that is itself *unconditional*. I underscore here this *unconditionality*. Husserl notes it more than once. We will have to return to it, for there is contained here the question of a certain honor of reason that governs but also exceeds theoretical or scientific reason. The Husserlian critique of the transcendental evil of a putatively rationalist objectivism is inscribed, in May 1935, in the critique of a certain irrationalism, one whose popularity and air of political modernity in the German and European atmosphere of the 1930s it seemed necessary to denounce. This was the first concern and the ultimate target of the author of the *Crisis*. He is thus going to reject at one and the same time both irrationalism *and* a certain rationalist naïveté that is often confused with philosophical rationality.

I said that the way of philosophy passes through naïveté. This is the place for the criticism offered by the irrationalism that is so highly esteemed [*des so hoch gerühmten Irrationalismus*], or rather the place to unmask the naïveté of that rationalism which is taken for philosophical rationality as such, which is admittedly characteristic of the philosophy of the whole modern period since the Renaissance and which takes itself to be the true, i.e., universal, rationalism. In this naïveté, then, unavoidable as a beginning stage, are caught all the sciences whose beginnings were already developed in antiquity. To put it more precisely, the most general title for this naïveté is *objectivism*, taking the form of the various types of naturalism, of the naturalization of the spirit. Old and new philosophies were and remain naïvely objectivist. In fairness we must add, though, that the German Idealism proceeding from Kant was passionately concerned with overcoming this naïveté, which had already become very troublesome, though it was unable to attain the higher stage of reflexivity which is decisive for the new form of philosophy and of European humanity. (*Crisis*, 292)

Husserl knows it and says it: objectivist naïveté is no mere accident. It is produced by the very progress of the sciences and by the production of ideal objects, which, as if by themselves, by their iterability and their necessarily technical structure, cover over or consign to forgetting their historical and subjective origin. Scientific reason, in its very progress, spontaneously produces the crisis. It is reason that throws reason into crisis, in an autonomous and quasi-autoimmune fashion. It could be shown that the ultimate "reason," in the sense of cause or foundation, the *raison d'être* of this transcendental phenomenological autoimmunity, is located in the very structure of the present and of life, in the temporalization of what Husserl called "the Living Present" (*die lebendige Gegenwart*). The Living Present is produced only by altering and dissimulating itself. I don't have the *time*, precisely, to pursue this path here, but I would like to note its necessity whenever the question of the development or the becoming [*devenir*], and thus of the time, of reason appears inseparable from the enormous question, the old and completely new question, of life (*bios* or *zōē*), which is at the very heart of the question of being, of presence and of beings, and thus of the question of "being and time," of *Sein und Zeit*—a question accentuated this time on the side of life rather than death, if this still makes, as I am tempted to believe it does, something of a difference.

2. Let us try to sharpen the paradox of this critical moment of the *Crisis*. Husserl's *critique* takes aim at those things that are responsible for the

crisis: the irrationalism in vogue, the objectivist irrationalism born on the inside of reason itself, the danger of a certain perverse and amnesic use of reason that stems, as we have just heard, from the specialization of multiple knowledges, indeed of regional ontologies. This irrationalist effect also resembles a certain development or becoming [*devenir*] of plural logics and rationalities, and thus a certain future or to-come [*avenir*] of reason that resists the *teleological* unity of reason, and thus the idea of an infinite task that presupposes, at least as its horizon, an organized totalization of truths, that "totality of truths" that I cited a moment ago and that philosophical responsibility would consist in making effective. It is necessary— and this is the infinite, teleological task—to effectuate, to make effective, "to realize this totality of truths [*die Allheit der Wahrheiten zu verwirklichen*]" (*Crisis*, 291). What, in the name of rationalities in the process of becoming [*en devenir*], resists this teleological unity, which is none other, in the end, than the ideal pole of philosophy as transcendental phenomenology, resembles to some extent—and this is hardly fortuitous—that which, in the Kantian antinomies, resisted the architectonic design. Moreover, the teleology or teleologism that so powerfully governs the transcendental idealisms and rationalisms of Kant and Husserl is also that which limits or neutralizes the event. Teleologism seems always to inhibit, suspend, or even contradict the eventfulness of what comes, beginning with the scientific event, the technoscientific invention that "finds" what it seeks, that finds and finds itself finding, and thus is possible as such, only when invention is impossible, that is, when it is not programmed by a structure of expectation and anticipation that annuls it by making it possible and thus foreseeable.

This teleology is not only a general and universal teleology. It can also be that which orients a determined configuration: *paradigm*, in Kuhn's sense, or *episteme* in Foucault's sense, along with so many other supposed infrastructures of technoscientific discovery. Whenever a *telos* or teleology comes to orient, order, and make possible a historicity, it annuls that historicity by the same token and neutralizes the unforeseeable and incalculable irruption, the singular and exceptional alterity of *what* [*ce qui*] comes, or indeed of *who* [*qui*] comes, that without which, or the one without whom, nothing happens or arrives. It is not only the question of the *telos* that is being posed here but that of the horizon and of any horizontal *seeing-come* in general. And it is also the question of the Enlightenment of Reason. For the critical denunciation of objectivist irrationalism

born out of the forgetting of subjective origins and out of the specialization of the technosciences is not the only paradox in the *Crisis*. Indeed it
is at this same moment and with this same gesture that Husserl also
wishes to distance himself from a certain enlightenment and a certain rationalism. He does not want to present himself as a conservative and reactionary rationalist. He struggles against a certain misunderstanding that
would reduce phenomenology to this "old rationalism [*der alte Ra-
tionnalismus*]" (*Crisis*, 298) incapable of a radical and universal self-under-
standing (*Selbstverständigung*) of spirit in the form of a responsible universal science. He even goes so far as to disavow, giving in to the prevailing
atmosphere of the time, the Enlightenment, the *Aufklärung*, and in an
even more denigrating and pejorative fashion, the *Aufklärerei*. This word,
which in fact goes back to Hegel, designates a sort of mechanical mania or
fetishism of the *Aufklärung*, of this *must* of the Enlightenment. To deny
that he is proposing a rehabilitation of rationalism and of the Enlightenment, Husserl uses an interesting word for my argument here. Granel
translates it well as "*réhabilitation.*" It is, in truth, *Ehrenrettung*: rehabilitation, an apology or defense, but literally a salvation or rescuing of
honor, an attempt to save the honor of rationalism, a rationalism that had
been compromised in the affair of the *Aufklärerei* (*Crisis*, 289). Husserl
does not want to save the honor of *that* rationalism; he wants nothing to
do with this *Ehrenrettung des Rationalismus, der Aufklärerei*. He considers
it a point of honor not to save the honor of a cheap *Aufklärung*, of an
Aufklärerei, of an *Ehrenrettung des Rationalismus, der Aufklärerei*. (I again
resist the temptation of taking a detour here through Heidegger's way of
interpreting and recalling the meaning of *retten*: to save, immunize, but
also to economize, save, spare, or liberate, to make free and open up the
openness of freedom.) In any case, Husserl at this time would rather pass
for a radical revolutionary than a reactionary. He marks this by diagnos-
ing the error or the errancy of a certain rationalism. We must consider the
historical and political climate between the two world wars, the rise of
Nazism as well as European fascism. This is absolutely necessary if we are
to hear today what Husserl said then, if we are to understand him as historians and philosophers concerned about our current responsibilities.
These responsibilities are at once different and analogous. Husserl said,
for example:

> I would like to think that I, the supposed reactionary [*der vermeintliche Reak-
> tionär*], am far more radical and far more revolutionary than those who in

their words proclaim themselves so radical today [*als die sich heutzutage in Worten so radikal Gebärdenden*]. I too am certain that the European crisis has its roots in a misguided rationalism [*in einem sich verirrenden Rationalismus wurzelt*]. But we must not take this to mean that rationality as such is evil. . . . On the other hand we readily admit (and German Idealism preceded us long ago in this insight) that the stage of development of *ratio* represented by the rationalism of the Age of Enlightenment was a mistake [*eine Verirrung*], though certainly an understandable [*begriffliche*] one. (*Crisis*, 290)

3. If this crisis remains ambiguous, if this double critique calls into question a certain rationalism *and* a certain irrationalism, the only possible conclusion is that the crisis can be overcome. It is not an irreversible failure. The failure of which we are speaking, if it indeed fails or goes aground (the event of an accidental running aground or the event of an intentional grounding, linked, therefore, to some freedom or transcendental evil), fails only in appearance and indicates only the *apparent failure* of rationalism. An apparent failure of rationalism—that is precisely Husserl's conclusion. It is going to inspire a call not to save the honor of reason (Husserl wants no such rescue) but to endure a heroism of reason, which, I think you will grant me, is not too far away. In any case, it is a question of undoing an appearance, of doing away with this nothing that the appearance is:

> In order to be able to comprehend the disarray [the word here is *Unwesen*, which my friend Gérard Granel, whose memory and work I would here like to honor, translates precisely by "*renversement de l'essence*," that is, the nothing or the negligible, indeed the degradation of being in the insignificant or apparent] of the present "crisis," we had to work out the *concept of Europe as the historical teleology of the infinite goals of reason*; we had to show how the European "world" [Husserl puts "world (*Welt*)" in quotation marks] was born out of ideas of reason, i.e., out of the spirit of philosophy. The "crisis" could then become distinguishable as the *apparent failure of rationalism* [deutlich werden als das scheinbare Scheitern des Rationalismus]. The reason for the failure [*Der Grund des Versagens*] of a rational culture, however, as we said, lies not in the essence of rationalism itself but solely in its being rendered superficial [*Veräusserlichung*], in its entanglement in [or in the cocoon of] "naturalism" and "objectivism" [*in seiner Versponnenheit in "Naturalismus" und "Objektivismus*,*"* which Granel translates as *dans le fait qu'il s'enrobe du cocon du "naturalisme" et de "l'objectivisme*"]. (*Crisis*, 299)

I would be tempted to take somewhat seriously this metaphor of the cocoon, of the *Versponnenheit* that objectivizes, animalizes, indeed naturalizes a nonnatural movement: reason spontaneously envelops itself in the web and threads that it itself weaves, after having itself secreted them—like a silkworm. The threads of this web come at once to reveal and veil the unveiling of truth. This reason resembles the *physis* of a silkworm, which, from the inside, on its own, produces and objectivizes on the outside the veil of naturalism and objectivism in which it will shut itself up for a time. Up until the point when the heroism of reason makes it appear, resuscitates it, and lets it be reborn. Like a phoenix, now, coming into the light.

A few lines later, and these are the last words of the text, Husserl in fact invokes the phoenix: "the phoenix of a new life-inwardness and spiritualization as the pledge of a great and distant future for man: for the spirit alone is immortal" (*Crisis*, 299).

In the interval, Husserl will have appealed to the responsibility of a "heroic" decision: not to save honor but to save us from night and from death, there where we might ask ourselves yet again, as if for the sake of honor, whether the heroism of reason indeed stems, in an immanent fashion, from reason, and whether faith in reason remains something rational through and through—something reasoned or reasonable.

Before specifying why, in Husserl's eyes, the answer has to be "yes," let me cite him again. It is indeed a question of life and death: "There are only two escapes from the crisis of European existence: the downfall of Europe in its estrangement from its own rational sense of *life* [my emphasis], its fall into hostility toward the spirit [*Geistfeindschaft*] and into barbarity; or the rebirth of Europe from the spirit of philosophy through a heroism of reason [*Heroismus der Vernunft*] that overcomes naturalism once and for all" (*Crisis*, 299).

Why does this heroism of the responsible decision remain, for Husserl, a heroism *of reason*? It is not because faith in reason would exceed reason. It is because theoretical reason is first of all, and finally, for him as for Kant, a prescriptive or normative task through and through, a practical reason, or, as others might say, a metaphysics of free will. In *Philosophy as Mankind's Self-Reflection*, certain lines recall this in an at once constative and prescriptive mode (as do certain statements in the *Cartesian Meditations*): "It is rational to seek to be rational. . . . Reason allows for no differentiation into 'theoretical,' 'practical,' 'aesthetic,' or whatever. Being human is teleological being and an ought-to-be."[7]

We will have to ask later whether this idea of an "ought"—of "duty"—exhausts the ethical law, the practical law, and especially the law of unconditional justice. Long before Husserl, Kant had also claimed the inseparable unity of theoretical reason and practical reason. He too had especially marked the inflexible subordination of theoretical to practical reason. This is even the title of one of the subsections of the *Critique of Practical Reason*, on the subject of the sovereign good: "On the Primacy [*Von dem Primat*] of Pure Practical Reason in Its Association [*Verbindung*] with Speculative Reason." Kant there insists: "But if pure reason of itself can be and really is practical, as the consciousness of the moral law shows it to be, it is only one and the same reason which judges a priori by principles, whether for theoretical or for practical purposes."[8] And just a few lines later: "Thus in the combination of pure speculative with pure practical reason in one cognition, the latter has primacy [*Primat*]. . . . Without this subordination [*Unterordnung*], a conflict [*Widerstreit*] of reason with itself would arise."

It is here that this singular "interest" of reason is rooted, the one we spoke of earlier and to which I will return in a moment.

4. If naturalism and objectivism are critical perversions of reason, the risk that is run has to do with what links the ideality of the ideal object to *exactitude*, and thus to a certain type of *calculability*. Husserl, as we know, distinguished with all possible rigor between *rigor* and *exactitude*. Certain types of objects might, for phenomenological science and for science in general, give rise to a rigorous knowledge and even, for what concerns a phenomenological *cogito*, an indubitable knowledge, even though, in essence, this knowledge *can*not and thus *must* not claim exactitude. In renouncing calculability in this way, such knowledge actually loses nothing of its rationality or its indubitability. I will not develop here, for lack of time and because I have treated this elsewhere, the logico-mathematical question of indecidables and Gödel's theorem of 1931, which I tried long ago to trace in Husserl's thought of the transcendental historicity of geometry, for example. For reasons that will later lead us outside phenomenology, outside the "as such" of ontology and phenomenology, outside transcendental idealism, outside its determination of beings as objects for an egological subject, for the consciousness of an indubitable "I think," outside its teleology and the very idea of idea (light and intelligible visibility of the *eidos*, the idea in the Kantian sense, the idea of an infinite task), I

am simply situating at this point the possibility of an incalculable that is neither irrational nor dubitable. I am simply noting that a rational and rigorous incalculability presented itself *as such* in the greatest tradition of rationalist idealism. The rationality of the rational has never been limited, as some have tried to make us believe, to calculability, to reason as calculation, as *ratio*, as account, as an account to be settled or an account to be given. We will later draw some of the consequences of this. The role that "dignity" (*Würde*), for example, plays in the *Groundwork of the Metaphysics of Morals* belongs to the order of the incalculable. In the kingdom of ends, it is opposed to what has a price on the market (*Marktpreis*) and so can give rise to calculable equivalences. The dignity of a reasonable being (the human person, for example, and this is, for Kant, the only example) is incalculable as an end in itself. It is at once universal and exceptional. "Morality, and humanity so far as it is capable of morality, is the only thing which has dignity."[9]

Leaving aside whatever questions this might raise, we must recognize that this incalculable dignity, which Kant sometimes calls "sublime," remains the indispensable axiomatic, in the so-called globalization [*mondialisation*] that is under way, of the discourses and international institutions concerning human rights and other modern juridical performatives. Consider, for example, the concept of a crime against humanity, or else the project of the International Criminal Court that this concept inspired, a project that is still opposed by the interests of so many sovereign nation-states (from the United States to Israel, and sometimes even France), who, by reason of these interests, are intent on holding on to their sovereignty.

How is one to relate this just incalculability of dignity to the indispensable calculation of law? How is one to articulate together a justice and a law that are equally rational? These are just some of the questions that await us. Since I intend to speak later, in another register, of sovereignty, of calculation and the world, of the world in the worldwide movement [*mondialisation*] under way, I am simply indicating here the direction in which we should continue to accompany this Kantian concept of a dignity that is incalculable and thus transcends the marketplace at all costs. For Kant, the world of rational beings, the *mundus intelligibilis* as kingdom of ends (*Reich der Zwecke*), a kingdom he calls "possible," depends, as he himself says, on both an "as if" and the *logos* of an analogy, that is, a *logos* as proportion. First, the formal principle of maxims for every reasonable being who acts *as if* (*als ob*) he were legislator is, "[A]ct *as if* [*als ob*] your maxims had to serve at the same time as a universal law (for all rational beings)" (*G*, 106). Second, the kingdom of ends, and thus of incalculable dignity, is possible only by analogy (*nach der Analogie*) with a kingdom of nature (*Reich der Natur*) where this kingdom is considered as a machine (*als Machine*), that is, subject to the constraints of calculable laws.

5. Finally, for the same reasons, and because I will later, as I often do, make great use of the theme of unconditionality, let me recall here two additional traits. On the one hand, unconditionality remains, and in this name, in German translated from Greek, the ultimate recourse, the absolute principle of pure reason, for Kant as well as for Husserl. On the other hand, unconditionality remains, and in this name, what binds practical reason to the theoretical reason it subordinates. It is the ultimate truth of an "interest of reason." I cite as proof or indication of this the frequent, literal recourse to unconditionality *both* in the texts of the *Crisis* (if philosophy must exercise an archontic function in humanity, Husserl tells us, it is because it requires an "unconditional truth": the idea of the truth of science "wants to be unconditional truth [*Sie will unbedingte Wahrheit sein*]" (*Crisis*, 278)—this essential association of truth and unconditionality thus attesting in truth to the fact that unconditionality is the truth of truth) *and* in the *Critique of Pure Reason*, where Kant explains to us that the subordination of speculative to practical reason is an irreversible hierarchy because what is at stake is the very "interest" (*Interesse*) of reason. The interest of speculative reason is thus only conditioned (*nur bedingt*), whereas that of practical reason is unconditioned (*unbedingt*) (*CPR*, 126–28).

Up until now we have relied on what I have called a first hearing of the phrase "to save the honor of reason." Before trying to hear it in a completely different way, I would like, from within the very resonance of this first hearing, to lend an ear to an even more distant provenance of this *unconditional* rationalism *of the unconditional* in the great, exacting, respectable, and singular forms it took in transcendental idealism, whether in Kant or in Husserl. As the responsible guardians we must be of this heritage, we also have the duty to recognize in it, in both cases, and within the horizon of an infinite *idea* as an infinite task for practical reason, a powerful *teleology*. It is precisely in relation to this supremacy of idea and of telos, the reason or *logos* that is ordered by them or that orders them, *ideo-logy* and *teleo-logy* themselves, this reason of ideality and this reason of the telos, that we will have to pose the question of the event, of the coming and of the to-come, that is, the future, of the event. We must ask ourselves whether, in their very historicity (for there is an undeniable thought of history in Kant and in Husserl, and even a place for a certain history of reason), these great transcendental and teleological rationalisms grant a thought of—or expose themselves to—that which *comes*, the event of *what* comes and of *who* comes, of what arrives or happens *by* reason and *to* reason, according to this *coming*, according to this verbal noun that links such notions as event, advent, future, and mutation to a vocabulary of the *coming*, a verbal noun twice inscribed—in a phrase that is rather untranslatably French—in the title of our conference, "la raison et son *avenir*, le *devenir* des rationalités" [reason and its to-come, the becoming of rationalities].

Let us stay with the resonances of this first hearing, but so as to make out, in a more genealogical or more archaeological fashion, the vibration of an even older marking of the bow. If I allow myself to play a bit with this sonorous register, it is in order to get closer to this essence of the event, of *what comes to pass* only once, only one time, a single time, a first and last time, in an always singular, unique, exceptional, irreplaceable, unforeseeable, and incalculable fashion, of *what* happens or *who* happens by precisely there where—and this is the end of the horizon, of teleology, the calculable program, foresight, and providence—one no longer *sees it coming*, no longer horizontally: *without prospect or horizon.*

To indicate it already in advance, it will be a matter for me of asking whether, in thinking the event, in thinking the coming [*venir*], the to-come [*avenir*], and the becoming [*devenir*] of the event, it is possible and in truth necessary to distinguish the experience of the unconditional, the desire and the thought, the exigency of unconditionality, the very reason and the justice of unconditionality, from everything that is ordered into a system according to this transcendental idealism and its teleology. In other words, whether there is a chance to think or to grant the thought of the unconditional event to a reason that is other than the one we have just spoken about, namely, the classical reason of what presents itself or announces its presentation according to the *eidos*, the *idēa*, the ideal, the regulative Idea or, something else that here amounts to the same, the telos.

Let us not abandon this first hearing. Let us listen from further away in order to try to be more responsible for our reason as well as for our heritage and to try to attune ourselves to them in a more responsible manner.

"To save the honor of reason": what, we have been asking ourselves, might this first mean? What might it signify? Would this question of signification be the first question of a philosopher worthy of this name? Committed to the question, such a philosopher would feel that he or she first of all had to understand, analyze, give reasons, and be responsible for the supposed meaning of his or her language. Unless, even before understanding and knowing the meaning thus signified or assigned, he or she would have to ask what this might or should *signify or assign to him or her*, as we say of a task or of a mission, of an obligation or a responsibility: not only that they mean, that they have some assigned meaning or that they designate something, but that they assign, notify, or serve notice, like an order, like a legal performative. But how are we to hear this?

I had called this, perhaps a bit too quickly, a *hypothesis*, a series of hypotheses. Now there's a word, *hypothesis*, that I must be content, at least for the moment and for lack of time, simply to salute in passing without stopping at all the signals it sends us toward the future of reason and the development of rationalities. But one will not treat this subject without speaking of the Greek *hypothesis*.

Hypothesis in Greek will have signified before all else the base or basis, the infrastructure *posed* beneath or at the bottom of a foundation. As such, it will have been a figure for the bottom or the basement, the groundwork or the foundation, and thus the principle of a thing, the reason of an institution, the raison d'être of a science or a reasoning, of a *logos* or a logic, of a theory, rationalization, or ratiocination. It will have also done this as the subject, substance, or supposition of a discourse, as a proposition, design, or resolution, but most often as a *condition*. The rationality of reason is forever destined, and universally so, for every possible future and development, every possible to-come and becoming, to contend *between*, on the one hand, all these figures and conditions of the hypothetical and, on the other hand, the absolute sovereignty of the anhypothetical, of the unconditional or absolute principle, a principle that I qualify as *sovereign* so as at once to give one of the notes, and not just a political note, of my words today, but also so as to recall in advance, having already had to cite it, whether I wanted to or not, a moment within the canonical text of Plato's *Republic* that I would be tempted to consider quasi-inaugural. It is the moment when, for the first time, in Greek, the *question* is posed, when the *demand*, rather, is made, in Greek, a demand that just might be, still today, here and now, at once our postulation and our common, inflexible, and demanding interrogation. It is the question of or demand for knowledge as power, for truth and for capacity (*dynamis*, *Vermögen*), namely, for the power to know, for power-knowledge, for the power *of* knowledge, for knowledge *as* power. We must let this question resonate right up to us, here and now, yesterday, today, and tomorrow, this question about *dynamis*, about a force and a power but also about the possible and its limits, about the possible and the impossible, about a sovereign "I can" and an "I cannot," about the potential and the virtual; we must let this question resonate wherever what is at stake is the calculable and the incalculable in ethical, juridical, and political reason, to be sure, but also, inseparably, in the technical reason of what is called a bit too quickly today the "virtual" in the technosciences, biopolitics, and so on.

We have not yet left Plato. Will we ever leave him? This interrogation concerning *dynamis* in the *Republic*, this concern about power and capacities, about the power of knowing, about a power assured *of* knowing or assured *by* knowledge, is first of all an interrogation concerning the *cause* of science and truth (*aitian d'epistēmēs ousan kai alētheias*) insofar as they are known (508e). Now, this cause, namely, that which gives us the capacity, the force, the power, the potential (*dynamis*) of knowing and that thus gives truth (*alētheia*) to the things to be known, is, we must not forget, an idea of the good (*idéa tou agathou*). It is thus necessary at least to recall, for what orients or disorients our *here and now*, the *four* following traits, which are so many markers or sendings, so many opening gestures [*coups d'envoi*].

1. The idea of the Good is situated, at once inscribed and deinscribed, on a divided *line* cut into two unequal parts, each of which is itself cut according to the calculable reason of a *logos*, and this is Plato's word, a *logos* that divides things up according to the *analogy* between the sensible visible, the mathematical (which itself, from the inside, will have ordered the line and its *logos*), the intelligible visible, and the invisible as the source of the visible, the invisible visibility of the visible, the condition of visibility that is itself invisible and unconditional.

2. For this idea of the Good, which at once orders and is itself ordered by the *logos* and the calculation that it exceeds, is an *anhypotheton*, the first

figure of the "unconditional," the principle and anhypothetical archon toward which the soul ascends (*to ep'arkhēn anupotheton*) (510b), without
icons and on the basis of hypothetical conditions.

3. It is to this idea of the Good that, in accordance with political or
politicizable figures, the ultimate sovereign power is granted. I specify and
emphasize *sovereign*. I do so not only to get a bit more quickly and literally to the concerns that guide me here but because Plato speaks throughout this famous passage about force and dialectical power, about what the
logos touches through its dialectical power (*ho logos haptetai tēi tou di-
alegesthai dunamei*) (511b), about the sun and the good, which, analogically, have the *power* and *right to reign* (*basileuein*), each one as a king
(*basileus*) over his realm or over his visible world, the one over the sensible
visible world, the other over the intelligible visible world. The word *sovereign* is further justified by the fact that Plato actually qualifies as *kurion*
(508a) this Sun and this Good, which produce, analogically, sensible visibility and intelligible visibility. But it is also, and especially, justified by the
fact that, at the moment of defining the idea of the Good in a literally hyperbolic fashion as *epekeina tēs ousias* (beyond being or beingness), Plato
couches this idea in the language of power or, rather, superpower. It is a
question of a power more powerful than power, conveyed in a sovereign
superlative that undercuts in an exceptional fashion the analogy and hierarchy it nonetheless imposes. That is the essence without essence of sovereignty. Besides *basileus* and *kurion*, the words Plato uses are those that
will have named sovereignty throughout the whole complicated, rich, and
differential history of the political ontotheology of sovereignty in the
West. It is the superpowerful origin of a reason that gives reason or proves
right [*donne raison*], that wins out over [*a raison de*] everything, that
knows everything and lets everything be known, that produces becoming
or genesis but does not itself *become*, remaining withdrawn in an exemplary, hyperbolic fashion from becoming or from genesis. It engenders
like a generative principle of life, like a father, but it is not itself subject to
history. A single quotation concerning the Good and the image of the sovereign Good will here suffice:

> The sun, I presume you will say, not only furnishes to visibles the power of
> visibility [*tēn tou horasthai dunamin*] but it also provides for their generation
> and growth and nurture though it is not itself generation [*ou genesin auton
> onta*]. . . . In like manner, then, you are to say that the objects of knowledge
> not only receive from the presence of the good their being known, but their

very existence [*to einai*] and essence [*tēn ousian*] is derived to them from it, though the good itself is not essence but still transcends essence in dignity [or majesty] and surpassing power [*ouk ousias ontos tou agathou, all' eti epekeina tēs ousias presbeia kai dunamei huperekhontos*]. (509b)[10]

Chambry's French translation of *presbeia kai dunamei* as *majesté et puissance*, "majesty and power," is right, to be sure; I would not add anything to the translation of *dunamis* as *puissance* or as *pouvoir*. But I will insist on the word *presbeia*, quite rightly translated as *majesté*. For *presbeia* is the honor and dignity attached to age, to what precedes and comes first, to seniority and primogeniture, but also to the principate, to the precedence of *what* or *who* has the privilege of the predecessor or forebear, of the ancestor, the father or grandfather—and thus of that which begins and commands, of the *arkhē*, if you will. *Presbeion*, I also note, since honor has from the very beginning held the place of honor here, is also the honor conferred on the oldest, the dignity that distinguishes the archaic or the archontic, the firstborn in a filiation, in what is called in testamentary law not the *principium* but, still in Roman law, the *praecipuum*, from *praecipuus* (the right accorded to the first heir, from *caput* and from *capital*, yet again). In French law we have the word *préciput*. But the translation of *presbeia* as *majesté* seems to me not only right but more fecund. Again in Roman political law, *majestas*, the grandeur of what is absolutely grand, superior to comparative grandeur itself, a grandeur most high, higher than height itself, more elevated than magnitude itself, is the word most often translated as *sovereignty*. Bodin recalls this in the beginning of his chapter "On Sovereignty," where, next to the Latin *majestas*, he cites the Greek family of *kurion* and of *arkhē*.

Although the majestic sovereignty of the idea of the Good is not the law (*nomos*), it would be easy, I think, to link its necessity to the Platonic thought of the state, of the *polis* or the *politeia*. One could argue, to put it all too briefly in the interest of time, that all these great rationalisms are, in every sense of this term, rationalisms of the state, if not state rationalisms. There is nothing fortuitous in the fact that none of these great rationalisms, with the exception perhaps of certain words of Marx, ever really confronted the "state" form of sovereignty.

4. Finally, in order to reconstitute just a couple of the different links in the chain of this genealogical filiation, this panoramically European and philosophical filiation of a discourse that, in this passage from the *Republic*, was also a discourse about patrimonial and capital filiation (the sun or

the Good was also defined, you will recall, as a father and as a capital), I limit myself to a single indication. It is in the *Crisis*, and once again in the Vienna Lecture, that Husserl cites or summons to appear a certain sun of Descartes, although he could have just as well replaced it by the sun of Plato. (But can one really replace the sun? Can one think an original technical prosthesis of the sun? That is perhaps the question underlying everything I'm saying here.) Husserl writes, in order to grant force to reason, if not actually to acknowledge that a certain reason, the reason of the strongest [*la raison du plus fort*], is right [*donner raison*]:

> Though the development [or the becoming of infinite ideals and tasks] weakened in antiquity, it was nevertheless not lost. Let us make the leap to the so-called modern period. With a burning enthusiasm the infinite task of a mathematical knowledge of nature and of knowledge of the world in general is taken up. The immense successes in the knowledge of nature are now supposed to be shared by the knowledge of the spirit [*der Geisteserkenntnis zuteil werden*]. Reason has demonstrated its force in relation to nature [*Die Vernunft hat ihre Kraft in der Natur erwiesen*]. (*Crisis*, 294)

Husserl then continues by citing Descartes to support what he has just advanced: "'Just as the sun is the one all-illuminating and warming sun, so reason is also the one reason' (Descartes)" (*Crisis*, 294).

§ 2 To Arrive—At the Ends of the State (and of War, and of World War)

What would this history of reason have taught us? How are we to think this at once continuous and differentiated becoming of reason, this essential link between, on the one hand, what will have dominated, it seems to me, the philosophical genealogy in its most powerful institution, and, on the other hand, reason in more than one European language, reason as the reason and raison d'être of philosophy?

It would thus be, or at least this is the hypothesis or argument I submit to you for discussion, a certain inseparability between, on the one hand, the exigency of sovereignty in general (not only but including political sovereignty, indeed state sovereignty, which will not be challenged, in fact quite the contrary, by the Kantian thought of cosmopolitanism or universal peace) and, on the other hand, the unconditional exigency of the unconditioned (*anhypotheton, unbedingt, inconditionné*).

Calculative reason (*ratio*, intellect, understanding) would thus have to ally itself and submit itself to the principle of unconditionality that tends to exceed the calculation it founds. This inseparability or this alliance between sovereignty and unconditionality appears forever irreducible. Its resistance appears absolute and any separation impossible: for isn't sovereignty, especially in its modern political forms, as understood by Bodin, Rousseau, or Schmitt, precisely unconditional, absolute, and especially, as a result, indivisible? Is it not exceptionally sovereign insofar as it retains the right to the exception? The right to decide on the exception and the right to suspend rights and law [*le droit*]?

My question would thus be, in short: can we still, and in spite of all this, separate these two exigencies? Can we and *must* we separate them in the name, precisely, of reason, but also in the name of the event, of the arrival [*venue*] or the *coming* [*venir*] that is inscribed in the to-*come* [à-*venir*] as well as in the be-*coming* [de-*venir*] of reason? Is not this exigency faithful to one of the two poles of rationality, namely, to this postulation of unconditionality? I say *postulation* in order to gesture toward the demand, the desire, the imperative exigency; and I say *postulation* rather than *principle* in order to avoid the princely and powerful authority of the first, of the *arkhē* or the *presbeia*; and, finally, I say *postulation* rather than *axiomatic* in order to avoid a comparative and thus calculable scale of values and evaluations.

Let us thus ask ourselves whether it is *today* possible, in the daylight of today, to think and put to the test a separation that seems impossible and unthinkable, irreducible to *logos*, or at least to *legein* interpreted as gathering or as the gathering of the self, as collecting oneself? Is this possible when the thought of the world to come and, first of all, of what is called man's terra firma is undergoing terror, the fears and tremblings of an earthquake whose every jolt is in some way overdetermined and defined by forces *in want of sovereignty* [*en mal de souveraineté*]—sovereignty in general but, more visibly, more decipherably, indivisible nation-state sovereignty. Can we not and *must* we not distinguish, even when this appears impossible, between, on the one hand, the compulsion or autopositioning of sovereignty (which is nothing less than that of *ipseity* itself, of the selfsame of the oneself [*meisme*, from *metipsissimus*], an ipseity that includes within itself, as the etymology would also confirm, the androcentric positioning of power in the master or head of the household, the sovereign mastery of the lord or seigneur, of the father or husband, the power of the *same*, of *ipse* as the selfsame self) and, on the other hand, this postulation of unconditionality, which can be found in the critical exigency as well as the (forgive the expression) deconstructive exigency *of* reason? In the name of reason? For deconstruction, if something of the sort exists, would remain above all, in my view, an unconditional rationalism that never renounces—and precisely in the name of the Enlightenment to come, in the space to be opened up of a democracy to come—the possibility of suspending in an argued, deliberated, rational fashion, all conditions, hypotheses, conventions, and presuppositions, and of criticizing unconditionally all conditionalities, including those that still found the critical idea, namely, those of the *krinein*, of the *krisis*, of the binary or dialectical decision or judgment.

I will risk going even further. I will push hyperbole beyond hyperbole. It would be a question not only of separating this kind of sovereignty drive from the exigency for unconditionality as two symmetrically associated terms, but of questioning, critiquing, deconstructing, if you will, one in the name of the other, sovereignty in the name of unconditionality. This is what would have to be recognized, thought, reasoned through, however difficult or improbable, however im-possible even, it might seem. Yet what is at issue is precisely another thought of the possible (of power, of the masterly and sovereign "I can," of ipseity itself) and of an im-possible that would not be simply negative.

The first thing to be unconditioned would be the event, the event in its essential structure, in its very eventfulness. If I insist so much on the Latin resources of the French language, it is not only to honor the motivating idea behind our conference and to take responsibility for it from the start. It is because, in the event or the advent, in the invention of what happens or arrives, the semantic link between the *avenir*—the future—of reason, the *devenir*—the becoming—of rationalities, and the "*viens*," the *venir*, or the *venue*—that is, the "come," the coming, or the arrival—is best marked in Latin. This link is sometimes untranslatable in all its idiomatic connections. We will thus think the *avenir* or the *devenir* in its rational necessity, we will take it into account, only when we will have given an account [*rendra compte*] of what in this "—*venir*" appears first of all *unforeseeable*, visible or seeable perhaps but unforeseeable, assuming that we can ever see without in some way foreseeing and without seeing come from out of some horizon. A foreseen event is already present, already presentable; it has already arrived or happened and is thus neutralized in its irruption. Everywhere there is a horizon and where we can see something coming from out of some teleology or ideal horizon, some horizon of an idea, that is, from out of the seeing [*voir*] or the knowing [*savoir*] of an *eidos*, everywhere that ideality is possible (and there is neither science nor language nor technique nor, and we must recognize this, experience in general, without the production of some ideality), this horizontal ideality, the horizon of this ideality, will have neutralized in advance the event, along with everything that, in any historicity worthy of this name, requires the eventfulness of the event.

As unforeseeable, any event worthy of its name must not only exceed all teleological idealism and elude the ruses by which teleological reason conceals from itself what might come or happen to it and affect it in its ipseity in an autoimmune fashion. (And, notice, it is reason itself that orders us to say this, reason that gives us such a thought of the event, not some obscure irrationalism.) The event must also announce itself as im-possible; it must thus announce itself without calling in advance, without fore-warning [*prévenir*], announcing itself without announcing itself, without any horizon of expectation, any telos, formation, form, or teleological pre-formation. Whence its always monstrous, unpresentable character, de-monstrable *as* un-monstrable. Thus never as such. One thus says, one ex-claims, "without precedent!" with an exclamation point. Whenever the event of, for example, a technoscientific invention, as I tried to show at the beginning of *Psyché: Inventions de l'autre*,[11] is made possible by a set of conditions for which we can give an account and that we can identify or determine in a saturable fashion, as is done and must be done after the fact by epistemology, by the history or philosophy of the technosciences (politico-economic infrastructure, epistemic configuration, paradigm, and so on), we are no longer talking about an invention or an event. An event or an invention is possible only as im-possible. That is, nowhere *as such*, the phenomenological or ontological "as such" annulling this experience of an im-possible that never appears or announces itself *as such*.

To think this and to say this is not to go against reason. To be worried about an ideocracy or a teleologism that tends to annul or neutralize the eventfulness of the event, and that does so precisely to immunize itself against it, is not to go against reason. It is in fact the only chance to think, rationally, something like a future [*venir*] and a becoming [*devenir*] of rea-son. It is also, let us not forget, that which should free not only thought but scientific research from the control or conditioning to which it is sub-jected by all sorts of political, military, technoeconomic, and capitalist powers or institutions (for example, in the appropriation through patents of biogenetic discoveries). The same goes for "state" control of knowledge, sometimes, to cite just one example, in the distinguished and respectable form of so-called ethics committees. For just as no power (whether polit-ical, juridical, religious, ideological, or economic) will ever be able to jus-tify through reason the control or limitation of scientific research, of a re-search for the truth, of a critical or deconstructive questioning, and thus of a rational and unconditional research in the order of knowledge and of thought, so also (or reciprocally), no knowledge as such, no theoretical reason, if you will, will ever be able to found a responsibility or a decision in any kind of a sustained manner, like a cause that would produce an effect, like a raison d'être or a sufficient reason that would provide an account of what follows from it. It *is necessary to know*, to be sure, to know that knowledge is indispensable; we need to have knowledge, the best and most comprehensive available, in order to make a decision or take responsibility. But the moment and structure of the *"il faut*," of the "it is necessary," just like the responsible decision, are and must remain heterogeneous to knowledge. An absolute interruption must separate them, one that can always be judged "mad," for otherwise the engagement of a responsibility would be reducible to the application and deployment of a program, perhaps even a program under the refined form of teleological norms, values, rules, indeed duties, that is to say, debts to be acquitted or reappropriated, and thus annulled in a circle that is still implicitly economic. That is why what I say here, I'm well aware, involves a serious risk.

A "responsibility" or a "decision" cannot be founded on or justified by any *knowledge as such*, that is, without a leap between two discontinuous and radically heterogeneous orders. I say rather abstractly "responsibility" and "decision" here rather than "practical," "ethical," "juridical" or "political" reason by reason of the difficulties that I will address, albeit all too briefly, in a moment.

In coming too slowly or too quickly toward my conclusion, I must share with you at this point a hesitation I had to overcome. In preparing for this session I asked myself how to solve the problem of time in the most economic and least unreasonable, if not most rational, way possible. I thus went over my accounts and updated my *livre de raison*. (You know that in French a *livre de raison* is a book of accounts [*rationes*] in which revenues and expenses are recorded and tallied.) One of my working hypotheses, which I later abandoned, was thus to sacrifice the main line of this noble rationalist and teleological tradition, the one that runs from Plato to Kant to Husserl, along with its French offshoot (running from Descartes to the Enlightenment to all those who were more attentive to a history or a becoming, that is, to a certain plasticity, of reason: Brunschvicg, Bachelard, Canguilhem, Foucault, Lacan, and so on), so as to focus everything on an example from today, on some concrete figure, some metonymy of all the urgencies that confront us. This example, I said to myself, would force me to mobilize indirectly the philosophemes we have just been questioning so as to allow them all to converge in the great question of reason and of life. (For we must not forget that Plato determines the Good, *to agathon*, the *epekeina tēs ousias*, which is the reason of *logos*, as the source of life, the figure of paternity or of patrimonial capital, the nongenetic origin of all genesis; and Aristotle speaks of the life of pure Actuality or of the Prime Mover; and the *logos* of Christianity defines itself as the life of the living, which is also true, and literally so, of the Hegelian *logos*.) A well-chosen example on the side of life, I told myself, would allow me to tie together, in as rigorous and tight a fashion as possible, reflections of an ethical, juridical, political, and, inseparably, technoscientific nature—and precisely in a place where technicity, the great question of the technical and the logic of the prosthesis, would be not accessory but essential and intrinsic to the problematic of reason. In this hypothesis, my choice would have gravitated toward the terrible dilemma of *cloning*— whether therapeutic or reproductive. For we would there find, I said to myself, the best and the worst of reason, the newest and most terrifying in the realm of the calculable as well as the incalculable, the powers and the impotence of reason confronted with some of the most advanced research into the essence of the living being, birth and death, the rights and dignity of the human person, the rights, laws, and powers of the sovereign state in these domains, the reason of state [*raison d'état*] that gives itself the right to rise above all other rights, the ongoing and future development of international law (for we know that the decisions being made today by Western heads of state on this subject are determining an international jurisprudence). In summoning the two major axiomatics that are authoritative today in so many circles (in science, politics, law, the media, and so on), we would find the opposition between the calculable and the incalculable. To generalize, the proponents of cloning, and especially of therapeutic cloning, claim the rational necessity of not limiting theoretical and technoexperimental research whenever the results can be calculated and the anticipated benefits programmed, even if this calculability risks, without any assurance, exposing us to the incalculable. On the other side, one opposes not only the improbable programmation of countless armies of threatening clones in the service of an industrial, military, or market rationality, whether demonic or mad (for a certain reason can of itself become mad), but also, and more often, therapeutic cloning (whose limits would not be rigorously secured) or even cautious experimentation in the area of reproductive cloning (whose technical possibility has not even been proven). One thus objects to all cloning in the name of ethics, human rights, what is proper to humanity, and the dignity of human life, in the name of the singularity and *nonrepetitive* unicity of the human person, in the name of an ethics of desire or a love of the other—which we some-times believe or try to make others believe, with an optimistic confidence, must always inspire the act of procreation. And, finally, one objects to cloning in the name of that incalculable element that must be left to birth, to the coming to light or into the world of a unique, irreplaceable, free, and thus nonprogrammable living being.

What, then, does this currently prevailing ethical axiomatic in the law and politics of the West keep out of rational examination? First of all, the fact that so-called identificatory repetition, the duplication that one claims to reject with horrified indignation, is already, and fortunately, present and at work everywhere it is a question of reproduction and of her-itage, in culture, knowledge, language, education, and so on, whose very conditions, whose production and reproduction, are assured by this du-plication. But what is also, and especially, overlooked is the fact that this militant humanism, this discourse concerned about ethics, about human freedom and human specificity, seems to assume that two so-called genet-ically identical individuals will have identical fates, that they will be indis-tinguishable and subservient to the calculation that has given them birth. This is yet another way of ignoring what history, whether individual or not, owes to culture, society, education, and the symbolic, to the incalcu-lable and the aleatory—so many dimensions that are irreducible, even for "identical" twins, to this supposedly simple, genetic naturalness. What is the consequence of all this? That, in the end, this so-called ethical or hu-manist axiomatic actually shares with the axiomatic it claims to oppose a certain geneticism or biologism, indeed a deep zoologism, a fundamental but unacknowledged reductionism.

The problem thus calls for (and here is the reason of the Enlightenment to come) a completely different elaboration. I say this not so as to come down on one side or the other, and not out of some wide-eyed optimism in a reproductive cloning for which I see little interest, attraction, or prob-ability. Yet I find few rational and justifiable objections to therapeutic cloning, assuming that one can in fact distinguish it from the other kind. For hasn't the path already been cleared for this, and approved in princi-ple, by so many prosthetic techniques, by recent developments in gene therapy using interfering RNA, by so-called information tele-technolo-gies, structures or organizations that are themselves prosthetic and that ac-tually situate, along with what I call iterability, the true place of the prob-lem of reason today: that of technicity, of what is proper to humanity or to the living body, of the proper in general? In every field. The presuppositions shared by both parties in this debate over cloning thus call for a systematic re-elaboration, one for which the vigilance of reason must be without respite, courageous and upright, determined not to give in to any dogmatic intimidation. But I said that I will not speak about cloning.

How shall I present my concluding propositions in as brief and economic a fashion as possible? To the value of this unforeseeable im-possibility I would associate the value of *incalculable* and *exceptional singularity*. I appeal here again to good sense itself, to common sense, that most widely shared thing in the world. A calculable event, one that falls, like a case, like the object of some knowledge, under the generality of a law, norm, determinative judgment, or technoscience, and thus of a power-knowledge and a knowledge-power, is not, *at least in this measure*, an event. Without the absolute singularity of the incalculable and the exceptional, no thing and no one, nothing *other* and thus *nothing*, arrives or happens. I say "no thing and no one" so as to return to a thought of the event that awakens or is awakened before distinguishing or conjoining the "what" and the "who." It is a matter of thinking reason, of thinking the coming of its future, of its to-come, and of its becoming, as the experience of *what* and *who* comes, of what happens or who arrives—obviously as other, as the absolute exception or singularity of an alterity that is not reappropriable by the ipseity of a sovereign power and a calculable knowledge.

1. *The unconditionality of the incalculable* allows or gives the event to be thought. It gives or lends itself to thought as the *advent* or *coming* of the other in experiences for which I will name just a few metonymic figures. My recourse to the lexicon of *unconditionality* has proven useful to me because tradition and translation (*anhypotheton, unbedingt, inconditionnel*) facilitate its intelligibility, indeed its pedagogy. But I am not sure that an elaboration to come will not impose another term, one that has been freed to a greater extent from these traditional semantic implications, which in fact differ from one language to the next: *anhypotheton, unbedingt, inconditionnel*—these are not exactly the same thing. Another language will perhaps one day help us to say better what still remains to be said about these metonymic figures of the unconditional. But whatever this other language may be, this word or this trope, it will have to inherit or retain the memory of that which, in the unconditionality of reason, relates each

singularity to the universalizable. It will have to require or postulate a universal beyond all relativism, culturalism, ethnocentrism, and especially nationalism, beyond what I propose naming, to refer to all the modern risks that these relativisms make reason run, *irratio-nationalism* or *irratio-nation-state-ism*—spell them as you will.

Among the figures of unconditionality without sovereignty I have had occasion to privilege in recent years, there would be, for example, that of an *unconditional hospitality* that exposes itself without limit to the coming of the other, beyond rights and laws, beyond a hospitality conditioned by the right of asylum, by the right to immigration, by citizenship, and even by the right to universal hospitality, which still remains, for Kant, for example, under the authority of a political or cosmopolitical law.[12] Only an unconditional hospitality can give meaning and practical rationality to a concept of hospitality. Unconditional hospitality exceeds juridical, political, or economic calculation. But no thing and no one happens or arrives without it.

Another example would be the unconditionality of the *gift* or of *forgiveness.* I have tried to show elsewhere exactly where the unconditionality required by the purity of such concepts leads us. A gift without calculable exchange, a gift worthy of this name, would not even appear *as such* to the donor or donee without the risk of reconstituting, through phenomenality and thus through its phenomenology, a circle of economic reappropriation that would just as soon annul its event. Similarly, forgiveness can be given *to* the other or come *from* the other only beyond calculation, beyond apologies, amnesia, or amnesty, beyond acquittal or prescription, even beyond any asking for forgiveness, and thus beyond any transformative repentance, which is most often the stipulated condition for forgiveness, at least in what is most *predominant* in the tradition of the Abrahamic religions.

In the open series of these examples, we have to think together two figures of rationality that, on either side of a limit, at once call for and exceed one another. The incalculable unconditionality of hospitality, of the gift or of forgiveness, exceeds the calculation of conditions, just as justice exceeds law, the juridical, and the political. Justice can never be reduced to law, to calculative reason, to lawful distribution, to the norms and rules that condition law, as evidenced by its history and its ongoing transformations, by its recourse to coercive force, its recourse to a power or might that, as Kant showed with the greatest rigor, is inscribed and justified in the purest concept of law or right. For "strict right," says Kant, implies the faculty or the possibility of a reciprocal use of coercion (*wechselseitigen Zwanges*), and thus of force, of a reason of the strongest following universal, and thus rational, laws, in accordance with the freedom of each.[13] To grant this heterogeneity of justice to law, it is not enough to distinguish, as Heidegger did, *dikē* from the legality of Roman *jus*; it is also necessary, as I tried to indicate in *Specters of Marx*, to question the Heideggerian interpretation of *dikē* as harmony or as gathering—indeed, ultimately, as *logos*.[14] The interruption of a certain unbinding opens the free space of the relationship to the incalculable singularity of the other. It is there that justice exceeds law but at the same time motivates the movement, history, and becoming of juridical rationality, indeed the relationship between law and reason, as well as everything that, in modernity, will have linked the history of law to the history of critical reason. The heterogeneity between justice and law does not exclude but, on the contrary, calls for their inseparability: there can be no justice without an appeal to juridical determinations and to the force of law; and there can be no becoming, no transformation, history, or perfectibility of law without an appeal to a justice that will nonetheless always exceed it.

To think *together both* this heterogeneity *and* this inseparability is to recognize, and so bear witness to, an *autodelimitation* that divides reason and that is not without relation to a certain autoimmunity. What is called reason, from one language to another, is thus found on both sides. According to a transaction that is each time novel, each time without precedent, reason goes through and goes between, on the one side, the reasoned exigency of calculation or conditionality and, on the other, the intransigent, nonnegotiable exigency of unconditional incalculability. This intractable exigency wins out [*a raison de*] and *must* win out over everything. On both sides, then, whether it is a question of singularity or universality, and each time both at once, *both* calculation *and* the incalculable *are necessary.* This responsibility of reason, this experience that consists in keeping within reason [*à raison garder*], in being responsible for a reason of which we are the heirs, could be situated with only the greatest difficulty. Indeed I would situate it precisely within this greatest of difficulties or, rather, in truth, within the autoimmune aporia of this impossible transaction between the conditional and the unconditional, calculation and the incalculable. A transaction without any rule given in advance, without any absolute assurance. For there is no absolutely reliable prophylaxis against the autoimmune. By definition. An always perilous transaction must thus invent, each time, in a singular situation, its own law and norm, that is, a maxim that welcomes each time the event to come. There can be responsibility and decision, if there are any, only at this price. If I had to attribute a meaning, the most difficult, least mediocre, least moderate meaning, to this well-worn, indeed long-discredited, word *reasonable*, I would say that what is "reasonable" is the reasoned and considered wager of a transaction between these two apparently irreconcilable exigencies of reason, between calculation and the incalculable. For example, between human rights, such as the history of a certain number of juridical performatives has determined and enriched them from one declaration to the next over the course of the last two centuries, and the exigency of an unconditional justice to which these performatives will always be inadequate, open to their perfectibility (which is more and something other than a regulative Idea) and exposed to a rational deconstruction that will endlessly question their limits and presuppositions, the interests and calculations that order their deployment, and their concepts—beginning with the concepts of law and of duty, and especially the concept of the human, the history of the concept of the human, of what is proper to humankind, to the human as *zoon logon ekhon* or *animal rationale*. It is rational, for example, at the very moment of endorsing, developing, perfecting, and determining human rights, to continue to interrogate in a deconstructive fashion all the limits we thought pertained to life, the being of life and the life of being (and this is almost the entire history of philosophy), between the living and the dead, the living present and its spectral others, but also between that living being called "human" and the one called "animal." Although I cannot demonstrate this here, I believe—and the stakes are becoming more and more urgent—that none of the conventionally accepted limits between the so-called human living being and the so-called animal one, none of the oppositions, none of the supposedly linear and indivisible boundaries, resist a rational deconstruction—whether we are talking about language, culture, social symbolic networks, technicity or work, even the relationship to death and to mourning, and even the prohibition against or avoidance of incest—so many "capacities" of which the "animal" (a general singular noun!) is said so dogmatically to be bereft, impoverished.

I just referred in passing to the distinction between the *constative* (the language of descriptive and theoretical knowledge) and the *performative*, which is so often said to produce the event it declares (as with, for example, the juridical performative that instituted in 1945, against the backdrop of human rights, the concept of a crime against humanity, the ferment of a laborious transformation in international law and of everything that depends on it). Now, just like the constative, it seems to me, the performative cannot avoid neutralizing, indeed annulling, the eventfulness of the event it is supposed to produce. A performative produces an event only by securing for itself, in the first-person singular or plural, in the present, and with the guarantee offered by conventions or legitimated fictions, the power that an ipseity gives itself to produce the event of which it speaks—the event that it neutralizes forthwith insofar as it appropriates for itself a calculable mastery over it. If an event worthy of this name is to arrive or happen, it must, beyond all mastery, affect a passivity. It must touch an exposed vulnerability, one without absolute immunity, without indemnity; it must touch this vulnerability in its finitude and in a nonhorizontal fashion, there where it is not yet or is already no longer possible to face or face up to the unforeseeability of the other. In this regard, autoimmunity is not an absolute ill or evil. It enables an exposure to the other, to *what* and to *who* comes—which means that it must remain incalculable. Without autoimmunity, with absolute immunity, nothing would ever happen or arrive; we would no longer wait, await, or expect, no longer expect one another, or expect any event.

What must be thought here, then, is this inconceivable and unknowable thing, a freedom that would no longer be the power of a subject, a freedom without autonomy, a heteronomy without servitude, in short, something like a passive decision. We would thus have to rethink the philosophemes of the decision, of that foundational couple activity and passivity, as well as potentiality and actuality. It is thus rational, legitimately rational, to interrogate or deconstruct—without however discrediting—the fertile distinction between constative and performative. Similarly, beyond law, debt, and duty, it would be necessary to rethink rationally a hyperethics or hyperpolitics that does not settle for acting simply "according to duty" (*pflichtmässig*) or even (to take up the Kantian distinction that founds practical reason) "from duty" or "out of pure duty" (*eigentlich aus Pflicht, aus reiner Pflicht*).[15] Such a hyperethics or hyperpolitics would carry us unconditionally beyond the economic circle of duty or of the task (*Pflicht* or *Aufgabe*), of the debt to be reappropriated or annulled, of what one *knows* must be done, of what thus still depends on a programmatic and normative knowledge that need only be carried out.

The hiatus between these two equally rational postulations of reason, this excess of a reason that of itself exceeds itself and so opens onto its future, its to-come, its becoming, this ex-position to the incalculable event, would also be the irreducible spacing of the very faith, credit, or belief without which there would be no social bond, no address to the other, no uprightness or honesty, no promise to be honored, and so no honor, no faith to be sworn or pledge to be given.

This hiatus opens the rational space of a hypercritical faith, one without dogma and without religion, irreducible to any and all religious or implicitly theocratic institutions. It is what I have called elsewhere the awaiting without horizon of a messianicity without messianism. It goes without saying that I do not detect here even the slightest hint of irrationalism, obscurantism, or extravagance. This faith is another way of *keeping within reason* [*raison garder*], however mad it might appear. If the minimal semantic kernel we might retain from the various lexicons of reason, in every language, is the ultimate possibility of, if not a consensus, at least an address universally promised and unconditionally entrusted to the other, then reason remains the element or very air of a faith without church and without credulity, the raison d'être of the pledge, of credit, of testimony beyond proof, the raison d'être of any belief *in* the other, that is, of their belief and of our belief in them—and thus also of any perjury. For as soon as reason does not close itself off to the event that comes, the event of what or who comes, assuming it is not irrational to think that the worst can always happen, and well beyond what Kant thinks under the name "radical evil," then only the infinite possibility of the worst and of perjury can grant the possibility of the Good, of veracity and of sworn faith. This possibility remains infinite but as the very possibility of an autoimmune finitude.

2. As for *the unconditionality of the exception*, reason is found in equal measures on both sides each time that a responsibility engages or commits us before what is called, in the West and in a Latin language, *sovereignty*. Each time, which is to say, more than ever in today's world and today's day and age—in truth, at every moment. For it happens that sovereignty is first of all one of the traits by which reason defines its own power and element, that is, a certain unconditionality. It is also the concentration,

into a single point of indivisible singularity (God, the monarch, the people, the state or the nation-state), of absolute force and the absolute exception. We did not have to wait for Schmitt to learn that the sovereign is the one who decides exceptionally and performatively about the exception, the one who keeps or grants himself the right to suspend rights or law; nor did we need him to know that this politico-juridical concept, like all the others, secularizes a theological heritage. I don't think I have to illustrate, and moreover time will not permit it, everything that is at stake—for Europe and the world—in this problematic of sovereignty, today and tomorrow. To conclude, then, I will settle for two telegraphic and programmatic indications.

In the first place, why did I underscore at the outset the date of Husserl's *Crisis*? This date is inscribed between two events considered to be without precedent, two events called *world wars*, even though they were at first intra-European wars, waged by sovereign states or coalitions of sovereign states whose supposed rationality formed the very horizon of the *Crisis*. The lecture of 1935 alluded, we recall, not only to Europe and to the rest of the world but to the national communities and nation-states that formed the horizon of that lecture. Is such a warning transposable or translatable today, at a time when the concept of nation-state sovereignty as indivisible and thus unshareable is being put to an even more than critical test? This test testifies more and better than ever (for we are not talking about something absolutely new) to the fragility of nation-state sovereignty, to its precariousness, to the principle of ruins that is working it over—and thus to the tense, sometimes deadly, denials that are but the manifestations of its convulsive death throes. But at the same time, through what remains, as I said earlier, *in want of sovereignty*, where the rationality of universal human rights encroaches on nation-state sovereignty (in the form of humanitarian initiatives, nongovernmental organizations, the laborious establishment of an International Criminal Court, and so many other vehicles of international law), what then loses its pertinence, in this phase of what is so obscurely called "globalization" or *mondialisation*, is the concept of *war*, and thus of *world war*, of *enemy* and even of *terrorism*, along with the distinction between civilian and military or between army, police, and militia. What is called just as obscurely "September 11" will have neither created nor revealed this new situation, although it will have surely media-theatricalized it. And this media-theatricalization is in fact an integral and co-determining part of the event. Calculated from both sides, it calls for just as many questions and analyses as that which it seems simply to "report" through a straightforward and neutral informational process.

Consider the context we've inherited from the end of the Cold War: a so-called globalization or *mondialisation* that is more inegalitarian and violent than ever, a globalization that is, therefore, only simply alleged and actually less global or worldwide than ever, where *the* world, therefore, is not even there, and where we, we who are worldless, *weltlos, form* a world only against the backdrop of a nonworld where there is neither world nor even that poorness-in-world that Heidegger attributes to animals (which would be, according to him, *weltarm*). Within this abyss of the without-world, this abyss without support, indeed on the condition of this absence of support, of bottom, ground, or foundation, it is as if one *bore* the other, as if I felt, without support and without hypothesis, *borne* by the other and *borne* toward the other, as if, as Celan says, *Die Welt ist fort, ich muss dich tragen*: the world goes away; the world disappears; I must bear you, there where the world would no longer or would not yet be, where the world would distance itself, get lost in the distance, or be still to come. It is this so-called globalization that then confiscates to an unprecedented degree and concentrates into a small part of the human world so many natural resources, capitalist riches, technoscientific and even teletechnological powers, reserving also for that small part of the world those two great forms of immunity that go by the names public health and military security. It is precisely in this context, then, at the end of the Cold War, that clashes of force in view of hegemony no longer oppose the sovereign state to an enemy that takes either an actual or virtual state form. The United States and its allies, as well as the international institutions that depend largely on them in their actual operations (the Security Council, if not the entire United Nations), no longer face an identifiable enemy in the form of a "state" territory with whom they would wage what would still be called a "war," even if it be a war on international terrorism. Air or surface missiles, chemical, bacteriological, or nuclear weapons, covert infiltrations into computer networks ("cyber attacks")—all these weapons can destabilize or destroy the most powerful apparatuses of the state. Yet such weapons now escape all control and all state oversight. They are no longer at the sole disposal of a sovereign state or coalition of sovereign states that protect one another and maintain a balance of terror, as was the

case during the Cold War, where everyone was held in check by a reasoned game theory that calculated the risks of escalation so as to exclude,
in principle and according to the greatest probability, any suicidal operation. All that is over. A new violence is being prepared and, in truth, has
been unleashed for some time now, in a way that is more visibly suicidal
or autoimmune than ever. This violence no longer has to do with *world*
war or even with *war*, even less with some right to wage war. And this is
hardly reassuring—indeed quite the contrary. It is a matter, in essence,
neither of classical, international war, that is, a war between nation-states,
declared in accordance with old *jus europeanus*, nor of intranational civil
war, nor even of what Schmitt called "partisan war," since even this latter,
just like terrorism in its classical sense, resorted to violence or terror only
with a view toward the liberation or foundation, in the short or longer
term, of some nation-state community, some nation-state territory, in
short, some sovereignty. There is essentially no longer any such thing today that can be called in all rigor "war" or "terrorism," even if there can
still be, here and there, in a secondary sense, as the surviving vestiges of
this paradigm, wars or terrorism in these three senses; and even if, by
means of loaded rhetorical gestures, one sometimes needs to make others
believe that one is going to war or preparing for war against some enemy
force organized into a state or into some state structure that supports the
enemy. The stir created by these war mobilizations can be terribly effective, to be sure; concrete, rational, and real, it can define and deafen the
entire earth. But it cannot make us forget that we are dealing here with
useful projections and ultimate denegations, with what psychoanalysis
calls "rationalizations" (as when it speaks of "sexual theory"). A powerful
"rationalization" would thus be under way, its calculation fully conscious
or not. It consists in accusing and mounting a campaign against so-called
rogue states, states that do in fact care little for international law. This rationalization is orchestrated by hegemonic states, beginning with the
United States, which has quite rightly been shown for some time now
(Chomsky was not the first to do so) to have been itself acting like a rogue
state. Every sovereign state is in fact virtually and a priori able, that is, in
a state [*en état*], to abuse its power and, like a rogue state, transgress international law. There is something of a rogue state in every state. The use of
state power is *originally* excessive and abusive. As is, in fact, the recourse
to terror and fear, which has always been—indeed it's as old as the world,
as Hobbes theorized so well—the ultimate recourse for the sovereign

power of the state, in an implicit or explicit, blatant or subtle, form, and even when it is contractual and protective. To claim the contrary involves always a denegation, a denial, a rationalization, sometimes a ratiocination that must not be allowed to take us unawares.

This reminds us that we must sometimes, in the name of reason, be suspicious of rationalizations. Let it thus be said in passing, albeit all too quickly, that the Enlightenment to come would have to enjoin us to reckon with the logic of the unconscious, and so with the idea, and notice I'm not saying here the doctrine, arising out of a psychoanalytic revolution. Which, I might add, would have had no chance of emerging in history without, among other things, this poisoned medicine, this *pharmakon* of an inflexible and cruel autoimmunity that is sometimes called the "death drive" and that does not limit the living being to its conscious and representative form.

It is thus no doubt necessary, in the name of reason, to call into question and to limit a logic of nation-state sovereignty. It is no doubt necessary to erode not only its principle of indivisibility but its right to the exception, its right to suspend rights and law, along with the undeniable ontotheology that founds it, even in what are called democratic regimes, and even when this is denied—in what is to my eyes a questionable fashion—by such experts as Bodin, Hobbes, and Rousseau.

In speaking of an ontotheology of sovereignty, I am referring here, under the name of God, this One and Only God, to the determination of a sovereign, and thus indivisible, omnipotence. For wherever the name of God would allow us to think something else, for example a vulnerable nonsovereignty, one that suffers and is divisible, one that is mortal even, capable of contradicting itself or of repenting (a thought that is neither impossible nor without example), it would be a completely different story, perhaps even the story of a god who deconstructs himself in his ipseity.

In any case, such a questioning of sovereignty is not simply some formal or academic necessity for a kind of speculation in political philosophy, or else a form of genealogical, or perhaps even deconstructive, vigilance. It is already under way. It is at work today; it is what's *coming*, what's *happening*. It *is* and it *makes* history through the anxiety-provoking turmoil we are currently undergoing. For it is often precisely in the name of the universality of human rights, or at least of their perfectibility, as I suggested earlier, that the indivisible sovereignty of the nation-state is being more and more called into question, along with the immunity of sovereigns, be they heads of state or military leaders, and even the institution of the death penalty, the last defining attribute of state sovereignty.

And yet, in the second place, it would be imprudent and hasty, in truth hardly *reasonable,* to oppose unconditionally, that is, head-on, a sovereignty that is itself unconditional and indivisible. One cannot combat, *head-on, all* sovereignty, sovereignty *in general,* without threatening at the same time, beyond the nation-state figure of sovereignty, the classical principles of freedom and self-determination. Like the classical tradition of law (and the force that it presupposes), these classical principles remain inseparable from a sovereignty at once indivisible and yet able to be shared. Nation-state sovereignty can even itself, in certain conditions, become an indispensable bulwark against certain international powers, certain ideological, religious, or capitalist, indeed linguistic, hegemonies that, under the cover of liberalism or universalism, would still represent, in a world that would be little more than a marketplace, a rationalization in the service of particular interests. Yet again, in a context that is each time singular, where the respectful attention paid to singularity is not relativist but universalizable and rational, responsibility would consist in orienting oneself without any *determinative* knowledge of the rule. To be responsible, to keep within reason, would be to invent maxims of transaction for deciding between two just as rational and universal but contradictory exigencies of reason as well as its enlightenment.

The invention of these maxims resembles the poetic invention of an idiom whose singularity would not yield to any nationalism, not even a European nationalism—even if, as I would like to believe, within today's geopolitical landscape, a new thinking and a previously unencountered destination of Europe, along with another responsibility for Europe, are being called on to give a new chance to this idiom. Beyond all Eurocentrism. This idiom would again be a singular idiom of reason, of the *reasonable* transaction between two antinomic rationalities. At the utmost point of its extreme difficulty, indeed of its im-possibility, what I call here—in these sentences and not others—the *reasonable* would be that which, in bearing within it pre-ference itself, will always be *preferable*—and thus irreducible—to the rational it exceeds. In such sentences as these the *rational* would certainly have to do with the *just* and sometimes with the justness or exactitude of juridical and calculative reason. But the *reasonable* would do yet more and something else; it would take into account the accounting of juridical *justness* or exactitude, to be sure, but it would also strive, across transactions and aporias, for *justice*. The reasonable, as I understand it here, would be a rationality that takes account of the incalculable so as to give an account of it, there where this appears impossible, so as to account for or reckon *with* it, that is to say, with the event of *what* or *who* comes.

It remains to be known, so as to save the honor of reason, how to *translate*. For example, the word *reasonable*. And how to pay one's respects to, how to salute or greet [*saluer*], beyond its latinity, and in more than one language, the fragile difference between the *rational* and the *reasonable*.

Reason reasons, to be sure, it is right [*elle a raison*], and it gives itself reason [*se donner raison*], to do so, so as to protect or keep itself [*se garder*], so as to keep within reason [*raison garder*]. It is in this that it is and thus wants to be *itself*; that is its sovereign ipseity.

But to make its ipseity see reason, it must be reasoned with.

A reason must let itself be reasoned with.

Notes

Preface

1. Jean de la Fontaine, *The Complete Fables of Jean de la Fontaine*, trans. Norman B. Spector (Evanston, IL: Northwestern University Press, 1988), 23. Derrida works throughout these two essays with the phrase "*la raison du plus fort,*" famously portrayed in La Fontaine's fable "The Wolf and the Lamb." The first two lines run: "*La raison du plus fort est toujours la meilleure / Nous l'allons montrer tout à l'heure.*" *La raison du plus fort* can be literally rendered "the reason of the strongest," but the closest English equivalent is probably "might makes right." The phrase suggests that the reason, reasoning, or argumentation of the strongest always wins out over or gets the best of those of its rivals and so, as in the fable, is always "best," meaning final, unimpeachable, sovereign. Here are two additional English versions of the opening lines of La Fontaine's fable: "Might is right: the verdict goes to the strong. / To prove the point won't take me very long" (*La Fontaine: Selected Fables*, trans. James Michie [New York: Viking, 1979], 18); "Force has the best of any argument: / Soon proved by the story which I present" (*The Fables of La Fontaine*, trans. Marianne Moore [New York: Viking, 1964], 21).—Trans.

2. The French *le droit* can mean either "right" or "law," an individual or collective "right" or else a "system of law." In cases where these two meanings cannot be easily distinguished we have either given both meanings or opted for one and added the French. *Le droit du plus fort* means literally "the law of the strongest," more colloquially, "the law of the jungle."—Trans.

3. This book brings together two related essays initially presented as lectures during the summer of 2002. The first, "The Reason of the Strongest (Are There Rogue States?)," was delivered at Cerisy-la-Salle on July 15, 2002. Directed and organized by Marie-Louise Mallet, the ten-day conference, which ran July 9–18, 2002, bore the general title "The Democracy to Come (Around Jacques Der-

rida)." The second essay, "The 'World' of the Enlightenment to Come (Exception, Calculation, and Sovereignty)," was presented at the opening of the twenty-ninth Congrès de l'Association des Sociétés de Philosophie de Langue française [ASPLF] at the University of Nice, August 27, 2002. This conference, which ran from August 27 to September 1, 2002, had as its general title "Avenir de la raison, devenir des rationalités" [The Future of Reason, the Development of Rationalities]. It was organized under the directorship of André Tosel.

In both cases it seemed to me more appropriate to publish these texts as such in order to respect not only the constraints and limits imposed on them but also their original audiences. None of the distinguishing features provided by the original contexts have thus been edited out or modified: on such a day, in such a place, before such an audience. Only a few notes were added after the fact (see 166–67n36, 172–73n12).

4. "'[E]cquis adest?' et 'adest' responderat Echo. / hic stupet, utque aciem partes dimittit in omnis, / voce 'veni!' magna clamat: vocat illa vocantem" (Ovid, *Metamorphoses* 3.380–82). Although translation is more or less impossible, requiring each time an idiomatic reinvention of the simulacrum in each language, I cite here, with just a few modifications, a couple of French attempts and one English one. Each partially inadequate, they sometimes seem to complete one another.

"*N'y a-t-il pas quelqu'un ici?'—'Si, quelqu'un,' avait répondu Echo. Narcisse stupéfait porte ses regards de tous côtés: 'Viens' crie-t-il à pleine voix. A son appel répond un appel d'Echo, 'Viens'*" (Ovide, *Les Métamorphoses*, trans. Joseph Chamonard [Paris: Garnier-Flammarion, 1966], 99).

"*Y a-t-il quelqu'un près de moi?' 'Moi' répondit Echo. Plein de stupeur, il promène de tous côtés ses regards. 'Viens!' crie-t-il à pleine voix. A son appel elle répond par un appel*" (Ovide, *Les Métamorphoses*, trans. George Lafaye [Paris: Budé, 1961], 1:81–82).

"'Is anyone here?' and 'Here!' cried Echo back. Amazed, he looks around in all directions and with loud voice cries 'Come!'; and 'Come!' she calls him calling" (Ovid, *Metamorphoses*, trans. Frank Justus Miller [Cambridge, MA: Harvard University Press, 1984], 1:151).

5. What is called an *état de droit*, that is, a "constitutional state" or "state of law," is, it should be emphasized, a conventional *system*, at once logical and social. It *prescribes* or grants predominance to a certain type of reasoning, the one that subjects to law the consensus that is sought and the conclusions of a debate or conflict, which is to say, in truth, all that is at issue in a litigation. Is the reason of the state always subject to the state of law? Does sovereignty itself stem from the state of law? Or does it exceed it and betray it, in an always exceptional way, at the very moment it claims precisely to found it? These are the *types* of questions brought together in this book.

6. In its relation to what has been called for close to forty years now "decon-

struction," the problematic of this "American" dimension has been admirably taken up, rethought, and formalized in an original way by Peggy Kamuf in "Event of Resistance," her introduction to Jacques Derrida, *Without Alibi*, trans. Peggy Kamuf (Stanford, CA: Stanford University Press, 2002), 1–27.

7. See Jacques Derrida, "The University Without Condition," in *Without Alibi*, 202–37.

8. Allow me to refer here to a few of my works that form the context for these claims, works that, after *Khōra*, *Sauf le nom*, and *Passions*, will have marked out a certain path (see Jacques Derrida, *On the Name*, ed. Thomas Dutoit [Stanford, CA: Stanford University Press, 1995]—Trans.): *Specters of Marx: The State of the Debt, the Work of Mourning, and the New International*, trans. Peggy Kamuf (New York: Routledge, 1994); *Politics of Friendship*, trans. George Collins (New York: Verso, 1997); "Faith and Knowledge: The Two Sources of 'Religion' at the Limits of Reason Alone," trans. Samuel Weber, in *Religion*, ed. Jacques Derrida and Gianni Vattimo (Stanford, CA: Stanford University Press, 1998), 1–78; *The Gift of Death*, trans. David Wills (Chicago: University of Chicago Press, 1995).

Part I

9. The French *décennie* means "decade," that is, a period of ten years, whereas *décade* means a period of ten days. Derrida is referring here to the fact that conferences at Cerisy typically run for a full ten days, a full *décade*. In the following paragraphs Derrida plays on the fact that English has no corresponding distinction and that *decade*, which usually means a period of ten years, can also be used, although it is rare, to designate a period of ten days.—Trans.

10. The dictionary *Le Robert* labels as "abusive" the use of the word *décade* to denote a period of ten years, a use that has come into the French language "often under the influence of the English." *Girodet* phrases the criticism even more strongly: "This very incorrect use must be absolutely condemned; one must instead say *décennie*."—Trans.

11. See Jean-Luc Nancy, *The Sense of the World*, trans. Jeffrey S. Librett (Minneapolis: University of Minnesota Press, 1997).

12. Derrida is referring to the title of a conference organized in the summer of 2002 at Cerisy by François Chaubet, Edith Heurgon, and Claire Paulhan: "Pontigny, Cerisy dans le S.I.E.C.L.E. (Sociabilités intellectuelles: Echanges, Coopérations, Lieux, Extensions)." The conference celebrated a century of intellectual encounters, exchanges, and collaborations, first at Pontigny and, later, at Cerisy.—Trans.

13. In English in the original.—Trans.

14. *Revenance*, meaning to return or come back, is related to *revenant*, ghost or specter. See Peggy Kamuf's translator's note in Derrida, *Specters of Marx*, 177.—Trans.

15. D. H. Lawrence, *The Portable D. H. Lawrence*, ed. Diana Trilling (New York: Viking, 1947), 482, 484.

16. Published as a book in French (*Schibboleth—pour Paul Celan* [Paris: Galilée, 1986]), the English version, translated by Joshua Wilner as "Shibboleth—For Paul Celan," is included in *Word Traces*, ed. Aris Fioretis (Baltimore, MD: Johns Hopkins University Press, 1994), 3–72. The following quotes all come from the first page of the English text.

17. Alexis de Tocqueville, *Democracy in America*, trans. George Lawrence (New York: Harper and Row, 1966), 51–53. Hereafter cited as *DA*. Chapter 4, "The Principle of the Sovereignty of the People in America," begins by telling us with what we must begin: "Any discussion of the political laws of the United States must always begin with the dogma of the sovereignty of the people" (51). Tocqueville does not use the word *dogma*, which comes up more than once, haphazardly. He analyzes the more or less hidden history of this dogma, which is gradually being brought "out into the daylight," having long been "buried" in the obscurity of nonrecognition. It is the dogma of "the will of the nation," sometimes "discovered in a people's silence." There are even those who thought that "the *fact* of obedience justified the *right* to command" (51).

America is the moment when sovereignty comes fully into the light. This light simply illuminates, in return, in a circular fashion, what turned out to have always been there: "In America the sovereignty of the people is neither hidden nor sterile as with some other nations; mores recognize it, and the laws proclaim it; it spreads with freedom and attains unimpeded its ultimate consequences. . . . The dogma of the sovereignty of the people . . . the war was fought and victory obtained in its name; it became the law of laws" (51–52).

18. Aristotle, *The Metaphysics*, trans. Hugh Tredennick (Cambridge, MA: Harvard University Press, 1935).

19. Homer, *Iliad*, trans. A. T. Murray (Cambridge, MA: Harvard University Press, 1978).

20. Derrida is alluding here to Emmanuel Levinas's use of this phrase in works such as *De Dieu qui vient à l'idée* (Paris: Librairie Philosophique J. Vrin, 1986), translated by Bettina Bergo as *Of God Who Comes to Mind* (Stanford, CA: Stanford University Press, 1998).—Trans.

21. Hesiod, *Theogony*, trans. Hugh G. Evelyn-White (Cambridge, MA: Harvard University Press, 1943), 461–62.

22. Louis de Rouvroy Saint-Simon, *The Memoirs of the Duke of Saint-Simon on the Reign of Louis XIV and the Regency*, vol. 2, trans. Bayle St. John (New York: Willey, 1936), 183, 322.

23. Voltaire, *The Works of Voltaire*, vol. 30, trans. William F. Fleming (New York: E. R. DuMont, 1901), 46.

24. The French *hypothèque*, most commonly translated as "mortgage," is derived from a Greek word meaning "to deposit as a pledge." The English *hypothec*,

from the same Greek word, is defined by the *OED* as "a security established by law in favor of a creditor over a subject belonging to his debtor, while the subject continues in the debtor's possession." In the following chapter Derrida emphasizes the relationship between *hypothec* and *hypothesis.*—Trans.

25. Aristotle, *Politics*, trans. H. Rackham (Cambridge, MA: Harvard University Press, 1932).

26. Giorgio Agamben, *Homo Sacer: Sovereign Power and Bare Life*, trans. Daniel Heller-Roazen (Stanford, CA: Stanford University Press, 1998), 1–3, 7–8.

27. Derrida is referring to the French presidential elections of spring 2002. In the first round of those elections Jean-Marie Le Pen, leader of the extreme right-wing party the National Front, scored a surprising victory over Lionel Jospin, then prime minister and candidate for the Socialist Party. The second round of the elections, held a couple of weeks later, pitted Le Pen against the incumbent president Jacques Chirac, who ended up winning in a landslide.—Trans.

28. Derrida, "Faith and Knowledge," 51.

29. Derrida is referring to the title of John Caputo's paper, which was distributed for discussion during the Cerisy conference.—Trans.

30. *De la grammatologie* (Paris: Editions de Minuit, 1967) (*Of Grammatology*, trans. Gayatri Chakravorty Spivak [Baltimore, MD: Johns Hopkins University Press, 1976]); "Différance," in *Marges de la philosophie* (Paris: Editions de Minuit, 1968), 1–29 (*Margins of Philosophy*, trans. Alan Bass [Chicago: University of Chicago Press, 1982], 1–27).

31. Jean-Luc Nancy, *The Experience of Freedom*, trans. Bridget McDonald (Stanford, CA: Stanford University Press, 1993). Hereafter cited as *EF*. Nancy was himself present at the Cerisy conference when Derrida delivered this paper.—Trans.

32. *Le partage* is both a "sharing in" and a "sharing out," both a "partaking in" and a "partitioning out." The English *share* or *to share* also carries both connotations, even if the latter is less audible. *Le partage* might thus be translated as the "sharing (out)."—Trans.

33. Among the many other reasons for citing the magnificent passage that follows is the question of "negotiations," which constitute, in my view, the very place of the aporia. Nancy must give in to these negotiations, and he does so once again, as if it were a concession, between two dashes:

> The *justice* necessarily in question here—because it is a question of sharing and of measure—is not that of a just mean, which presupposes a given measure, but concerns a just measure of the incommensurable. For this reason—regardless of the negotiations that at the same time must be conducted with the expectations and reasonable hopes for a just mean—*justice* can only reside in the renewed decision to challenge the validity of an established or prevailing "just measure" *in the name of the incommensurable.* The political space, or the political as spacing, is given from the outset in the form— always paradoxical and crucial for what is neither the political nor the community, but

the management of society—of the common (absence of) measure of an incommensurable. Such is, we could say, the first thrust of freedom. (*EF*, 75)

34. See *EF* 72, 76 (there, instead of "if it must be said," we have a "not to mention": "freedom, equality, not to mention fraternity . . . "), 78, 168 (see *infra*, 166–67n36), 169.

35. François Furet and Mona Ozouf, *A Critical Dictionary of the French Revolution*, trans. Arthur Goldhammer (Cambridge, MA: Belknap Press of Harvard University Press, 1989), 696.

36. In this note, which I am adding a few weeks after the conference, I would like to mention two invaluable fragments that Nancy appends to his book (which was first a dissertation that gave rise to a "defense" during which, if memory serves, I already raised this Freudian-Christian question of the father and the brother). Two of these fragments are glances back or retrospections that resemble to some extent repentances or regrets. They open the way ("half the path" is still to be traveled, says Nancy) to other forays, to what is perhaps something other than "half the path," something more like another destination. They thus deserve to be reread here *in extenso*, and not just because they refer to Arendt and Blanchot:

> The motto "liberty, equality, fraternity" seems to us somewhat ridiculous and difficult to introduce into philosophical discourse, because in France it remains official (a lie of the State) and because it is said to summarize an obsolete "Rousseauism." But for Heidegger, does not "being-there also with others" (§26, *Being and Time*) determine itself according to "an equality [*Gleichheit*] of being as being-in-the-world?" Such an equality is unbreachable: it belongs precisely to freedom.
>
> As for fraternity, which gives one even more to smile about: should it be suspected of coming from a relation to murdering the Father, and therefore of remaining a prisoner as much of the sharing of hatred as of a communion with an identical substance/essence (in the totemic meal)? This interpretation of the community as "fraternal" must indeed be carefully dismantled. But it is possible, even with Freud, to interpret it otherwise: as a sharing of a maternal thing which precisely would not be substance, but sharing—to infinity. In this respect, Chapter 7 [the chapter we have just been talking about] has traveled only half the path. Perhaps the "mother" must also be abandoned, if we cannot avoid her being "phallic" (but is this certain?). We must also think of the fraternity in abandonment, of abandonment.
>
> ⁓
>
> *"Fraternity: we love them, we cannot do anything for them, except help them to reach the threshold."* Blanchot's fragment ascribes to fraternity a love without effect, without affect, without communion. A strange restraint of love, yet still named "love." (Regarding fraternity, Hannah Arendt could be invoked in the same sense.) What, in these conditions, does "help" mean: not a support, not a consolation, but the communal exposure of freedom. (*EF*, 168)

To be sure. But then why not simply *abandon* the word *fraternity as well*, now that it has been stripped of all its recognizable attributes? What does *fraternity* still name when it has no relationship to birth, death, the father, the mother, sons and brothers?

If the link to the traditional word and concept is so arbitrary that one can abandon it, then why say nothing of the daughter and the sister—or the wife? Where have they gone? I tried to work out these questions in relation to Blanchot and Nancy in *Politics of Friendship*, 46–47n15, 296–99.

37. Even though the French dictionary *Littré* makes reference in the entry on the adjective *rogue* to the English word of the same spelling ("In English, *rogue* means rascally as well as mischievous"), and even though the two words probably share the same origin in the Scandinavian *hrok* or *hrokr*, the French usage seems to emphasize the sense of arrogance, rudeness, or haughtiness. In English, as we will see, the emphasis is rather on the sense of defiance and offence, on an infraction against or an indifference to the law. Hence the translation into French as *voyou*.

38. Cited by Walter Benjamin in *The Arcades Project*, trans. Howard Eiland and Kevin McLaughlin (Cambridge, MA: Belknap Press of Harvard University Press, 1999), 739, and there translated: "The Paris purebred is this pale guttersnipe / Stunted growth, yellowed like an old penny."—Trans.

39. Gérard de Nerval, "Les Nuits d'octobre X," in *Oeuvres*, vol. 1 (Paris: Bibliothèque de la Pléiade, 1960), 94. Translated by Richard Sieburth in *Gerard de Nerval: Selected Writings* (New York: Penguin, 1999), 219, as "that hoarse whisper characteristic of Parisian toughs."

40. Walter Benjamin, "Critique of Violence," in *Reflections*, trans. Edmund Jephcott (New York: Schocken Books, 1978), 281.

41. The *OED* gives these two meanings for the term "alligation": "1. The action of attaching; the state of being attached. 2. The 'Rule of Mixtures'; the arithmetical method of solving questions concerning the mixing of articles of different qualities of values."—Trans.

42. The expression translated here as "in four easy steps" is "*en quatre temps et trois mouvements*," which means "quickly," "in short order," but which translates literally as "in four times and three movements." Although Derrida essentially wishes to underscore the way in which the wolf in La Fontaine's fable dispenses with the lamb's arguments or pleas "quickly," "in short order," it is worth recalling that the wolf makes exactly *four* different allegations against the lamb, which defends itself against the first *three* but is devoured by the wolf before it has a chance to answer the fourth.—Trans.

43. The italicized words are all in English in the original.—Trans.

44. Jean-Jacques Rousseau, "On Democracy," bk. 3, chap. 4 of *On the Social*

Contract, trans. Donald A. Cress (Indianapolis, IN: Hackett, 1987), 56. Hereafter cited as *SC*.

45. Aristotle's reference to the story of Antisthenes ends here, the response of the lions being no doubt so well known that it did not have to be cited. We have lost Antisthenes' exact words, but H. Rackham's interpolation in a note to his translation of the *Politics* sounds about right: "Where are your claws and teeth?"—Trans.

46. Immanuel Kant, *Perpetual Peace*, trans. Lewis White Beck (Indianapolis: Bobbs-Merrill, 1957), 20. Hereafter cited as *PP*.

47. At the foot of this word for sovereignty, *Majestas*, I add a *footnote*: like the word *sovereignty*, its synonym *majesty* suggests the greatest in size (*majestas* comes from *majus*, for *magius*, major, greatness, height, superiority, the supreme or supremacy, that which, like the *superanus* of the sovereign, comes *above*). Sovereign majesty: a question of size, therefore, as in the democratic majority that assures sovereignty. But it is a question of calculable-incalculable size, for if the majority is numerical, the general will of the sovereign or of the monarch cannot be divided. And the One (of God, of the monarch, or of the sovereign) is not greater, very great (comparatively or superlatively), superiorly great or supremely high. It is absolutely great and thus above measurable greatness. Higher than height, incommensurable in any case, even if it can sometimes take the form and have the supreme power of the smallest and most invisible. In a modernity of nanotechnological sciences, power is also measured in terms of how it measures up to the potency of the smallest possible. The sovereign One is a One that can no longer be counted; it is *more than one* [*plus d'un*] in the sense of being *more than a one* [*plus qu'un*], beyond the more than one of calculable multiplicity.

48. Jacques Derrida, *Du droit à la philosophie* (Paris: Editions Galilée, 1990), 53. Translated in *Who's Afraid of Philosophy: Right to Philosophy I*, trans. Jan Plug (Stanford, CA: Stanford University Press, 2002), 29.

49. Jacques Derrida, "Force of Law: The 'Mystical Foundation of Authority,'" trans. Mary Quaintance, in Jacques Derrida, *Acts of Religion*, ed. Gil Anidjar (New York: Routledge, 2002), 281.

50. Jacques Derrida, "*Sauf le Nom (Post-Scriptum),*" trans. John P. Leavey Jr., in Derrida, *On the Name*, 83. Hereafter cited as *ON*.

51. "Appendix to the Transcendental Dialectic; The Regulative Employment of the Ideas of Pure Reason," in Immanuel Kant, *Critique of Pure Reason*, trans. Norman Kemp Smith (New York: St. Martin's, 1965), 547; A 666/B 694. Hereafter cited in the text as *CPR*.

52. Kant, *Critique of Pure Reason*, 533; A 644/B 672. We know the decisive and enigmatic role played by the *als ob* in all of Kant's thought; this is especially true of the regulative Idea. It is a matter of considering the connections between phenomena "*as if* they were the ordinances of a supreme reason, of which our reason

is but a faint copy [*als ob sie Anordnungen einer höchsten Vernunft wären, von der die unsrige ein schwaches Nachbild ist*]" (*CPR*, 555; A 678/B 706); "*as if* this being, as supreme intelligence, acting in accordance with a supremely wise purpose, were the cause of all things [*als ob diese als höchste Intelligenz nach der weisesten Absicht die Ursache von allem sei*]" (*CPR*, 561; A 688/B 716). "For the regulative law of systematic unity prescribes that we should study nature *as if* systematic and purposive unity, combined with the greatest possible manifoldness, were everywhere to be met with, *in infinitum* [*als ob allenthalben ins Unendliche systematische und zweckmäßige Einheit bei der größtmöglichen Mannigfaltigkeit angetroffen würde*]") (*CPR*, 568; A 700/B 728).

To continue in the direction I indicated above by distinguishing a "reservation" from an "objection," let's just say that I am sometimes tempted to make "as if" I had no objections to Kant's "as if's." In "The University Without Condition" I treat the difficult question of the "as if" in Kant and elsewhere, and I propose another way of thinking it.

53. "The second regulative idea of merely speculative reason is the concept of the world in general [*Die zweite regulative Idee der bloß spekulativen Vernunft ist der Weltbegriff überhaupt*]" (*CPR*, 558; A 684/B 712).

54. Jacques Derrida, *The Other Heading*, trans. Pascale-Anne Brault and Michael Naas (Bloomington: Indiana University Press, 1992), 78.

55. Derrida, *Specters of Marx*, 169.

56. Derrida, *Politics of Friendship*, 64. Hereafter cited as *PF*.

57. Blaise Pascal, *Pensées, The Provincial Letters*, trans. W. F. Trotter (New York: Random House, 1941), in sec. 5, "Justice and the Reason of Effects," 103.

58. Immanuel Kant, *The Metaphysics of Morals*, trans. Mary Gregor (New York: Cambridge University Press, 1996), pt. 1, "Metaphysical First Principles of the Doctrine of Right, Introduction to the Doctrine of Right," §§D–E, 25–26. German text: *Kantswerke*, Akademische Textausgabe (Berlin: Walter de Gruyter, 1968), 6:231–33. Hereafter cited as *AK*, followed by volume and page number.

59. Mark Strauss, "A Rogue by Any Other Name," *Chronicle of Higher Education*, Dec. 15, 2000, B11.

60. Noam Chomsky, *Rogue States: The Rule of Force in World Affairs* (Cambridge, MA: South End Press, 2000); *9–11* (New York: Seven Stories Press, 2001).

61. Robert S. Litwak, *Rogue States and U.S. Foreign Policy* (Baltimore, MD: Johns Hopkins University Press, 2000).

62. This appears to be Mark Strauss's summary of Litwak's argument rather than a direct quote from Litwak. See Strauss's aforementioned article in the *Chronicle of Higher Education* (note 59 above).—Trans.

63. These are the words of Robert Wright, author of *NonZero: The Logic of Human Destiny* (New York: Pantheon, 2000), cited by Mark Strauss in the aforementioned article in the *Chronicle of Higher Education* (see note 59 above).—Trans.

64. William Blum, *Rogue State: A Guide to the World's Only Superpower* (Monroe, ME: Common Courage Press, 2000).

65. Over the past few weeks the authority of the Security Council has been invoked by the United States in an attempt to continue to forestall the establishment of the International Criminal Court, which certain states (such as the United States and Israel—the motivating force behind all this) find threatening. The United States thus requested through the Security Council that the tribunal defer for twelve months any investigation into or any indictment of the personnel of states that contribute to operations mandated or authorized by the United Nations. For example the operations against "international terrorism." The same Security Council then "decided that this request shall be renewed every year, on July 1, for the following twelve months." This amounted to asking for a de facto exemption from the jurisdiction of the International Criminal Tribunal for so-called peacekeeping forces. It is not hard to imagine where all this might lead or what ambiguities it might foster. It is in this context that the United States has itself been accused of acting like an "outlaw."

66. See notes 60 and 64 above. One might now wish to add to the list Clyde Prestowitz's *Rogue Nation: American Unilateralism and the Failure of Good Intentions* (New York: Basic Books, 2003).—Trans.

67. In English in the original.—Trans.

68. Chomsky, *Rogue States*, 4.

69. See Derrida's interview on 9-11 with Giovanna Borradori in *Philosophy in a Time of Terror: Dialogues with Jürgen Habermas and Jacques Derrida*, ed. Giovanna Borradori (Chicago: University of Chicago Press, 2003), 85–136.—Trans.

70. From an interview with Martin Heidegger in *Der Spiegel*. "Only a God Can Save Us," trans. Maria P. Alter and John D. Caputo in *Philosophy Today* 20, no. 4 (Winter 1976): 277. Hereafter cited as *DS*. Translation slightly modified to suit the context of Derrida's argument.—Trans.

71. Martin Heidegger, *Contributions to Philosophy*, trans. Parvis Emad and Kenneth Maly (Bloomington: Indiana University Press, 1999), 289, 293.

72. Martin Heidegger, "The Question Concerning Technology," in *Basic Writings*, ed. David Farrell Krell, revised and expanded edition (New York: HarperCollins, 1993), 311–41.

73. "Building Dwelling Thinking," in Heidegger, *Basic Writings*, 351. Hereafter cited as "BDT." Translation slightly modified to suit the context of Derrida's argument.—Trans.

74. "What Are Poets For?" in Martin Heidegger, *Poetry, Language, Thought*, trans. Albert Hofstadter (New York: Harper and Row, 1975), 141. Hofstadter's translation runs: "The unholy, as unholy, traces the sound for us. What is sound beckons to the holy, calling it. The holy binds the divine. The divine draws the god near."

75. As Derrida has made clear throughout the essay, *salut* must be understood as both a greeting and a farewell, a hello and a good-bye, a salutation that wishes well. In the present context, it might even be translated "Godspeed!"—Trans.

Part II

1. 1. Dominique Janicaud, *Powers of the Rational*, trans. Peg Birmingham and Elizabeth Birmingham (Bloomington: Indiana University Press, 1994), 260 (Janicaud's emphasis). Translation slightly modified. Hereafter cited as *PR*. Originally published as *La puissance du rationnel* (Paris: Editions Gallimard, 1985), 375.

2. Janicaud, *Powers of the Rational*, 46 (Janicaud's emphasis). This proposition belongs to the development of a reading of Heidegger. It is neither totally endorsed nor, it seems to me, explicitly criticized by Janicaud.

3. Immanuel Kant, *Critique of Pure Reason*, trans. Norman Kemp Smith (New York: St. Martin's, 1965), 2nd div., bk. 2, chap. 2, sec. 3, "The Interest of Reason in These Conflicts," 422–30; A 462/B 490–A 476/B 504. It would appear, although I knew nothing about this or else had buried it in forgetting, that Kant had used the expression "to save the honor of reason" in an early work. Jean Ferrari, president of the Association des Sociétés de Philosophie de Langue française, told me this just after my presentation, promising to send me the reference. In his *Les sources françaises de la philosophie de Kant* (Klincksieck, 1980), Ferrari, whom I here thank again, refers twice (pp. 27, 247) to the young Kant's expression "*die Ehre der menschlichen Vernunft verteidigen*": "to defend [to support, plead for, rather than 'to save'] the honor of human reason."

Amnesia, symptom, the work of the unconscious, or coincidence, the *necessity* of this recurrence is here confirmed in its *meaning*; it attests, in any case, and in more than one way, to an undeniable rationality. The expression, like the question it opens up, is all the more justified by reason of the fact that, once more *after the fact*, I came across it again in Husserl (see pages 129–30 below).

4. Kant, *Critique of Pure Reason*, 429; A 474/B 502. This thesis is more historical than it appears for someone interested in the development or the historicity of reason. For if the concern for synthetic and synchronic coherence, the concern for the *arkhē* (as foundation, cause, or principle), has always associated reason with *architectural* organization and all its metaphors, the project of an *architectonic system*, in the strict sense of the term, is a relatively modern form of this concern. Architecture is not architectonic. All coherence is not and has not always been systemic. It seems to me that Heidegger was right to insist on this in several places.

5. Had I the time, I would be tempted to follow the thread that runs from *Vom Wesen des Grundes* (1929), in particular in relation to the concept of "world" and its history, up to *Der Satz vom Grund* (1957).

6. Edmund Husserl, *The Crisis of European Sciences and Transcendental Phenomenology*, trans. David Carr (Evanston, IL: Northwestern University Press, 1970), 269–99. Hereafter cited as *Crisis*. [The French translation Derrida is working with is that of Gérard Granel, *La crise des sciences européennes et la phénoménologie transcendantale* (Paris: Gallimard, 1976).—Trans.] German text: *Husserliana 6* (The Hague: M. Nijhof, 1954).

7. Edmund Husserl, "Philosophy as Mankind's Self-Reflection," appendix 4 in *Crisis*, 341.

8. Kant, *Critique of Practical Reason*, bk. 2, chap. 2, sec. 3, "On the Primacy of Pure Practical Reason in Its Association with Speculative Reason," trans. Lewis White Beck (New York: Macmillan, 1993), 126–28. Hereafter cited as *CPR*. German text: *Kantswerke*, Akademische Textausgabe (Berlin: Walter de Gruyter, 1968), 5:121. Hereafter cited as *AK*, followed by volume and page number.

9. Immanuel Kant, *Groundwork of the Metaphysics of Morals*, trans. H. J. Patton (New York: Harper and Row, 1964), 102. Hereafter cited as *G. AK* 4:435.

10. Plato, *The Republic*, trans. Paul Shorey (Cambridge, MA: Harvard University Press, 1987).

11. See the essay "Psyché: Inventions de l'autre," in *Psyché: Inventions de l'autre* (Paris: Galilée, 1987). An excerpt from this essay has been translated into English in *A Derrida Reader: Between the Blinds*, ed. Peggy Kamuf (New York: Columbia University Press, 1991).

12. *Unconditional hospitality*, I emphasize. Several friends recently brought to my attention a recent publication ("a pathetic Parisian tabloid in the style of *Gala*," as one of them put it) whose author pontificates, without verifying anything, on what I've written and taught for a number of years now under the name *unconditional hospitality*. Obviously understanding nothing, the author even gives me, as if still back in high school, a bad grade and exclaims peremptorily in the margins of my paper: "Absurd!" Well, what can I say? . . .

I have always, consistently and insistently, held *unconditional hospitality*, as *impossible*, to be *heterogeneous* to the *political*, the *juridical*, and even the *ethical*. But the impossible is not nothing. It is even that which happens, which comes, by definition. I admit that this remains rather difficult to think, but that's exactly what preoccupies what is called thinking, if there is any and from the time there is any.

Perhaps I should have given in to the temptation simply to "click off" and ignore such brazen rumors and ineptitudes. The benefits to be derived from such things have been all too obvious for some time now. But for whoever is still honest enough to do his or her *homework* (as one sometimes asks American students who have not put in the effort to read and so arrogantly say whatever they want), here are a few references for starters. There are, it is true, paradoxical or aporetic relations between two concepts that are at once *heterogeneous and inseparable*, *unconditional* hospitality and *conditional* hospitality (that is, the only one, let me repeat it, that belongs to the order of laws, rules, and norms—whether ethical, juridical, or political—at a national or international level): *Of Hospitality*, trans. Rachel Bowlby (Stanford, CA: Stanford University Press, 2000), esp. 23, 55, 65, 75, 133, 147; *On Cosmopolitanism and Forgiveness*, trans. Mark Dooley and Michael Hughes (New York: Routledge, 2001), esp. 16–23; *Adieu—to Emmanuel Levinas*, trans. Pascale-Anne Brault and Michael Naas (Stanford, CA: Stanford University Press, 1999), 21, 45, 67, 91.

If one wants to read no more than five pages, see "Le principe d'hospitalité," in *Papier Machine* (Paris: Galilée, 2001), 273–77 (esp. 277). With a bit more patience see also 296, 342, 351, 361; for the first of these references see *Negotiations: Interventions and Interviews, 1971–2001*, ed. and trans. Elizabeth Rottenberg (Stanford, CA: Stanford University Press, 2002), 353–63. See also *De quoi demain . . .* , with Elizabeth Roudinesco (Paris: Fayard/Galilée, 2001), 100–104; and *Manifeste pour l'hospitalité—aux Minguettes (Autour de Jacques Derrida)* (Grigny: Editions Paroles d'Aube, 1999).

As for the notion of *sacrifice*, which the same newspaper confusedly throws into the mix, I've written so much on the subject that a whole page of references would not suffice. One last bit of advice—uttered out of desperation: read everything! And then, if need be, reread it!

13. Immanuel Kant, *The Metaphysics of Morals*, trans. Mary Gregor (New York: Cambridge University Press, 1996), pt. 1, "Metaphysical First Principles of the Doctrine of Right, Introduction to the Doctrine of Right," §§D–E, 25–26. *AK*, 6:231–33.

14. This is perhaps the place to provide, after the fact, and all too briefly, a few clarifications on the question of what might link "deconstruction," or at least the one that has seemed necessary to me in my work for so long now, to reason as *logos*.

These clarifications are called for because of a discussion at the end of the conference around "metaphysical and postmetaphysical reason." There was a great deal of talk there about *logos* and deconstruction. For several different reasons, I was unable to take part in the discussion. I thus take this opportunity to recall a few facts that seem to have been oddly omitted from the discussion.

1. Heideggerian deconstruction (*Destruktion*) never really opposed logocentrism or even *logos*. Indeed it is often, on the contrary, in the name of a more "originary" reinterpretation of *logos* that it carried out the deconstruction of classical ontology or ontotheology.

2. The "deconstruction" that I attempt or that tempts me is not only distinct (in ways too numerous and too widely discussed elsewhere for me to recall here) from the one practiced by Heidegger. First and foremost, it never

took the objectifying form of a knowledge as "diagnosis," and even less of a "diagnosis of diagnosis," since it has always been, and has always acknowledged itself to be, inscribed, undertaken, and understood in the very element of the language it calls into question, struggling at the heart of metaphysical debates that are themselves in the grips of autodeconstructive movements. Hence I never associated the theme of deconstruction with the themes that were constantly being brought up during the discussion, themes of "diagnosis," of "after" or "post," of "death" (death of philosophy, death of metaphysics, and so on), of "completion" or of "surpassing" (*Überwindung* or *Schritt zurück*), of the "end." One will find no trace of such a vocabulary in any of my texts. This is not fortuitous, as you might well believe, and it is not without enormous consequence. It is not fortuitous that, as early as *Of Grammatology* (1965), I explicitly declared that it was not a question of the end of metaphysics and that the closure was certainly not the end. And such a closure, I very quickly clarified, did not surround or enclose something like "Metaphysics" in general and in the singular but instead traversed its heterogeneous space following a grid of complex and noncircular limits.

3. One must not only say, as was said, and not without audacity, "*Luther qui genuit Pascal*," but perhaps also "*Luther qui genuit Heidegger*." Which has completely other consequences. I have recalled in several different places that the theme and word *Destruktion* designated in Luther a desedimentation of instituted theology (one could also say ontotheology) in the service of a more originary truth of Scripture. Heidegger was obviously a great reader of Luther. But despite my enormous respect for this great tradition, the deconstruction that concerns me does not belong, in any way, and this is more than obvious, to the same filiation. It is precisely this difference that I attempt, although not without difficulty, to be sure, to articulate.

I would say more or less the same thing with regard to the privilege I constantly grant aporetic thought. I know and recognize quite well what this thought no doubt owes to the Aristotelian aporia, as well as, and I recall this in this very text, to the Kantian antinomies, but it seems to me always to mark them with a wholly other wrinkle. It is precisely this limit of analogy that decides everything and so requires the most vigilant attention. I would again say the same thing with regard to the hyper- or ultratranscendentalism (which is thus also a hyperrationalism) to which, in order to avoid empiricist positivism, I expressly appealed as early as *Of Grammatology*.

4. Finally, I hesitate to insist yet again on the difference between deconstruction and destruction, or between deconstruction and critique. Decon-

struction does not seek to discredit critique; it in fact constantly relegitimates its necessity and heritage, even though it never renounces either a genealogy of the critical idea or a history of the question and of the supposed privilege of interrogative thought.

All these themes, dare I say, have been the objects of long developments in numerous publications over the course of the last four decades.

15. See bk. 1, chap. 3, "Of the Drives of Pure Practical Reason," in Kant, *Critique of Practical Reason*, esp. 84–85.

MERIDIAN

Crossing Aesthetics

Jacques Derrida, *Rogues: Two Essays on Reason*

Peggy Kamuf, *Book of Addresses*

Giorgio Agamben, *The Time that Remains: A Commentary on the Letter to the Romans*

Jean-Luc Nancy, *Multiple Arts: The Muses II*

Alain Badiou, *Handbook of Inaesthetics*

Jacques Derrida, *Eyes of the University: Right to Philosophy 2*

Maurice Blanchot, *Lautréamont and Sade*

Giorgio Agamben, *The Open: Man and Animal*

Jean Genet, *The Declared Enemy*

Shosana Felman, *Writing and Madness: (Literature/Philosophy/Psychoanalysis)*

Jean Genet, *Fragments of the Artwork*

Shoshana Felman, *The Scandal of the Speaking Body: Don Juan with J. L. Austin, or Seduction in Two Languages*

Peter Szondi, *Celan Studies*

Neil Hertz, *George Eliot's Pulse*

Maurice Blanchot, *The Book to Come*

Susannah Young-ah Gottlieb, *Regions of Sorrow: Anxiety and Messianism in Hannah Arendt and W. H. Auden*

Jaques Derrida, *Without Alibi*, edited by Peggy Kamuf

Cornelius Castoriadis, *On Plato's 'Statesman'*

Jacques Derrida, *Who's Afraid of Philosophy? Right to Philosophy 1*

Peter Szondi, *An Essay on the Tragic*

Peter Fenves, *Arresting Language: From Leibniz to Benjamin*

Jill Robbins, ed. *Is It Righteous to Be? Interviews with Emmanuel Levinas*

Louis Marin, *Of Representation*

Daniel Payot, *The Architect and the Philosopher*

J. Hillis Miller, *Speech Acts in Literature*

Maurice Blanchot, *Faux pas*

Jean-Luc Nancy, *Being Singular Plural*

Maurice Blanchot / Jacques Derrida, *The Instant of My Death / Demeure: Fiction and Testimony*

Niklas Luhmann, *Art as a Social System*

Emmanual Levinas, *God, Death, and Time*

Ernst Bloch, *The Spirit of Utopia*

Giorgio Agamben, *Potentialities: Collected Essays in Philosophy*

Ellen S. Burt, *Poetry's Appeal: French Nineteenth-Century Lyric and the Political Space*

Jacques Derrida, *Adieu to Emmanuel Levinas*

Werner Hamacher, *Premises: Essays on Philosophy and Literature from Kant to Celan*

Aris Fioretos, *The Gray Book*

Deborah Esch, *In the Event: Reading Journalism, Reading Theory*

Winfried Menninghaus, *In Praise of Nonsense: Kant and Bluebeard*

Giorgio Agamben, *The Man Without Content*

Giorgio Agamben, *The End of the Poem: Studies in Poetics*

Theodor W. Adorno, *Sound Figures*

Louis Marin, *Sublime Poussin*

Philippe Lacoue-Labarthe, *Poetry as Experience*

Ernst Bloch, *Literary Essays*

Jacques Derrida, *Resistances of Psychoanalysis*

Marc Froment-Meurice, *That Is to Say: Heidegger's Poetics*

Francis Ponge, *Soap*

Philippe Lacoue-Labarthe, *Typography: Mimesis, Philosophy, Politics*

Giorgio Agamben, *Homo Sacer: Sovereign Power and Bare Life*

Emmanuel Levinas, *Of God Who Comes to Mind*

Bernard Stiegler, *Technics and Time, 1: The Fault of Epimetheus*

Werner Hamacher, *pleroma—Reading in Hegel*

Serge Leclaire, *Psychoanalyzing: On the Order of the Unconscious and the Practice of the Letter*

Serge Leclaire, *A Child Is Being Killed: On Primary Narcissism and the Death Drive*

Sigmund Freud, *Writings on Art and Literature*

Cornelius Castoriadis, *World in Fragments: Writings on Politics, Society, Psychoanalysis, and the Imagination*

Thomas Keenan, *Fables of Responsibility: Aberrations and Predicaments in Ethics and Politics*

Emmanuel Levinas, *Proper Names*

Alexander García Düttmann, *At Odds with AIDS: Thinking and Talking About a Virus*

Maurice Blanchot, *Friendship*

Jean-Luc Nancy, *The Muses*

Massimo Cacciari, *Posthumous People: Vienna at the Turning Point*

David E. Wellbery, *The Specular Moment: Goethe's Early Lyric and the Beginnings of Romanticism*

Edmond Jabès, *The Little Book of Unsuspected Subversion*

Hans-Jost Frey, *Studies in Poetic Discourse: Mallarmé, Baudelaire, Rimbaud, Hölderlin*

Pierre Bourdieu, *The Rules of Art: Genesis and Structure of the Literary Field*

Nicolas Abraham, *Rhythms: On the Work, Translation, and Psychoanalysis*

Jacques Derrida, *On the Name*

David Wills, *Prosthesis*

Maurice Blanchot, *The Work of Fire*

Jacques Derrida, *Points . . . : Interviews, 1974–1994*

J. Hillis Miller, *Topographies*

Philippe Lacoue-Labarthe, *Musica Ficta (Figures of Wagner)*

Jacques Derrida, *Aporias*

Emmanuel Levinas, *Outside the Subject*

Jean-François Lyotard, *Lessons on the Analytic of the Sublime*

Peter Fenves, *"Chatter": Language and History in Kierkegaard*

Jean-Luc Nancy, *The Experience of Freedom*

Jean-Joseph Goux, *Oedipus, Philosopher*

Haun Saussy, *The Problem of a Chinese Aesthetic*

Jean-Luc Nancy, *The Birth to Presence*